Cruel and Unusual Punishment:

Comparative Perspective in International Conventions, the United States and Iran

Cruel and Unusual Punishment:

Comparative Perspective in International Conventions, the United States and Iran

By

Sanaz Alasti
LL.B, LL.M, S.J.D.

Vandeplas Publishing
United States of America

Cruel and unusual punishment: comparative perspective in international conventions, the United States and Iran

Alasti, Sanaz

Published by:

Vandeplas Publishing - March 2009

801 International Parkway, 5th Floor
Lake Mary, FL. 32746
USA

www.vandeplaspublishing.com

All Rights Reserved

ISBN: 978-1-60042-068-9
© 2009 Sanaz Alasti

Dedication

This book is dedicated to my lovely father and mother. Without their support, none of my advanced legal studies would have been possible.

Acknowledgements

I consider myself exceptionally fortunate in having enjoyed the intellectual stimulation and support of my supervisor Dr. Professor Sompong Sucharitkul and three excellent advisers Professor Franklin E. Zimring, Professor Myron Moskovitz and Dr. Professor Christian Okeke in the space of the last four years, and I am glad to have an opportunity to say that.

Above all, I owe thanks to Daniel Hewera and my other friends and colleagues for their constant encouragement criticism, and number of individuals who took the trouble to read the entire draft.

Finally, and as always, John Pluebell deserves special thanks for his help and support who extensive criticism and commentaries have done much to enhance the quality of what is offered here.

Table of Contents

Introduction *1*

Chapter 1 .... *7*

Origins of Cruel and Unusual Punishment *7*

I **The Concept of Cruel and Unusual Punishment** 7
    1 Prohibition of Cruel and Unusual Punishment under International Law 7
        A International Instruments 7
        B Customary International Law 13
        C Peremptory norms 15
    2 Prohibition of Cruel and Unusual Punishment under National Laws 18
        A United States 18
        B Iran 26

II **Definition** 30
    1 Terminology 30
        A From Torture to Cruel and Unusual Punishment 30
        B Relationship between Cruel and Unusual Punishment 36
    2 What Constitute Cruel and Unusual Punishment 38
        A Modes of Punishment 38
        B Essential Elements 39

III **Harshness v. Mildness** 41
    1 Socio-historical Perspective 41
    2 Harshness and Penological Objectives 44

Chapter 2 .... *47*

Death Penalty *47*

I **History** 47
    1 History of Death Penalty in the United States from Colonial Times to Twentieth Century 47
        A The Colonial Period (1597-1740) 47
        B The Revolutionary times (1718-1797) 48
        C Death Penalty in the New Nation (1777-1857) 49
        D Civil War Era (1856-1876) 50
        E Death Penalty in Victorian America (1870-1901) 50
        F Progressive era (1898-1938) 51
        G Mid-century (1941-1959) 52
        H In to the Modern Era 52
    2 History of Death Penalty in Iran from the Ancient Times to Revolutionary Restatement of Capital Punishments 56
        A Capital punishment in the ancient era 56
        B Capital punishment in the Islamic era 56
        C Capital Punishment under the Pahlavi Monarchy (1925-1979) 57

		D	Capital Punishment Post-Islamic Revolution (1979)	57

II   Cruel and Unusual Per Se 62
- 1 Arbitrary Infliction 62
- 2 Pain Infliction 63
- 3 Legislative and Judicial Approval 64

III   International Aspect 71
- 1 The Right to Life under International Law 72
  - A The Universal Declaration of Human Rights 72
  - B The International Covenant on Civil and Political Rights ... 73
  - C The Second Optional Protocol to the International Covenant on Civil and Political Rights 75
  - D Convention Against Torture 77
  - E The American Convention on Human Rights 77
  - F The European Convention for the Protection of Human Rights 79
  - G The Universal Islamic Declaration of Rights 80
  - H United Nations Resolutions 81
- 2 Death Penalty and International Law in U.S. Courts 84
- 3 Fundamental Conflict between Theocracy and Principles of Human Rights 87
  - A Cultural Relativism in International Law 88
  - B Can Islamic Law Evolve? 90

Chapter 3 95

Execution Methods 95

I   Biblical Times to Modern Era 95
- 1 History of Execution Methods 97
- 2 Legislative Endorsement of the Execution Methods in the United States and Iran 98
  - A Hanging 99
  - B Crucifixion 103
  - C Stoning 103
  - D Shooting 103
  - E Electrocution 105
  - F Lethal gas 106
  - G Lethal injection 108

II   Stoning, Harshness and Abolition 110
- 1 Definition 111
  - A Definition of stoning in Islam 111
  - B Definition of stoning in Judaism 116
- 2 Stoning crimes 118
  - A In Islam 118
  - B In Judaism 119
- 3 Evidentiary & Execution Procedure 121
  - A In Islam 121
  - B In Judaism 122
- 4 Stoning Location 126
- 5 Reversal of Punishment 127

		A	In Islam	127
		B	In Judaism	128
	6		Stoning and contemporary standards of societies	128
	7		Abolition of stoning or moratorium	131
III	**Challenging the Various Methods of Inflicting the Death Penalty**			**137**
	1		Considerable Factors	138
		A	Duration of Procedure	138
		B	The Pain Involved in the Execution Method	138
		C	The Reliability & mutilation caused by Execution Method	139
		D	The Degrading Preparation Involved in the Method	140
	2		Socio-Humanity Perspective	140
		A	Unacceptable to Society	140
		B	Public Executions	141
		C	International Human Rights Perspective	144

Chapter 4 147

Cruel and Unusual due to the Doctrine of Proportionality 147

I	**When the Death Penalty is Appropriate?**			**147**
	1		The Death Penalty as Excessive	147
	2		Proportionality Doctrine & 8th Amendment in the United States	150
	3		Proportionality Doctrine v. Islamic Laws in Iran	154
		A	Hodoud Offenses	154
		B	Qisas (Retaliation)	156
		C	Taazir (Discretionary Punishments)	157
II	**Juvenile Death Penalty**			**158**
	1		The Efficacy of Death Penalty for Juvenile Crimes & Violation of International Law	162
		A	Penology View	162
		B	International View	166
	2		The Story of Juvenile Death Penalty Abolition in the United States	172
		A	Legal Background	173
		B	Diminished Responsibility	177
		C	Facts behind the Juvenile Death Penalty in the United States	181
	3		Juvenile Death Penalty in Iran	184
		A	Legal Background	185
		B	Rational behind the Juvenile Death Penalty in Iran	187
III	**Miscellaneous Conditions & Proportionality**			**190**
	1		Mandatory Death Sentences	190
	2		Mentally Retarded Offenders	193
	3		Challenging the Imprisonment as Excessive	196
	4		Cruel and Unusual due to the Status of Offender	202

Chapter 5 209

Corporal Punishment 209

I	**History**	210

		1	History of Corporal Punishment in the United States from Colonial Times to Twentieth Century...210

        1   History of Corporal Punishment in the United States from Colonial Times to Twentieth Century...210
            A   Corporal Punishment in Early America (1597-1740)..211
            B   Corporal Punishment in Revolutionary Times (1718-1797) 212
            C   Corporal Punishment in the New Nation (1777-1857)...213
            D   Corporal Punishment in the Civil War Era (1856-1876)..213
            E   Corporal Punishment in the Young Nation 214
        2   History of Corporal Punishment in Iran from the Ancient Times to the Revolutionary Restatement of Corporal Punishment 215
            A   Corporal Punishment in the Ancient Era...215
            B   Corporal punishment in the Islamic Era..216
            C   Corporal Punishment under the Pahlavi Monarchy (1925-1979).........................216
            D   Corporal Punishment after Islamic Revolution (1979)...217
        3   Contemporary Corporal Punishment...219

II   **From Different Methods to International Restrictions 223**
        1   Corporal Punishment Methods in the United States & Iran......................................223
            A   Whipping...223
            B   Branding..225
            C   Mutilation...225
            D   Ducking Stool..227
            E   Stocks & the Pillory 228
        2   International Aspect..229
            A   Treaties & International cases 229
            B   Amnesty International..231
            C   Applying International Norms in Domestic Courts..232

III   **Cruel & Unusual Analysis 239**
        1   Cruel & Unusual Per se...239
        2   Pain Infliction..241
        3   Legislative Story 242
        4   Judicial Story 247

IV   **Cruel & Unusual Due to the Doctrine of Proportionality 253**
        1   Proportionality Analysis 253
        2   When is Whipping Appropriate? 256
        3   Punishment Objectives v. Contemporary Standards 257
            A   Contemporary Standards of Decency...257
            B   Penological Objectives..259

Conclusion *266*

Table of Cases *271*

Table of Charts & Figures *275*

Bibliography... *277*

Introduction

During my experience as a law student, I developed my research on the issues related to the study of punishment. The research helped me understand many views that non-scholars do not have. I conducted research about cruel and unusual punishments. Later I developed my research on the origin of concept and interpretation of cruel and unusual punishment in International conventions, the United States Constitutional law (Federal and State level) and Iran law (statute, Sharia Law).

The main focus of inquiry in this research is to find out which kinds of punishments constitute cruel and unusual, whether these punishments are inherently cruel and unusual, excessive, disproportionate, or unnecessary to society; or inflicted arbitrary. This book will not discuss torture and administrative punishments, prison rules, practices and prison conditions outside of the meaning of judicial punishments.

Another issue, it is reasonable for judges to grant national standards greater influence when assessing what is cruel and unusual. In my view judges should allow international trends to shed light on the issue as well. That means the United States and Iran can apply International definition of cruel and unusual punishment. Because the United States and Iran are a party to International agreement that bear on the issue, it is necessary to consider International trends at least relevant in to contemporary standards of decency. Therefore, using International norms will not invade United States and Iran sovereignty but will provide a better guideline in deciding what cruel and unusual punishment is.

This book is a comparative study of cruel and unusual punishment in the United States and Iran based on the prohibition of these punishments in International conventions. This research as a comparative analysis identifies patterns of cruel and unusual punishment over space and time. The major limitation involves non-adequacy of available data and particular cases in Iran.

My primary motivation in this research is to demonstrate that harshness in the law of punishment such as corporal punishment, long sentences of imprisonment and harshness in the inflexibility of punishment (Applying unvarying punishments regardless of any sense of the individual deserts of offenders), contradicts with the universal declaration of human rights and, every other law concerning this matter.

My second goal is to use a comparative historical approach by illustrating the similarities and differences in cruel and unusual punishments over time and place. We will review the current practice of harsh punishments in both Iran and United States. Through this comparative historical perspective, the reader can gain appreciation of the western and Islamic nature of these punishment practices.

Finally the novelty and necessity of the research motivated me. Surprisingly little research has been done focusing on this issue, or they are far from comprehensive. My study should not be viewed as the ultimate source for reviewing inhuman punishment in the United States and Iran. I hope that I can follow this study by providing more intimate detailed analysis at the actual cases, other countries, and more in the way of anecdotal information.

The condemnation of cruel and unusual punishment is universal. In national and international law the definition of what constitute cruel and unusual punishment is highly subjective. Almost all countries prohibit inhuman punishments. Countries vary in the extent to which they legally permit what would commonly be considered cruel and degrading punishment or treatment. Most countries absolutely prohibit any form of torture.

The American concept of cruel and unusual punishment is traceable to early English history (English Bill of Rights). The prohibition against cruel and unusual punishment in the English Bill of Rights restricted the imposition of excessive degree of punishment. Upon introduction to North America, the concept took an expanded meaning and emphasis was placed upon restricting the kind of punishment that might be imposed. The Eighth Amendment to the U.S. Constitution provides that "cruel and unusual punishments" shall not be inflicted.

This provision is applicable to the states through the Due Process Clause of the Fourteenth Amendment, and similar provisions exist in some state constitutions. While some such state constitutional provisions are held to be of identical scope to that of the Eighth Amendment. Other provisions are deemed to afford greater protection than their federal counterpart. A textual parallelism between state and federal constitutional prohibitions against cruel and unusual punishment does not foreclose a more expansive interpretation of the state constitutional prohibition than of the similar federal provision. Conversely, textual dissimilarities between state and federal prohibitions do not bar a state court from looking to cases interpreting the federal provision for guidance in interpreting the state prohibition.

When discussing punishment in Iran one must keep in mind the relationship between the state and concept of justice is derived from the religious principle of Islam. The Sharia, general and particular rules of Islamic corpus juris, is not merely a code of law but a code of conduct of behavior and ethics, a combination of law and morality, one and inseparable. Evidence of this relationship can be seen in the Penal Code and punishments of Iranian law which imposes the death penalty on those who are deemed "Corrupt on earth." Also Iran is likely to execute offenders of major economic crimes with subversive intent..., impose corporal punishment and other inhuman punishments.

Throughout history, varying punishments were deemed cruel and unusual, including surgical castration, vasectomies, and certain forms of the death penalty. The meaning of "cruel and unusual" must draw from the evolving standards of decency that mark the progress of a maturing society. The test, then, will ordinarily be a cumulative one: If a punishment is unusually severe, if there is a strong probability that it is inflicted arbitrarily, if it is substantially rejected by contemporary society, and if there is no reason to believe that it serves any penal purpose more effectively than some less severe punishment, then the continued infliction of that punishment violates the idea that the State may not inflict inhuman and uncivilized punishments upon those convicted of crimes.

The exact meaning of the concept has vacillated from decade to decade, court to court, and place to place. Various tests have been suggested by United States scholars and jurists, the most elaborated being Justice Brennan's in Furman v. Georgia. The concept becomes more and more important with passing of each decade to the twentieth century.

This book is organized in five chapters. Chapter one has three sections, defining the cruel and unusual punishment at the national and International levels, using the United States and Iran as examples. It outlines the background of prohibition of cruel and unusual punishment under International Conventions from Convention Against Torture and other Cruel, Inhuman or Degrading Treatment or Punishment, the Universal

Declaration of Human Rights, the International Covenant on Civil and Political Rights (ICCPR), the African Charter to the American Convention of Human Rights.

Chapter two discusses the death penalty as a cruel and unusual punishment per se from the colonial period in United States and ancient era in Iran to modern time. The research questions in this chapter are based on two claims: 1- The interpretation of death penalty as a cruel and unusual punishment in national level still allows application of these punishments: 2- United States and Iran can apply the International definition of cruel and unusual punishment to avoid death penalty. We consider whether national courts adopt international standards in the application of cruel and unusual punishment? Does such application offend sovereignty?

Chapter three examines execution methods and challenges various methods of inflicting the death penalty. Execution methods in the United States (even lethal injection) and in Iran (sample among Islamic countries) are still harsh. What is going on in these countries? How cultural roots of harsh punishment have emerged in contemporary America and Iran? How harsh criminal punishments can develop in a society that belongs to the Western liberal tradition (United States) and a society which has old cultural roots (Iran)?

Chapter four challenges the proportionality doctrine and evolving standards concerning cruel and unusual death penalty in general, juvenile and mentally retarded executions, imprisonment as excessive and also describes how criminalization of status constitute cruel and unusual punishment. Many scholars argue that cruel and unusual punishment phrase was meant to prevent torture and inhuman physical punishment. Close examination of early English documents shows clearly that the clause was intended to prohibit excessive punishments rather than particular modes of inflicting them. Chapter four concludes with the five goals of punishment (deterrence, retribution, rehabilitation, incapacitation or expression of society's condemnation). And are these goals observable in the harsh system of punishment that executes juveniles or mild?

Chapter five focuses on corporal punishment and different scholarly debates regarding this issue. Much has been written regarding corporal punishment in schools. In this book corporal punishment is beyond the meaning of corporal punishment in schools and it includes judicial corporal punishment. Considering many factors we explain if corporal punishment can meet with the philosophical challenge of just punishment and can also go much of the way to solving the fiscal problem of criminal punishment or merely represents the "essence of barbarism".

Chapter 1

Origins of Cruel and Unusual Punishment

'I call upon you to remember that cruel punishments have an inevitable tendency to produce cruelty in the people'.

Sir Samuel Romilly 1813

I   The Concept of Cruel and Unusual Punishment

1 Prohibition of Cruel and Unusual Punishment under International Law

A International Instruments

The prohibition of torture and cruel, inhuman or degrading treatment or punishment is set out in all the major international instruments dealing with civil and political rights, including:

· Art. 5 of the Universal Declaration of Human Rights of 1948;
· Art. 3 of the European Convention of Human Rights of 1950;
· Art. 7 of the International Covenant on Civil and Political Rights of 1966;
· U.N. Convention against Torture and other Cruel, Inhuman or Degrading Treatment or Punishment of 1984;
· European Convention for the Prevention of Torture and Inhuman or Degrading Treatment or Punishment of 1987;
· Art. 37 (a) of the Convention on the Rights of the Child;
. Article 4 of the Charter of Fundamental Rights of the EU states;

It is also prohibited by the four Geneva Conventions of 12 August 1949 and their two Additional Protocols and in national Constitutions and domestic legislation throughout the world.

The *Universal Declaration of Human Rights*[1] is not legally binding in the sense that treaties or conventions bind parties under international law. Although such declarations qua declarations are not binding, they carry great weight and may be taken

---

[1] Universal Declaration of Human Rights, G.A. Res. 217A, U.N. Doc. A/810 at 71 (1948).

as evidence of binding customary international law. It is generally accepted that the Universal Declaration of Human Rights --which lacked legal obligation at the time of its adoption in 1948--has become part of customary international law as a result of subsequent state practice. [2]

The Universal Declaration of Human Rights indicates that "no one shall be subjected to torture or to cruel, inhuman, or degrading treatment or punishment."[3] This phrase is echoed in later international treaties, most notably the Convention Against Torture and the International Covenant on Civil and Political Rights. As will be seen, identical language is also repeated in a number of regional human rights instruments.

The *European Convention for the Protection of Human Rights and Fundamental Freedoms* and its Eight Protocols were signed in 1950, and entered into force in 1953.[4] The preamble to the Convention states that its aim is to secure the "universal and effective recognition and observance of the rights therein declared." Among the rights "therein declared" is the right not to be subjected to torture or to inhuman or degrading treatment or punishment.[5]

The *International Covenant on Civil and Political Rights*,[6] which entered into force in 1976, explicitly prohibits torture or other cruel, inhuman, or degrading treatment. A separate provision prohibits derogation from this standard.[7] In its general comments to article 7, the Human Rights Committee observed that the purpose of the article is to "protect the integrity and dignity of the individual."[8] Article 7 states: No one shall be

---

[2] Rosalyn Higgins, *The Development of International Law Through the Political Organs of the United Nations*, pp. 168-170, The American Journal of International Law, Vol. 59, No. 1 (Jan., 1965).

[3] *Supra* note 1, at Art 5.

[4] Convention for the Protection of Human Rights and Fundamental Freedoms, Nov. 4, 1950, 213 U.N.T.S. 221.

[5] *Id.* at Art. 3.

[6] G.A. Res. 2200, U.N. GAOR, 22d Sess., Supp. No. 16, at 52, U.N. Doc. A/6316 (1967).

[7] *Id,* at Art. 4,7.

[8] U.N. GAOR, 37th Sess., Supp. No. 40, at 94, U.N. Doc. A/37/40 (1982).

subjected to torture or to cruel, inhuman or degrading treatment or punishment. In particular, no one shall be subjected without his free consent to medical or scientific experimentation. However, the Covenant fails to define or explain the phrase cruel, inhuman, or degrading treatment.

The *Convention Against Torture and Other Cruel, Inhuman or Degrading Treatment or Punishment* (Convention Against Torture) was opened for signature in 1984.[9] Although the term "torture" is defined in the Convention but the Convention's is greatly limited by its failure to define "cruel, inhuman, and degrading treatment." Parties are merely obligated to undertake to prevent other acts of cruel, inhuman or degrading treatment or punishment which do not amount to torture as defined in article 1[10]: "The term "torture" means any act by which severe pain or suffering, whether physical or mental, is intentionally inflicted on a person for such purposes as obtaining from him or a third person information or a confession, punishing him for an act he or a third person has committed or is suspected of having committed, or intimidating or coercing him or a third person, or for any reason based on discrimination of any kind, when such pain or suffering is inflicted by or at the instigation of or with the consent or acquiescence of a public official or other person acting in an official capacity. It does not include pain or suffering arising only from, inherent in or incidental to lawful sanctions."

Article 16 Convention against torture calls upon each State Party to undertake to prevent "other forms of cruel, inhuman or degrading treatment or punishment not amount to torture" as that term is defined in the Convention, inter alia through many of the same educational and remedial measures.[11]

Also the Convention establishes a Committee Against Torture to monitor and enforce compliance with its provisions, on the basis of reports from States Party, its own inquiries, and consideration of complaints that other States Party or individuals submit.[12]

---

[9] Convention Against Torture and Other Cruel, Inhuman or Degrading Treatment or Punishment, opened for signature Dec. 10, 1984, G.A. Res. 46, U.N. GAOR, 39th Sess., Supp. No. 51, at 197, U.N. Doc. E/CN.4/1984/72, Annex (1984).

[10] *Id*, at Art. 1.

[11] The Convention Against Torture and Other Cruel, Inhuman or Degrading Treatment or Punishment, *supra* note 9, Art 16.

[12] *Id*, Arts. 17-24.

The scope of phrase "cruel, inhuman or degrading treatment or punishment" Article 16 of Convention against torture exceeds existing United States law. Because it is unclear how the Convention's terms will be interpreted, it was considered necessary to condition United States ratification of the convention on a formal reservation to the effect that the United States considers itself bound by the obligation under Article 16 only insofar as the term cruel, inhuman or degrading treatment or punishment means the cruel, unusual and inhumane treatment or punishment prohibited by the fifth, eighth and/or fourteenth amendments to the Constitution.[13]

Although the enforcement in the international arena is always problematic due to considerations of state sovereignty the Convention Against Torture requires parties to take "effective measures to prevent torture" and explicitly forbids parties from justifying acts of torture because of "political instability or public emergency."[14]

Enforcement of the provisions of the Convention Against Torture is accomplished through moral suasion and exposure to adverse public opinion rather than through particular sanctions. Parties are required to report within one year on measures taken to meet their obligations. Subsequent reports are required every four years.[15] Parties may, but are not required to, subject themselves to the competence of the United Nations Committee Against Torture to hear complaints against them from other state parties or from individuals. Even after the United Nations Committee Against Torture has received "reliable information which appears to it to contain well-founded indications that torture is being systematically practiced," the committee's authorization to act is quite limited.[16]

The *European Convention for the Prevention of Torture and Inhuman or Degrading Treatment or Punishment* was concluded in Strasbourg in 1987, and entered into force on February 1, 1989.[17] It provides the same definition of torture as the other

---

[13] David P. Stewart, **The Torture Convention and the Reception of International Criminal Law within the United States**, 15 Nova L. Rev. 449 (spring 1991).

[14] *Supra* note 9, at Art. 2.

[15] *Supra* note 9, at Art 19.

[16] *Supra* note 9, at Art. 20-22.

torture conventions, and likewise lacks an explanation of its prohibition of cruel, inhuman, or degrading treatment or punishment. Unlike its predecessors, however, the European Convention establishes a Committee for the Prevention of Torture and Inhuman or Degrading Treatment or Punishment, which has the right to conduct visits to member states' prisons.

The Organization of American States (OAS) developed a regional code of human rights protection in 1969. The *American Convention on Human Rights*[18] entered into force in 1978. Article 5, the Right to Humane Treatment, states that "no one shall be subjected to torture or to cruel, inhuman, or degrading punishment or treatment. All persons deprived of their liberty shall be treated with respect for the inherent dignity of the human person."[19] The American Convention does not expand on what "respect for the inherent dignity of the human person" entails, nor does it define "torture" or "cruel, inhuman, or degrading punishment or treatment."

The *African Charter on Human and Peoples' Rights* was signed in 1986. Article 5 provides: "Every individual shall have the right to the respect of the dignity inherent in a human being . . . . All forms of exploitation and degradation of man particularly . . . torture, and cruel, inhuman or degrading punishment and treatment shall be prohibited."[20] Neither the Article nor its commentary defines "exploitation," "degradation," or "cruel, inhuman or degrading punishment and treatment."

The *Inter-American Convention to Prevent and Punish Torture*, which entered into force in 1987, has more than twenty signatories.[21] The wording and structure of the Inter-American Torture Convention is parallel to the international Convention Against Torture. The same definition of torture is provided in article 2, and as with the international convention, it does not define "other cruel, inhuman, or degrading treatment." The preamble states: Reaffirming that all acts of torture or any other cruel,

---

[17] Council of Europe Doc. No. H (87)4, reprinted in 27 I.L.M. 1152 (1988).

[18] Nov. 22, 1969, O.A.S. Treaty Series No. 36, O.A.S. Official Records OEA/Ser. L/V/II, Doc. 21, rev. 6 (1970).

[19] *Id*, at Art. 5.

[20] Albert P. Blaustein, *Human Rights Sourcebook,* p 115, UNESDOC Documents and Publications (1987).

[21] Inter-American Convention to Prevent and Punish Torture, Dec. 9, 1985, 25 I.L.M. 51.

inhuman, or degrading treatment or punishment constitute an offense against human dignity and a denial of the principles set forth in the Charter of the Organization of American States and in the Charter of the United Nations and are violations of fundamental human rights and freedoms . . . . [22]

Art. 37 (a) of the *Convention on the Rights of the Child* States: Parties shall ensure that: No child shall be subjected to torture or other cruel, inhuman or degrading treatment or punishment. Neither capital punishment nor life imprisonment without possibility of release shall be imposed for offences committed by persons below eighteen years of age.

CRC has been ratified by 192 states, except Somalia and the U.S.A. In 1993 Iran joined the CRC with a precondition that wherever the provisions of the convention conflicted with Iranian Civil Code and Islamic laws the Iranian government would not be bound to comply with them. To presume that Iran can disregard the provisions of the Convention under the pretext that they conflict with the Iranian Law is wrong and a willful breach of the Convention, because in that case there was no need for the country to join the Child Rights Convention. Meanwhile we must not forget that international law (including the Child Rights Convention) must be considered as compulsory in the same way that domestic law is also compulsory in Iran, otherwise it is senseless for a government to join an international convention or treaty and declare that it would comply with or will not comply with it whenever it deems prudent.[23]

Article 4 of the *Charter of Fundamental Rights of the EU states* Prohibited torture and inhuman or degrading treatment or punishment:
"No one shall be subjected to torture or to inhuman or degrading treatment or punishment".

The four *Geneva Conventions* and Protocols, commonly known as the Geneva Conventions of 1949, have more or less codified the laws of war.[24] Article 3 of Geneva

---

[22] *Id.*

[23] Shirin Ebadi, *Children Rights*, Tehran, Iran: Kanoon publication, (1996) [In Farsi].

[24] Convention for the Amelioration of the Condition of the Wounded and Sick in Armed Forces in the Field, Aug. 12, 1949, 6 U.S.T. 3114, 75 U.N.T.S. 31; Convention for the Amelioration of the Condition of the Wounded, Sick, and Shipwrecked Members of Armed Forces at Sea, Aug. 12,

Convention[25] relative to the Treatment of Prisoners of War, Adopted on 12 August 1949 by the Diplomatic Conference for the Establishment of International Conventions for the Protection of Victims of War, held in Geneva from 21 April to 12 August, 1949 indicates: In the case of armed conflict not of an international character occurring in the territory of one of the High Contracting Parties, each party to the conflict shall be bound to apply, as a minimum, the following provisions: Persons taking no active part in the hostilities, including members of armed forces who have laid down their arms and those placed hors de combat by sickness, wounds, detention, or any other cause, shall in all circumstances be treated humanely, without any adverse distinction founded on race, colour, religion or faith, sex, birth or wealth, or any other similar criteria. To this end the following acts are and shall remain prohibited at any time and in any place whatsoever with respect to the above-mentioned persons: Violence to life and person, in particular murder of all kinds, mutilation, cruel treatment and torture.

B Customary International Law

The prohibition against cruel and unusual punishment is hardly a new development in international law. Indeed, it has been recognized so often and so widely that most scholars and practitioners consider it a principle of customary international law binding on all states.

The Statute of the International Court of Justice (ICJ) recognizes international custom as a source of international law. Article 38(1) (b) of the Statute of the ICJ defines international custom as "evidence of a general practice accepted by the law."[26] Customary international law is established by acts of States that are similar, repeated, and undertaken with the conscious conviction of the parties that their actions are required by international law.[27]

1949, 6 U.S.T. 3217, 75 U.N.T.S. 85; Geneva Convention Relative to the Treatment of Prisoners of War, Aug. 12, 1949, 6 U.S.T. 3316, 75 U.N.T.S. 135; Convention Relative to the Protection of Civilian Persons in Time of War, Aug. 12, 1949, 6 U.S.T. 3516, 75 U.N.T.S. 287.

[25] Article 3 of the four Geneva Conventions of 1949 prohibits "cruel treatment and torture," as well as "outrages upon personal dignity, in particular, humiliating and degrading treatment."

[26] Statute of the International Court of Justice, June 26, 1945, Art. 38(1) (b), 59 Stat. 1031, 1060, T.S. No. 993.

Thus, there are two elements necessary to establish a customary norm: state practice, and a sense of legal obligation, or opinio juris State practice consists of the duration, consistency, repetition, and generality of the particular custom, when there are few contrary rules to be surmounted and there is an overwhelming necessity to preserve a sense of regulation in international relations. [28] Opinio juris is more than mere acts of courtesy, fairness, or morality. It connotes a sense of legal obligation. Thus, not only must the acts concerned amount to a settled practice, states must believe that they are conforming to what amounts to a legal duty. [29]

Among the International instruments binding cruel and unusual punishment the Universal Declaration of Human Rights --which lacked legal obligation at the time of its adoption in 1948--has become part of customary international law as a result of subsequent state practice.[30] Although such declarations qua declarations are not binding, they carry great weight and may be taken as evidence of binding customary international law.

Although the International Covenant on Civil and Political Rights has not yet achieved the status of customary international law, nearly one hundred states have become parties to it. To explicitly binding the parties, the Convention Against Torture may fairly be taken as evidence of customary international law.

It is generally accepted that the Geneva Conventions have achieved the status of customary international law even if Protocol I and II have not.[31] At the end of 1990, there were 164 states parties to the Geneva Conventions, ninety-nine states parties to Protocol

---

[27] Lazare Kopelmanas, *Custom as a Means of the Creation of International Law*, 18 Brit. Y.B. Int'l L. 127, 129 (1937).

[28] Malcolm N. Shaw, *International Law*, p 61, Cambridge University Press, (1986) (customary law is grounded upon the performance of state activities and the convergence of practices).

[29] Rebecca M. Wallace, *International Law,* p 14, Sweet & Maxwell publication (1986).

[30] See, e.g., Rosalyn Higgins, *The Development of International Law Through the Political Organs of the United Nations* 2-10 (1963); John P. Humphrey, *The Universal Declaration of Human Rights, in Human Rights: Thirty Years After the Universal Declaration* 29 (B.G. Ramcharan ed., 1979); Louis Sohn, *The New International Law: Protection of the Rights of Individuals Rather than States*, 32 Am. U. L. Rev. 1, 17 (1982).

[31] Theodor Meron, *The Geneva Conventions as Customary Law*, 81 Am. J. Int'l L. 348 (1987).

I, and eighty-nine states parties to Protocol II.[32] The scope of Geneva Convention III's prisoner protections is a limited one: it applies only to prisoners of war. Protocol II has an even more limited application: to non-international armed conflicts. Nevertheless, both instruments provide basic definitions and relevant standards that clearly evince dawning norms of customary international law for all prisoners.

Customary International law barring cruel and unusual punishment is still evidence of present International societal mores. This prohibition requires that no one shall be subjected to torture and cruel, inhuman or degrading punishment apply universally and without any limitations in allegedly valid reservations or understandings during ratification of a relevant treaty. One might think that it should be relatively easy to convince a judge that this norm exist. But there is enormous difficulty in doing so. This difficulty is a political one and dose not arise because the prohibition on and degrading punishment dose not really exist in International law.[33]

The concepts of human dignity and the right not to be subjected to "cruel, inhuman, or degrading treatment" appear over and over in international treaties. Therefore the prohibition of cruel and unusual punishment constitutes customary international law, or at a minimum, a "general principle of law recognized by civilized nations" within the meaning of article 38(1) of the Statute of the ICJ.

C Peremptory norms

Certain rules of international law are of such importance that they are considered to be "peremptory norms", otherwise known as *jus cogens*, which all states must abide by under any circumstance. The Vienna Convention on the Law of Treaties defines a norm of *jus cogens* as "a norm accepted and recognized by the international community of States as a whole as a norm from which no derogation is permitted and which can be modified only by a subsequent norm of international law having the same character". Jus Cogens are those from which no derogation can be justified and which can only be changed by a subsequent norm of the same character.

---

[32] Status of Four Geneva Conventions and Additional Protocols I and II, Report of the International Committee of the Red Cross, I.C.R.C. No. DDM/JUR 91/51 CPS/5 (Dec. 31, 1990), reprinted in 30 I.L.M. 397, 402 (1991).

[33] Paul Hoffman, *The Blank Stare Phenomenon: Proving Customary International Law in U.S. Courts*, 26 Ga. J. Int'l & Comp. L. 181 (1995-1996).

The prohibition of cruel and unusual punishment has achieved the status of *jus cogens*: it is a non-derogable norm of international law which holds the highest hierarchical position among other norms and principle.[34]

Therefore, the prohibition against cruel and unusual punishment is also non-derogable under general human rights treaties and that, as such, cannot be suspended under any circumstance. Under the Geneva Conventions, the use of ill-treatment constitutes a grave breach giving rise to universal jurisdiction. The Rome Statute lists ill treatment as a separate category (in addition to torture) in its list of acts which may constitute crimes against humanity.[35] Similarly, ill-treatment is also considered by the Rome Statute as a war crime in both international and non-international armed conflict.[36]

Despite the considerable body of international law prohibiting such conditions, torture and cruel, inhuman, and degrading treatment are practiced in nearly every region of the world.[37] In 1990, such violations were reported by Africa Watch in Kenya, Liberia, Malawi, Mauritania, Nigeria, Somalia, South Africa, Sudan, and Zimbabwe; by Americas Watch in Argentina, Brazil, Chile, Guatemala, Honduras, Mexico, Panama, Paraguay, and Peru; by Asia Watch in Afghanistan, Burma, Cambodia, China, Indonesia, Nepal, South Korea, and Vietnam; by Helsinki Watch in Turkey, the U.S.S.R., and Yugoslavia; and by Middle East Watch in Algeria, Iran, Iraq, the Israeli Occupied

---

[34] Eur. Ct. H.R., Al Adsani v. The United Kingdom, Judgment of 21 November 2001, § 60-61; Eur. Ct. H.R., Ireland v. The United Kingdom, Judgment of 18 January 1978, § 163.

[35] Article 7 Crimes Against Humanity: (k) Other inhumane acts of a similar character intentionally causing great suffering, or serious injury to body or to mental or physical health, Rome Statute of the International Criminal Court, U.N. Doc. A/CONF.183/9.

[36] Article 8 War Crimes :a) Grave breaches of the Geneva Conventions of 12 August 1949, namely, any of the following acts against persons or property protected under the provisions of the relevant Geneva Convention: ii) Torture or inhuman treatment, including biological experiment ;c) In the case of an armed conflict not of an international character, serious violations of Article 3 common to the four Geneva Conventions of 12 August 1949, namely, any of the following acts committed against persons taking no active part in the hostilities, including members of armed forces who have laid down their arms and those placed hors de combat by sickness, wounds, detention or any other cause: (i) Violence to life and person, in particular murder of all kinds, mutilation, cruel treatment and torture;(ii) Committing outrages upon personal dignity, in particular humiliating and degrading treatment.

[37] Human Rights Watch World Report 1990 (1991).

Territories, Morocco, and Syria.[38] During the same year, Amnesty International received reports of torture and other ill treatment of detainees from more than ninety countries.[39]

The 1992 Amnesty International Annual Report recounted torture and ill treatment in at least 104 countries.[40] In 2005 this number has been decreased to following countries: Albania, Algeria, Brazil, Cameroon, Chile, China, Congo, Dominican Republic, Ecuador, Equatorial Guinea, Eritrea, Estonia, Georgia, Indonesia, Iran, Iraq, Jamaica, Jordan, Kenya, Korea (Democratic people's republic of), Latvia, Malaysia, Mauritania, Mexico, Moldova, Mongolia, Myanmar, Nepal, Peru, Saudi Arabia, Sudan, Swaziland, Syria, Tajikistan, Togo, Trinidad and Tobago, Tunisia, Turkey, Uganda, United Arab Emirates, United States.[41]

Figure 1-1 shows the changes over time (From 1985-2005) in the proportion of countries in the world that use cruel, inhuman, and degrading treatment. The trend over time was an increase from the early 1990s to the mid 1990, followed by a decrease in violation of cruel, inhuman, and degrading treatment in the late 1990 and this trend climbs during the recent years, and in 2005, Amnesty International Annual Report recounted torture and ill treatment in only 41 countries.

---

[38] *Id.*

[39] Amnesty International Annual Report Summary 1991 (1991).

[40] Amnesty International Annual Report Summary 1992 (1992).

[41] Amnesty International Annual Report Summary 2006 (2006).

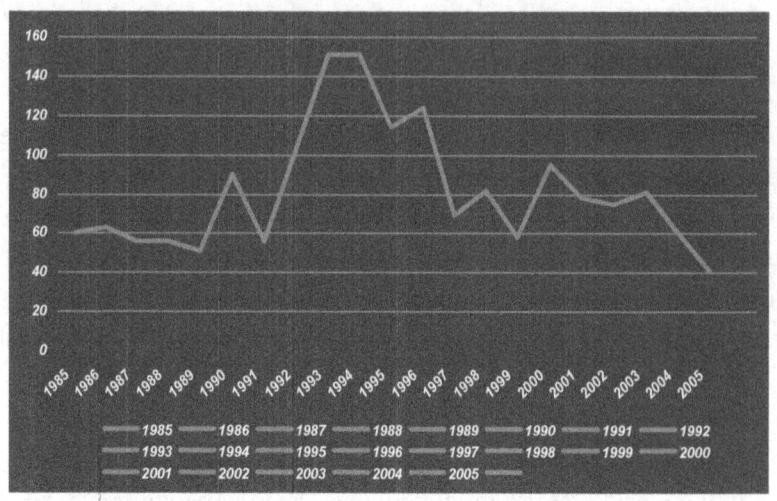

Figure 1. Practice of torture and cruel, inhuman, and degrading treatment in the world by year, 1985-2005. Source: Amnesty International Annual Report 1986-2006.

Figure 1-1

2 Prohibition of Cruel and Unusual Punishment under National Laws

A United States

The American concept of cruel and unusual punishment is clearly traceable to early English history.[42] First it seems that the phrase meant to prevent torture and inhuman physical punishment. However close examination of early documents shows that the clause was intended to prohibit excessive punishment rather than particular modes of inflicting them.[43]

---

[42] Larry Charles Berkson, *The Concept of Cruel and Unusual Punishment*, p 3, Lexington Books (1975).

[43] *Id.*

The present language of concept is first found in the ***English Bill of Rights*** (1689), in the late 17th century, England was at the end of the "shaky reign of King James II." Abuses during "the reign of James II, and to a lesser extent that of Charles II, provided the historical background of the provisions of the Bill of Rights."[44] After James II fled England, parliament drew up a declaration of rights "which the new monarchs, William and Mary, would ratify."[45] This document was designed "to prevent a recurrence of recent events" in England,[46] which stated: "Excessive bail ought not to be required, nor excessive fines imposed; nor cruel and unusual punishment inflicted." However, England did not abolish its most cruel punishments at early dates. In 1790 the burning of women was ended. In 1814, drawing and quartering was abolished. In 1841 Parliament prohibited the whipping of women, and pillorying in 1837. In 1870 beheading was abolished. Finally almost all methods of extinguishing life were abolished by Parliament in 1965. Despite some early retreat from cruel and unusual punishment, it was more than two centuries before most of the brutal forms of punishment began to disappear.[47]

The Claim of Right of 1689 stated "that the forcing of Leiges to depone against themselves in capital crimes, however the punishment be restricted is contrary to law."[48] Significantly, unlike the other "barbarous" punishments which occurred during the Bloody Assizes, and which continued after the Bill of Rights of 1689, inquisitorial proceedings ceased around this time.[49] By the turn of the eighteenth century, compelled confessions had largely disappeared.[50] In spite of this, scholars have relied upon the Oates case to conclude that the phrase "seems to have meant a severe punishment

---

[44] Anthony F. Granucci, *"Nor Cruel and Unusual Punishments Inflicted:" The Original Meaning*, 57 Cal. L. Rev. 839, 848 (1969).

[45] *Id.*

[46] David Ogg, ***England in the Reigns of James II and William III*** *175*, Oxford Univ. Press (1955).

[47] Larry Charles Berkson, *supra* note 42.

[48] ***Claim of Right***, pp 252-258, reprinted in Gordon Donaldson, Scottish Historical Documents, Barnes & Noble, Inc. (1970).

[49] M. Macnair, ***The Early Development of the Privilege Against Self-Incrimination***, 10 Oxford J. Legal Studies 66, (1990).

[50] Lawrence Herman, ***The Unexplored Relationship Between the Privilege Against Compulsory Self-Incrimination and the Involuntary Confession Rule*** (Part 1), 53 Ohio St. L. J. 101, 147 (1992).

unauthorized by statute and not within the jurisdiction of the court to impose"[51] and a "reiteration of the English policy against disproportionate penalties."[52]

The first detailed enactment by a colonial legislature on the subject of human rights was the ***Massachusetts Body of Liberties*** (1641). Its concern was about torture, brutality, and punishment and reflected in the six articles.[53]

Language reminiscent of the Eighth Amendment was first introduced into the laws of Massachusetts by Reverend Nathaniel Ward.[54] Ward, a minister, had also been trained in the law. After being "suspended, excommunicated and deprived of his benefice" in England, Ward came to Massachusetts[55]. While he was there, a period of political unrest ensued. Following some of this upheaval in the Massachusetts colony, a series of committees was established. Reverend Ward was appointed to one of these committees. In 1641, a proposed code which Reverend Ward drafted was circulated and ultimately enacted "under the title Body of Liberties."[56] This code has been recognized as "the most important as a forerunner of the federal Bill of Rights." The Body of Liberties prohibited "Barbarous and inhumane" torture and "bodilie punishments."[57]

The prohibition that Ward drafted for this code can be traced back to the writings of Englishman Robert Beale. This is well documented in Anthony Granucci's groundbreaking article on the subject. Sir Robert Beale had been a member of the High Commission which had been turned into an ecclesiastical court and had used "torture to

---

[51] Anthony F. Granucci, *supra* note 44.

[52] *Id.*

[53] Larry Charles Berkson, *supra* note 42.

[54] F.C. Gray, ***Remarks on the Early Laws of Massachusetts Bay***, p 193, reprinted in Collection of the Massachusetts Historical Society (3d Series 1843).

[55] Recent Cases, ***Constitutional Law - Cruel and Unusual Punishment Provision of Eighth Amendment as Restriction Upon State Action Through the Due Process Clause***, 34 Minn. L. Rev. 134, 135 (1950).

[56] *Id.*

[57] Massachusetts Body of Liberties (1641), reprinted in Bernard Schwartz, I The Bill of Rights, A Documentary History 71, Chelsea House (1971).

extract confessions." Beale objected to the use of torture "when authorized by the royal prerogative" and other inquisitorial methods.[58] Later Beale published a manuscript in which, among other things, he condemned the use of torture by the High Commission.[59] In response to this, Whitgift, the architect of the High Commission, had a "Schedule of Misdemeanors" drawn up against Beale for condemning such things as the use of the rack as "cruel, barbarous, contrary to law."[60]

In addition to concerns about torture that was used to extract confessions in the absence of a conviction and bodily punishments that were "inhumane Barbarous or cruel." [61] The meaning of this document is made clearer when considered along with the interpretations of the government officials attempting to implement it at the time.

In explaining the meaning of the proscriptions contained in the Body of Liberties, ministers to then Massachusetts governor Bradford specifically used the word "punishment" when referring to torturous interrogation.[62] Based on this historical record, it is clear that the Body of Liberties was motivated by and intended to prevent conduct that included such punishment as torturous interrogations.

With adoption of the *Virginia Declaration of Rights* on June 12, 1776, new era in the history of cruel and unusual punishment began. Less than one hundred years later, this language would be "transcribed verbatim into the Virginia Declaration of Rights and, with the substitution of 'shall' for "ought,'" [63] it became the Eighth Amendment. Because of this clear link, when interpreting the meaning of the Eighth Amendment, historians and courts alike have tried to discern the meaning of the phrase in England at the time it was adopted there.[64] Article 9 of Declaration stated: "Excessive bail ought not to be

---

[58] Larry Charles Berkson, *supra* note 42.

[59] *The Dictionary of National Biography*, Oxford Univ Press (1921-27).

[60] *Id.*

[61] Richard L. Perry, *Sources of Our Liberty*, p 222-23, American Bar Foundation (1959).

[62] R. Carter Pittman, *The Colonial Constitutional History of the Privilege Against Self-Incrimination in America*, 21 Va. L. Rev. 763, 768 (1935).

[63] *Id.*

[64] *Id.*

required, nor excessive fines imposed, nor cruel and unusual punishment inflicted." And, repeated exactly the phrase of the statement in the English Bill of Rights.

After American Revolution each colony except Rhode Island organized conventions to draft and adopt constitutions. From thirty states, Connecticut, Pennsylvania, Delaware, Virginia, North Carolina, Massachusetts, Maryland, and New Hampshire adopted constitutions that contained separate bills of rights[65]. Of these only Connecticut and Pennsylvania did not include prohibitions against cruel and unusual punishment.[66]

In 1777 the Continental Congress ratified the Articles of Confederation. In 1783 a committee chaired by Thomas Jefferson had been appointed to prepare plans for temporary government of the Northwest territory. Various committees sequently considered the governing of the area; they began to suggest that certain fundamental rights be guaranteed. The final document of 1783 contained the Bill of Rights that stated: 'No cruel or unusual punishment shall be inflicted.' In 1787 the Constitutional convention was held, but no bill of rights was attached to the proposal document.[67]

Finally by adoption of the Constitution commenced a new era in the history of cruel and unusual punishment. On June 1789, James Madison introduced the first draft of the Federal bill of rights in to the United States House of Representative. Part of his fourth Article stated: 'Excessive Bail shall not be required, nor excessive fines imposed, nor cruel and unusual punishment inflicted'[68]. There was no important change in the wording but the substitution of the imperative shall for the flaccid ought implies that the prohibition was considered stronger wording in compare to pervious documents.

The final unchanged version of Amendment was sent to Senate on August 24, 1789. The twelve amendments were accepted by the house on September 25, 1789,

---

[65] Four states: New Jersey, Georgia, New York and South Carolina scattered individual rights throughout the main text of their constitutions rather than including separate bills of rights.

[66] Bernard Schwartz, *The Bill of Rights: A Documentary History,* pp 231-79, New York: McGrew Hill Book Co. (1971).

[67] *Id.*

[68] *Annals of Congress*, vol. 1, column 434, Lancaster, PA (1974).

making it the second and third times those national legislative bodies has seen fit to guarantee the right.[69] Thus on December 15 1791, the cruel and unusual punishment clause became the eight Amendment and formally part of the law of the land.

The framers of **Eight Amendment** intended to consider a meaning far different from that of its English precursor. This time, the phrase of cruel and unusual punishment was interpreted much more broadly by prohibition of torture and other cruel punishments. Finally on December 15, 1791 the cruel and unusual punishment clause became the Eight Amendment and formally part of the law in the United States.

The Eighth Amendment deals only with criminal punishment, and has no application to civil processes. In holding the Amendment inapplicable to the infliction of corporal punishment upon schoolchildren for disciplinary purposes, the Court explained that the cruel and unusual punishments clause ''circumscribes the criminal process in three ways: First, it limits the kinds of punishment that can be imposed on those convicted of crimes; second, it proscribes punishment grossly disproportionate to the severity of the crime; and third, it imposes substantive limits on what can be made criminal and punished as such.''[70] These limitations, the Court thought, should not be extended outside the criminal process.

The Eighth Amendment that indicates "Excessive bail shall not be required, nor excessive fines imposed, nor cruel and unusual punishments inflicted" is based on traditional definitions, cruel and unusual punishment includes any uncommon penalty imposed by the court on a person in response to a crime, for the purposes of intentionally inflicting pain and of deterring illegal conduct in the future. Accordingly, the Cruel and Unusual Punishment Clause of the United States Constitution was interpreted to prohibit cruel and unusual sentences, such as drawing and punishments that are grossly disproportional to the actual or threatened harm and the offender's culpability.[71] For Instance, Life imprisonment may be constitutional for intentional murder but not for a strict liability offense of overtime parking. Justice Scalia indicates Cruel and Unusual Punishment Clause, prohibits only "always-and-everywhere 'cruel' punishments." A

---

[69] Kammen, Michael G, **Documentary History of Constitution**, pp 321-24, Washington: Department of State (1894).

[70] Ingraham v. Wright, 430 U.S. 651, 667 (1977).

[71] Sara L. Rose, Comment: **"Cruel and Unusual Punishment" Need Not Be Cruel, Unusual, or Punishment**, 24 Cap. U.L. Rev. 827 (1995).

punishment may qualify as "always-and-everywhere" unconstitutional if it is one of "'those modes or acts of punishment that had been considered cruel and unusual at the time that the Bill of Rights was adopted.'"[72]

Many legal scholars assert that the purpose of the Eighth Amendment was to prohibit certain punishments.[73] This view is supported by the earliest cases decided by the Supreme Court; until 1909, the prohibition of cruel and unusual punishment was interpreted as prohibiting only torture and mistreatment.[74]

At first, the case law was inclined to an historical style of interpretation, determining whether or not a punishment was "cruel and unusual" by looking to see if it or a sufficiently similar variant was considered "cruel and unusual" in 1789.[75] But in *Weems v. United States*[76] it was concluded that the framers had not merely intended to bar the reinstitution of procedures and techniques condemned in 1789, but had intended to prevent the authorization of "a coercive cruelty being exercised through other forms of punishment." The Amendment therefore was of an "expansive and vital character"[77] and, in the words of a later Court, "must draw its meaning from the evolving standards of decency that mark the progress of a maturing society."[78]

---

[72] Atkins, 536 U.S. at 349 (Scalia, J., dissenting). In Harmelin v. Michigan, Justice Scalia accordingly rejected a principle of proportionality as contrary to the original understanding.

[73] Anthony F. Granucci, *supra* note 44.

[74] Anthony A. Avey, Casenote, *Criminal Law -- Cruel and Unusual Punishments*.

[75] Wilkerson v. Utah, 99 U.S. 130 (1878); In re Kemmler, 136 U.S. 436 (1890); *cf.* Weems v. United States, 217 U.S. 349, 368–72 (1910). On the present Court, Chief Justice Rehnquist subscribes to this view (*see, e.g.*, Woodson v. North Carolina, 428 U.S. 280, 208 (dissenting)), and the views of Justices Scalia and Thomas appear to be similar. *See, e.g.*, Harmelin v. Michigan, 501 U.S. 957, 966–90 (1991) (Justice Scalia announcing judgment of Court) (relying on original understanding of Amendment and of English practice to argue that there is no proportionality principle in non-capital cases); and Hudson v. McMillian, 503 U.S. 1, 28 (1992) (Justice Thomas dissenting) (objecting to Court's extension of the Amendment "beyond all bounds of history and precedent" in holding that "significant injury" need not be established for sadistic and malicious beating of shackled prisoner to constitute cruel and unusual punishment).

[76] 217 U.S. 349 (1910).

[77] 217 U.S. at 376–77.

Difficulty would attend the effort to define with exactness the extent of the constitutional provision which provides that cruel and unusual punishments shall not be inflicted; but it is safe to affirm that punishments of torture [such as drawing and quartering, embowelling alive, beheading, public dissecting, and burning alive], and all others in the same line of unnecessary cruelty, are forbidden by that amendment to the Constitution.[79]

The state constitutions enacted during and shortly after the Bill of Rights' ratification also counsel against a literal interpretation. Pennsylvania and South Carolina each enacted constitutions during 1790, while ratification of the Bill of Rights was still pending. In addition, Delaware and Kentucky enacted constitutions in 1792 during the year following the Bill of Rights' ratification. All of these constitutions prohibited "cruel punishments," omitting entirely any reference to the term "unusual." Numerous state constitutions enacted after the Founding period used this same language.[80] There is no evidence that this formulation was understood to mean anything different from either the Eighth Amendment's proscription of "cruel and unusual punishments" or the ban of the many state constitutions enacted during the Revolutionary and post-Revolutionary periods against "cruel or unusual" punishments.

The obvious and marked difference in the literal meaning of the state constitutional formulations, the evident absence of any perceived difference, and the affirmative evidence in the history of the English Bill of Rights together point to the same conclusion: the Founders did not understand the Cruel and Unusual Punishment Clause in a literal fashion and did not mean for a punishment's unusual nature to be an invariable requirement of unconstitutionality. As then Chief Justice Burger remarked in his Furman dissent: "There was no discussion of the inter-relationship of the terms 'cruel' and 'unusual,' and there is nothing in the debates supporting the inference that the

---

[78] Trop v. Dulles, 356 U.S. 86.

[79] Wilkerson v. Utah, 99 U.S. 130, 135 (1878).

[80] Pa. Stat. Ann. Const. Art. 1, § 13 & Historical Note (2002) ("nor cruel punishments inflicted"); S.C. Const. Art. IX, § 4 (1790) ("nor cruel punishments inflicted"),. Ala. Const. Art. 1, § 16 (1819); Miss. Const. Art. 1, § 16 (1817); R.I. Const. Art. 1, § 8 (1843); S.D. Const. Art. VI, § 23 (1889); Wash. Const. Art. I., § 14 (1889); cf. Mich. Const. Art. I § 18 (1838) ("[C]ruel and unjust punishments shall not be inflicted.").

Founding Fathers would have been receptive to torturous or excessively cruel punishments even if usual in character or authorized by law." [81]

B   Iran

Iranian history[82] starts in the beginnings of human life on earth. The first Iranian ruling house was a dynasty of lawgivers. Iranian law began to take shape ever since humanity started forming itself, and indeed that happened far away in the past when we consider that man has been living on this globe for over ten million years, or probably for much more many ages than that huge period of time.[83]

The rulers of the first ancient royal house of Iran have all been distinguished as lawgivers. The first person to have framed and codified laws was Prince Uruvakhshaya. The prince was the brother of the immortal hero Krsaspa (Garshasp) and the son of King Thrita, the father of medicine. They were the immediate descendants of great Yima, the brilliant antediluvian monarch.[84] This definitely shows that Law started in Iran in the beginnings of human history.

---

[81] Furman v. Georgia, 408 U.S. 238, 377 (1972) (Burger, C.J., dissenting). See also Trop v. Dulles, 356 U.S. 86 (1957).

[82] The ancient nation of Iran was historically known to the West as Persia until March 21, 1935 (see also History of Persia, History of Levant). Once a major empire in its own right, it has been overrun frequently and has had its territory altered throughout the centuries. Invaded by Arabs, Seljuk Turks, Mongols, and others--and often caught up in the affairs of larger powers--Iran has always reasserted its national identity and has developed as a distinct political and cultural entity. Archeological findings have placed knowledge of Iranian prehistory at middle Paleolithic times (100,000 years ago). The earliest sedentary cultures date from 18,000-14,000 years ago. The sixth millennium BC saw a fairly sophisticated agricultural society and proto-urban population centers. Many dynasties have ruled Iran, the first of which was under the Achaemenids (559 - 330 BC), a dynasty founded by Cyrus the Great. After the Hellenistic period (300 - 250 BC) came the Parthian (250 BC - AD 226) and the Sassaniy (226 - 651) dynasties.

[83] Morteza Ravandi, *Revolution of Law and Administration of Justice*, Tehran, Iran (1988) [In Farsi].

[84] Hassan Pirnia, *History of Ancient Iran*, Donyaye Ketab Publication, Tehran, Iran, (1982) [In Farsi].

Jurisprudence is often said to have a very ancient history in all annals of humanity. Every civilized nation of antiquity must have had a fair system of laws to guide and govern it. The ancient civilizations of Iran, China, India and Egypt had early systems of law. The laws of the Vendidad among the Iranians and the laws of Manu among the early Indians are well-known. It is not well known that the laws of the Vendidad formed only a fragment of the vast jurisprudence of the ancient Iranians.[85] Since the days of Zarathushtra human knowledge was raised into the sanctity of religion and formulated into twenty-one Nasks or Holy Books. By clerics one third of that great knowledge comprised Law, one-third Science, and one-third pure Religion.[86] The Books of Law dealt with Court and Magisterial Law, Law of Accusations, Law for Injuries to Person and Property; Laws Pertaining to Theft, Misappropriation and Cruelty to Animals; Laws Applying to Soldiers and Military Organizations; Church Law, Family Law and Law of Pedigree and Descent; Law Applying to Medical Practice; Law of Business Transactions in Relation to Property, Animate and Inanimate; Laws Relating to Debt and Interest, the other Mutual Obligations; Laws of Purity, Health and Sanitation, Private and Public; Laws Applying to the Cultivation of the Soil and Colonizing Schemes; and finally, the Law of the Heavenly Kingdom and the Divine Government of the Universe.[87]

Law was founded on Religion and Divinity in the System of Zarathushtra. Law forms an essential part of the religious system of the Zarathushtra, one-third of their sacred literature comprises Law in its various phases and spheres.[88] Indeed Law in a wider sense would coincide with Religion. The domain of Religion covers the universal field of Law. Science stands on the foundation of Law. Science constitutes the middle third of the Religious system of the Zarathushtrians and forms an essential link between God and Man. In Zarathushtrian Theology the law abiding is one of the most meaningful names of the Supreme Being.[89]

---

[85] Majid Razi, *Avesta Era*, Asia Publication, Tehran, Iran, (1963) [In Farsi].

[86] Mary Bois, *History of Zarathushtrian Religion*, Translation by Homayoon sanatizadeh, Toos Publication, Tehran, Iran (1997) [In Farsi].

[87] *Matikan-e- Hazar Datastan: The Digest of a Thousand Points of Law*, translated by Sohrab Jams, Published by Houshang Anklesaria, Bombay, India (1937).

[88] Majid Razi, *supra* note 85.

[89] *Id.*

The aim of Law would be to promote Religion and Divinity in Mankind furthered by the Spread of Learning and Knowledge among Men. The aim of Law is to further the Mighty Word of the All-Knowing Creator and to defeat Falsehood, to compass in the end the immortal, the illustrious and the most Brilliant and Perfect Sovereignty of the Kingdom of God.[90] This would be possible, because Law-abidingness is imbedded in Humanity. The Divine Being has created the world and implanted man in it to live the Life of Righteous Progress. Law-abidingness is to prove useful and valuable in the distant end by means of knowledge and education, and discrimination and enlightenment and learning.[91]

It appears that all laws were enacted by the Imperial Legislature, and promulgated by the Decree of the Great King. While no one was allowed to defy or frustrate the principles of justice, severest penalties were held out to person who sat in judgment and violated its sanctity by an intentional miscarriage of justice. This rule prevailed in Iran from the days of the Achaemenian Empire and earlier, and was scrupulously maintained throughout the Sassanian sovereignty.[92]

In Persia the Judge warned against an intentional miscarriage of justice. He was also instructed to maintain absolute impartiality in balancing judgment between the parties standing in litigation before him, to allow himself to be swayed by the smallest inclination towards any one side. He was thus to cast out all consciousness of self in the judgment seat. If for personal reasons and unusual circumstances he felt any prejudice against the accused, he was to pass the case on directly to the higher court, and not handle it himself.[93]

In ancient Iranian era sever punishments for deterrence were in use.[94] Iran was not an exception, Zarathushtrian religion spread humanity in criminal justice system.

---

[90] Hashem Razi, ***Ancient Religion of Iran***, Asia Publication, Tehran, Iran (1963) [In Farsi].

[91] *Id.*

[92] Arastoo Aflatooni, ***Law of Ancient Iran***, Iran Publication, Tehran, Iran (1947) [In Farsi].

[93] ***Matikan-e- Hazar Datastan***, *Supra* note 87.

[94] Ava Vahedi, ***Criminal Justice System of Iran in Sassanian Era***, Mizan Publication, Tehran, Iran (2001) [In Farsi].

Origins of Cruel and Unusual Punishment

There was no specific indication regarding prohibition of cruel and unusual punishments. Enactment of cruel and inhuman punishments was common in the ancient world. Advent of religions caused its transformation to human modes of punishments. Moral standards do not easily tolerant these kind of cruelties. Islam emphasizes that in punishment, human dignity and veneration of the accused should be preserved. Moreover, the punishment should fit the crime considering Islamic penal standards.[95]

After the fall of Iranian Empire in 640 A.D., Islamic legal principles became the main source of law throughout the country. According to Muslim historians, the second Muslim Caliph, Umar, issued one of the earliest Islamic Instructions to an Arab judge. These instructions established a basis for Islamic law and judicial system. The Arab caliphates borrowed much of the administrative heritage of Persia.[96]

Following the Islamic revolution in Iran (1979), a modern legal system was replaced by an Islamic legal system based on Shiite version of Sharia law. This system of law formed in the early 1980s during the tenure of the Ayatollah Ruhullah Musavi Khomeini. It replaced the secular system that two Pahlavi monarchs established in Iran during their consecutive reigns. Shiism has been particularly influenced by the opinions of the sixth Imam, Abu Abdullah Jafar bin Mohammad Sadegh. Its legal school is known as the Jafari School of Jurisprudence. According to the Jafari School, sources of Islamic law are the Holy book, tradition (Hadith), the consensus of the jurist (Ijma), and reason (Aql). In the former Penal Code of Iran the death penalty was applied for specific crimes. After the Islamic revolution, the application of the death penalty was expanded. In addition, corporal punishment and other inhuman punishments became enforceable in Iran.

When discussing punishment in Iran during 1980s keep in mind the relationship between the state and concept of justice is derived from the religious principle of Islam. The Sharia, general and particular rules of Islamic corpus juris, is not just a code of law but a code of conduct of behavior and ethics, a combination of law and morality, inseparable. Evidence of this relationship can be seen in the Penal Code and punishments of Iranian law. Those who are deemed "Corrupt on earth" or those committed major

---

[95] Abas mousavi, *Torture: In the Iranian, UN and Criminal Policy,* pp 103-4, Khat-E-Sevom publishing, Tehran, Iran (2003) [In Farsi].

[96] Hassan Amin, *The History of Law in Iran,* p 12, The Encyclopedia of Iran Publications, Tehran, Iran (2004).

economic crimes with subversive intent... are often sentenced to die. Also corporal punishment and other inhuman punishments are in practice.

In Iran, torture is prohibited for the purpose of extracting information, cruel and degrading treatment of detainees is prohibited constitutionality. Principle 38 of Iran Constitution indicates "All forms of torture for the purpose of extracting confession or acquiring information are forbidden. Compulsion of individuals to testify, confess, or take an oath is not permissible; and any testimony, confession, or oath obtained under duress is devoid of value and credence. Violation of this article is liable to punishment in accordance with the law".[97]

Article 579 of Islamic Penal Code of Iran states "punishment of condemned sever than conviction sentence or punishment beyond conviction sentence requiring imprisonment and compensation of victim damages."[98] Other provisions emphasize the principle that punishment should fit the crime.[99] There is no specific provision regarding cruel and unusual punishment. The interpretation and application of cruel and unusual punishment is based on Sharia law. In Islam, God's will is the origin of criminal law. Islamic punishment is fixed based on justice and prudence, therefore in Islamic jurisprudence circles all Islamic punishments are usual and fair.

II Definition

1 Terminology

A From Torture to Cruel and Unusual Punishment

Distinction can be drawn between acts of torture, acts amounting to inhuman treatment and acts amounting to degrading treatment based upon a threshold of severity: the first one presents a higher degree of seriousness than the second one, which is more

---

[97] Constitution of Iran, Principle 38, 1995 [In Farsi].

[98] Islamic Penal Code of Iran, Article 579, 1991[In Farsi].

[99] Criminal procedure of Iran, Article 134, 1991[In Farsi].

severe than the last one.[100] The attempt to simplify terminology by using a single phrase is not meant to obscure semantic distinctions in the norms, although it certainly reflects the fact that by and large courts do not attempt to draw too fine a line between the various categories.

Torture means any act by which severe mental or physical pain or suffering is intentionally inflicted for purposes of punishment, coercion, intimidate or discrimination, by or at the instigation or with the consent or acquiescence of a public official or other person acting in an official capacity, excluding lawful sanctions.[101]

Most of international instruments, do not provide a definition of the concept of torture and ill-treatment except article 1 of the UN Declaration on the Protection of All Persons from Being Subjected to Torture and Other Cruel, Inhuman or Degrading Treatment or Punishment[102], article 2 of the Inter-American Convention to Prevent and Punish Torture (9 December 1985), article 7 of the Rome statute of the International Criminal Court (17 July 1998) but One of the major instruments dealing with torture that does provide a definition is the UN Convention against Torture. Consequently, when a definition of this concept is needed, it is usually referred to this treaty.

---

[100] Eur. Ct. H.R., *Tyrer v. The United Kingdom*, Judgment of 25 April 1978, § 29; Eur. Ct. H.R., *Ireland v. The United Kingdom*, Judgment of 18 January 1978, § 167.

[101] Art. 1(1) Convention against Torture and other Cruel, Inhuman or Degrading Treatment or Punishment states: "For the purposes of this Convention, the term "torture" means any act by which severe pain or suffering, whether physical or mental, is intentionally inflicted on a person for such purposes as obtaining from him or a third person information or a confession, punishing him for an act he or a third person has committed or is suspected of having committed, or intimidating or coercing him or a third person, or for any reason based on discrimination of any kind, when such pain or suffering is inflicted by or at the instigation of or with the consent or acquiescence of a public official or other person acting in an official capacity. It does not include pain or suffering arising only from, inherent in or incidental to lawful sanctions."

[102] Adopted by General Assembly resolution 3452 (XXX) of 9 December 1975: "1. For the purpose of this Declaration, torture means any act by which severe pain or suffering, whether physical or mental, is intentionally inflicted by or at the instigation of a public official on a person for such purposes as obtaining from him or a third person information or confession, punishing him for an act he has committed or is suspected of having committed, or intimidating him or other persons. It does not include pain or suffering arising only from, inherent in or incidental to, lawful sanctions to the extent consistent with the Standard Minimum Rules for the Treatment of Prisoners. 2. Torture constitutes an aggravated and deliberate form of cruel, inhuman or degrading treatment or punishment."

The UN Convention against Torture definition provides that torture is "any act by which severe pain or suffering, whether physical or mental, is intentionally inflicted on a person for such purposes as obtaining from him or a third person information or a confession, punishing him for an act he or a third person has committed or is suspected of having committed, or intimidating or coercing him or a third person, or for any reason based on discrimination of any kind, when such pain or suffering is inflicted by or at the instigation of or with the consent or acquiescence of a public official or other person acting in an official capacity. It does not include pain or suffering arising from, inherent in or incidental to lawful sanctions". This definition has been held to constitute customary international law.[103]

Punishment is a sanction such as a fine, penalty, confinement, or loss of property, right, or privilege -- assessed against a person who has violated the law.[104] In any event, the plain meaning of the word punishment must be addressed. Punishment is defined in the American Heritage Dictionary as 1. a. An act of punishing. b. The condition of being punished. 2. A penalty imposed for wrongdoing. 3. Informal rough handling; mistreatment. This definition is echoed in a number of other common dictionaries. For example, the Merriam-Webster's Collegiate Dictionary defines punishment as a 1: the act of punishing 2 a: suffering, pain, or loss that serves as retribution b: a penalty inflicted on an offender through judicial procedure 3: severe, rough or disastrous treatment.[105] The American Edition of the Oxford Essential Dictionary defines it as 1. act or instance of punishing; condition of being punished. 2. loss or suffering inflicted in this. 3. severe treatment or suffering.[106]

What each of these definitions reveals is that the word, as used in the common vernacular, encompasses two distinct sets of conduct: that which is inflicted in response to an offense and one that involves rough or severe treatment, neither necessarily following judicial procedure. In this research we define the term punishment more narrowly, limiting its application to a penalty inflicted upon a person by the authority of

---

[103] ICTY, 10 December 1998, *Prosecutor v. Anto Furundzija* [1998] ICTY 3, § 160.

[104] Bryan Garner, **Black's Law Dictionary,** West Publisher (8th ed. 2004), punishment.

[105] Merriam Webster, **Merriam-Webster's Collegiate Dictionary**, p 945, Merriam-Webster publisher (10th ed 2003.).

[106] **Oxford Essential Dictionary**, p 485, Oxford University Press (10th ed. 2006).

the law and the judgment and sentence of a court, for some crime or offense committed by him.

Thus as a legal term of, the word "punishment" was limited to post-conviction punishment because it was defined at the time as those actions undertaken as a "penalty for transgressing the Law."[107] However, this definition, on its own terms, is not limited to post-adjudication punishment, but rather to those penalties used against transgressors.

The word *cruel*, while it meant merciless in the seventeenth century, also had in common usage a less onerous significance as severe or rigorous.[108] Cruelty is the intentional and malicious infliction of mental or physical suffering on a living creature, esp. a human; abusive treatment; outrage.[109] In United States the Court has defined "cruel" punishment as involving "the gratuitous infliction of suffering."[110]

A "cruel" punishment is a harsh punishment, one that inflicts suffering. But harshness is a necessary, not a sufficient condition. Otherwise, virtually all punishments would be "cruel" simply because they impose unwelcome hardships.[111] In the United States the Court has correctly defined it as punishment that inflicts suffering without good reason.[112]

The word *unusual*, in common use from about 1630, meant uncommon or exceptional. An unusual punishment is one that is out of the ordinary, one that is not regularly employed.[113] "Unusual" was a synonym for "illegal" at common law because

---

[107] *Black's Law Dictionary*, *supra* note 104.

[108] Lois G. Schwoerer, *The Declaration of Rights*, p 92, Johns Hopkins U. Press (1981).

[109] *Black's Law Dictionary*, *supra* note 104, cruelty.

[110] 428 U.S. 153, 183(1976).

[111] 428 U.S. 153, 183(1976), see also 503 U.S. 1, 5(1992), 475 U.S. 312, 319 (1986).

[112] Gregg v. Georgia, 428 U.S. 153, 183 (1976) (plurality opinion). See also Hudson v. McMillian, 503 U.S. 1, 5 (1992) (upholding the rule that "'the unnecessary and wanton infliction of pain . . . constitutes cruel and unusual punishment'"

[113] Tom Stacy, *Cleaning up the Eighth Amendment Mess*, 14 Wm. & Mary Bill Rts. J. 475 (December 2005).

the common law doctrine of precedent insisted that judicial decisions could succeed in articulating law if and only if they served an underlying principle of moral-- and therefore legal--equality among litigants. Based on common law method if a particular punishment was distinguishable from its predecessors for good reason, then it reflected an evolved understanding of the common law rather than a departure from the common law. Therefore imposition of two different punishments for the same crime without any reason is unusual and illegal.[114] To determine whether a government action qualifies as unusual, we can look to such things as international standards.

The only International law instrument to use the term "unusual" is the American Declaration of the Rights and Duties of Man (adopted in May 1984). "Unusual" punishment is also prohibited by English Bill of Rights, the United States Constitution, and most of the state constitutions within the United States.

In the United States Virtually no punishments are "cruel" under the Court's definition. The Court thus may invalidate a punishment only by, first, characterizing it as "unusual" and, second, effectively defining the Eighth Amendment's meaning in terms of that requirement alone. The Court's cases, however, have been arbitrarily selective in their use of the term "unusual," permitting some unusual punishments and condemning some common prison conditions.[115]

"Unusual" meant illegal because a departure from common law precedent without morally sufficient reason. In other words, "unusual" meant intra-jurisdictionally novel.[116] One way to define unusualness is using inter-jurisdictional comparison by this methodology we can determine whether a punishment is in fact "too much." Inter-jurisdictional comparison may assist to decide whether a punishment is excessive, but it

---

[114] Laurence Claus, *The Antidiscrimination Eight Amendment*, 28 Harv. J.L. & Pub. Pol'y 119 (Fall 2004).

[115] Tom Stacy, *supra* note 113.

[116] Laurence Claus, *supra* note 114.

does not determine the issue. By the way the term is vague and that what might be considered "unusual" in one country might not be so viewed in another.[117]

There is no international legal definition of a cruel, inhuman or degrading treatment. The UN Human Rights Committee stated that it does not consider necessary to establish sharp distinctions between the different kinds of punishment or treatment; the distinctions depend on the nature, purpose and severity of the treatment applied.[118]

Based on the definition of Association for the prevention of torture some human rights experts consider that creating a hierarchy between torture and the different forms of cruel and unusual punishment should be avoided.[119] Despite this definition many describe torture as the highest point of a continuous development which comprises cruel, inhuman or degrading treatment.[120]

Inhuman treatment has been defined by the European Commission on Human Rights as being at least such treatment as deliberately causes severe suffering, mental or physical. The European Court of Human Rights in Ireland v. United Kingdom held that treatment was inhuman if it was premeditated, if it was applied for hours at time, and if it is resulted in intense physical and mental suffering, even if it dose not cause actual bodily injury.[121]

As a result, once a certain level of gravity is reached, an act can be qualified as *degrading* treatment. Degrading treatment, when it reaches a certain severity, can be re-

---

[117] William A. Schabas, *The death Penalty as Cruel Treatment and torture*, p 48, Northeastern University press (1996).

[118] U.N. Doc. HRI\GEN\1\Rev.1 at 30 (1994), Human Rights Committee, General Comment 20, Article 7, § 4.

[119] Association for the Prevention of Torture, *The Definition of Torture. Proceedings of an Expert Seminar*, p 18, APT, Geneva, 2001.

[120] Kersty McCourt and Manuel Lambert, *Interpretation of the Definition of Torture or Cruel, Inhuman or Degrading Treatment or Punishment in the Light of European and International case law*, A report presented to the EU Network of Independent Experts in Fundamental Rights (30 October 2004).

[121] William A. Schabas, *supra* note 117, pp 47-8.

classified as inhuman treatment which, in turn, if particularly serious can be classified as torture.[122]

Degrading punishment seems easier to distinguish, since it involves an element of humiliation. According to the Human rights Committee, "For punishment to be degrading, the humiliation or debasement involved must exceed a particular level and must, an any event; entail other elements beyond the mere fact of deprivation of liberty."

The degradation is one the obvious aspects of punishment that has been condemned by International conventions and at the European Court of Human Right. Degradation interpretation is complex in legal literature. Degrading is not coterminous with either violence or torture. Degrading act needs hardly be violent. There are many degrading punishments that have nothing to do with torture. Therefore degrading is neither violence nor torture, and scholars usually use degradation impressionistically.

B   Relationship between Cruel and Unusual Punishment

The phrases "cruel and unusual," "cruel or unusual," and "cruel" were instead understood as referring to a single concept of inhumane or cruel punishment. A punishment is "cruel" if it inflicts pain without reason.[123] One might plausibly believe that cruel punishments would be unusual in a democracy, which has the constraints of legislative authorization, publicity, and judicial review. But cruelty and frequency are separable concepts, and the relationship between them is contingent, not necessary.[124]

In fact, a harsh punishment's frequency is often thought to increase, not decrease, the need for condemnation and prohibition. The example of torture illustrates the point. Some philosophers and jurists maintain that torture can be justified in extremely limited circumstances.[125] The unusual nature of torture is said to be the key to its acceptability,

---

[122] Kersty McCourt and Manuel Lambert, *supra* note 120.

[123] See Gregg v. Georgia, 428 U.S. 153, 183 (1976).

[124] Jeffrie G. Murphy & Jules L. Coleman, **Philosophy of Law: An Introduction to Jurisprudence,** pp 75-82, 109-30, Westview press (rev. ed. 1990).

[125] Alan M. Dershowitz, **Why Terrorism Works**, pp 141-58, Yale University Press (2002).

prompting Professor Alan Dershowitz to call for "torture warrants" designed to sharply limit its use.[126] One of the main arguments advanced in support of a categorical prohibition against torture is the slippery slope fear that once legitimized in principle; torture will be too commonly employed.[127]

This history has particular salience because the Cruel and Unusual Punishment Clause was taken virtually verbatim from the English Bill of Rights.[128] The history of the English Bill of Rights reinforces that the phrases "cruel and unusual" and "cruel or unusual" were understood to capture the same meaning. Just months after the House of Lords approved the Bill's prohibition against "cruel and unusual punishments," a group of Lords filed a dissenting statement in the case of Titus Oates. The dissenting Lords concluded that the punishments imposed in Oates's case violated the Bill of Rights, which they described as providing that neither "cruel nor unusual punishments [be] inflicted."[129] Their mistake suggests that they understood prohibitions of "cruel and unusual" and "cruel or unusual" punishments as equivalents.

The relationship between these two terms raises interesting questions of interpretation. In United States the Justices sometimes have said that an unconstitutional punishment must be both cruel and unusual, just as the literal text provides. However, Justices have questioned "whether the term 'unusual' has any qualitative meaning different from 'cruel.'"[130]

The historical evidence regarding the relationship between cruel and unusual term is admittedly thin, but the Founders used the phrases "cruel and unusual punishment," "cruel or unusual punishments," and "cruel punishments" interchangeably to refer to a unitary concept.[131]

---

[126] *Id.*

[127] Oren Gross, *Are Torture Warrants Warranted? Pragmatic Absolutism and Official Disobedience*, *88 Minn. L. Rev. 1481, 1506 (2004).*

[128] Anthony F. Granucci, *supra* note 44.

[129] Philip B. Kurland & Ralph Lerner, *The Founders' Constitution*, p 369, University of Chicago Press (1987) (reprinting statement of dissenting Lords in the Titus Oates case).

[130] Trop, 356 U.S. at 100 n.32.

In the United States the Court's approach to inter-jurisdictional comparison belies the claim that such comparisons serve to establish "unusualness."[132] To call a punishment "unusual" was to call it immorally discriminatory. To call a punishment "cruel and unusual" was to call it immorally discriminatory in the direction of greater severity. Understanding the Cruel and Unusual Punishments Clause as a prohibition of discrimination most faithfully translates the historic text into a modern context[133] Therefore Punishments that are both immorally excessive (cruel) and inter-jurisdictionally novel (unusual) are cruel and unusual.

2 What Constitute Cruel and Unusual Punishment

A Modes of Punishment

We know that certain modes of punishment and excessive degrees of punishment can be defined as cruel and unusual. What guidelines help legal scholars understand when a statute or punishment is in cruel and unusual concept in kind or degree.

There are four situations in which a punishment may be struck down as cruel and unusual: 1) when the death penalty is imposed; or when an inhumane or barbarous type of punishment is imposed;2) when the punishment is based solely on the "status" of the offender;3) when a sentence is grossly disproportionate to the crime committed. And 4) when the punishment is unacceptable to society.

The first type limits legislative power to authorize means of punishment. Despite this limitation legislative authority imposes physical torture, like the rack, thumbscrew or drawing and quartering, as punishment for crime.

---

[131] Tom Stacy, *supra* note 113.

[132] Solem v. Helm, 463 U.S. 277, 291-92 (1983).

[133] James Compbell, **Revival of the Eight Amendment: Development of Cruel-Punishment Doctrine by the Supreme Court**, 16 Stand. L. Rev. 996 (July 1964).

The second type is power to criminalize the conduct or status. In this issue, "Is it possible for the government to impose any punishment on anyone for conduct?" It is violation of cruel and unusual clause to punish persons merely for their "status" as narcotics addicts, prostitutes or homosexuals.

The Third type of cruel and unusual punishment clause limits legislative power to authorize a means or amount of punishment for a particular crime and also limits judicial power to impose a means or amount of punishment on a specific criminal. Therefore it proportionate for government to impose punishment X on any offender found guilty of crime Y? The issue in this type takes the form, is it proportionate for the government to impose punishment X on offender N for crime Y, committed in a particular manner and under particular circumstances? Both cases require a proportionality inquiry, though at different levels of abstraction. Adjudication of this type involves consideration of the punishment, the crime and whether the punishment fits the crime. As evinced by objective indicia, the most important of which is legislation enacted by the country's legislatures. Thus Cruel and Unusual Punishment Clause does not prohibit punishments that are grossly disproportionate to the offense.

The fourth type outlaws modes of punishment that are inconsistent with modern standards of decency. The Cruel and Unusual Punishment Clause, derives its meaning from the "evolving standards of decency that mark the progress of a maturing society."[134] These standards, in turn, are defined "to the maximum possible extent"[135] by objective standards such as statutes passed by society's elected representatives.

B Essential Elements

The first considerable element is ***sever pain and arbitrary infliction***. An act of cruel and unusual punishment must attain a minimum level of seriousness to be held as a reprehensible act: an entry level threshold of severity must be reached to fit this particular qualification. The assessment of this minimum is relative: as the European Court of Human Rights deemed in the *Ireland v. The United Kingdom Case*, it depends

---

[134] Trop, 356 U.S. at 101. See, e.g., Atkins v. Virginia, 536 U.S. 304, 311-12 (2002); Hudson v. McMillian, 503 U.S. 1, 8 (1992); Stanford v. Kentucky, 492 U.S. 361, 369 (1989).

[135] Coker v. Georgia, 433 U.S. 584, 592 (1977) (plurality opinion). See also Harmelin, 501 U.S. at 1000 (quoting Rummel v. Estelle, 445 U.S. 263, 274-75 (1980)); Gregg, 428 U.S. at 173.

on the duration of the treatment, its physical or mental effects and on the sex, age and state of health of the victim.[136]

The second element of cruel and unusual punishment is its ***purpose***. An act of cruel and unusual must be inflicted for punishment. As far as some categories of disadvantaged people (children, women, minorities, indigent people,) are concerned, purpose as a component of cruel and unusual can be too restrictive. Because of their particular vulnerability, those categories require higher standards of protection than other groups and specific positive measures. In particular, the State must assume a higher degree of responsibility in cases of torture or cruel, inhuman or degrading treatment or punishment perpetrated against them. This means that, in some cases, it must be held responsible even though these acts may be perpetrated without any specific purpose.[137]

Also cruelty of punishment depends on the intentions of those who punish and not on the physical act of punishment or its impact on him who is punished. Moreover the mode of punishment and its effect on the condemned may be of a character allowing inference of the prohibited intention.[138]

The third element is ***inhumanity v. human dignity***. Although the essential understanding of cruel and unusual phrase is human dignity none of the relevant international or regional conventions define humane or inhumane treatment. Because the conventions are so general, the interpretation of what constitutes inhumane treatment is left within the discretion of those most likely to perpetrate it.

Dignity is enunciated in the following international instruments: the Universal Declaration of Human Rights, the Covenant on Civil and Political Rights, the European Convention for the Protection of Human Rights and Fundamental Freedoms, the American Declaration on the Rights and Duties of Man, and the American Convention on Human Rights.

---

[136] Eur. Ct. H.R., *Ireland v. The United Kingdom*, Judgement of 18 January 1978, § 162; Eur. Ct. H.R., *Soering v. The United Kingdom,* Judgment of 07 July 1989, § 100.

[137] Kersty McCourt and Manuel Lambert, *supra* note 120.

[138] James Compbell, *supra* note 133.

A similar phrase, "human dignity," is also repeated throughout the International instruments. The International Covenant on Civil and Political Rights demands treatment "with humanity and with respect for the inherent dignity of the human person." [139]

III *Harshness v. Mildness*

1   Socio-historical Perspective

Cruel and unusual punishment and social reactions about it is complex, and the history of harsh punishment linked to various patterns in human social development. Understanding cruel and unusual punishment depends on how different social traditions have emerged. Therefore, harshness and mildness of a punishment is completely different from culture to culture and from era to era. For instance flogging which is a harsh punishment in the western countries, in Islamic penal system is regarded as mild one, or while branding was a mild punishment in ancient era, in 21 century it is regarded as a harsh punishment.

Therefore cultural factors are important in evaluating whether punishment is cruel and unusual. Notions of cruel and unusual will depend on a number of personal elements that are socially conditioned. For example in *Tyrer v. United Kingdom* the continental judges of European Court of Human Rights were shocked at the practice of Birching but judge Fitzmaurice was not at all outraged. Because he was educated under a system according to which the corporal punishment of schoolboys was regarded as the normal sanction for serious or even less serious misbehavior. But there must be a limit to the role cultural factors may play. Otherwise the norm prohibiting cruel and unusual punishment ceases to have any international scope. Although a "margin of appreciation" in applying fundamental rights is recognized within the European system, such bodies as the Human Rights committee and the Committee against Torture have yet to elaborate a doctrine on just how broadly cultural factors may be invoked within the context of cruel treatment and torture.[140]

---

[139] International Convention on Civil and Political Rights, (1976) 999 U.N.T.S. 171, at Art. 10.

[140] William A. Schabas, *supra* note 117, pp 51-52.

Since Montesquieu, people have believed that harsh punishment is produced by strong states, with relatively unbridled power. Durkheim stated it as nothing less than a law: The intensify of punishment, he held, depended not only on the complexity of a society, but on the absolute character of its state power.[141]

Harsh criminal punishment has an overwhelming impact on a convict's life. Criminal punishment represents government at its most coercive. For affected individuals, the stakes are much higher with respect to other forms of governmental regulation. Criminal punishment may deprive a person of physical liberty for decades- and even of life itself.[142]

The common understanding of a "cruel" punishment is one that is unnecessarily harsh. But a punishment may be unnecessarily harsh for one purpose but not for another. For instance, in 21 century, ten years imprisonment at hard labor would be gratuitously harsh and therefore "cruel" for a libel offense, but not for murder. The same may be said of the term "unusual." For example life imprisonment for a minor shoplifting is unusual but life sentences for other offenses involving more aggravated culpability or harms such as kidnapping is usual.

Thus what constitutes cruelty differs from one society to another. For instance, European Court of Human Rights considered whether corporal punishment by birching violates "inhuman or degrading treatment or Punishment," Judge Fitzmaurice, who sat on behalf of the United Kingdom, admitted that in his view the fact that there was no violation was undoubtedly conditioned by his own youthful experience in English Public schools. His views were not shared by the majority of court, perhaps because the other judges could not empathize with his nostalgia for such brutality and had not been culturally conditioned to appreciate its alleged benefits.[143]

---

[141] Durkheim, *Two laws of Penal evolution*, 21, in M. Gane, ed., The Radical sociology of Durkheim and Mauss, London (1992).

[142] Tom Stacy, *supra* note 113.

[143] *Id.*

Respectful modes of punishment, for conception of humanity can ground a more humane penal system.[144] But the respectful treatment is dramatically absent in American and Iranian penal systems by contrast with International Conventions. How can a country that rhetorically portrays itself as 'the land of the free' maintains punitive practices that are so much harsher than those of other purportedly liberal states? Punishments in America (sample among Western nations) and Iran (sample among Islamic countries) are harsh. What is going on in these countries? How cultural roots of harsh punishment have emerged in contemporary America and Iran? How harsh criminal punishments can develop in a society that belongs to the Western liberal tradition (United States) and the society which has old cultural roots (Iran)?

These questions are, left aside by contemporary sociological theorists. They often talk in general terms about 'modernity' and 'post-modernity', but may not attend to such differences between countries, and by philosophers whose abstract theorizing about 'the justification of punishment', and about such issues as proportionality, fails to attend to those more particular, substantive features of penalty that distinguish penal systems from each other and that are so central to the reality and meaning of criminal punishment.

In defining harshness, we will focus on harshness in criminalization of status and harshness in punishment.[145] To bolster these hypothesis that the punishments in United States and Iran are harsh, status criminalized in the United States includes high-level some sex or morals offenses.[146] Since some sex offenses have been decriminalized,[147] and in Iran status statutes include sex and moral offenses,[148] vagrancy,[149] drunkenness[150] and addiction.[151]

---

[144] R.A. Duff, **Punishment, Dignity and Degradation**, 25 Oxford J. Legal Stud. 141 (spring 2005).

[145] James Whiteman, **Harsh Justice: Criminal Punishment and the Widening divide between America and Europe**, p 33, New York: Oxford University Press (2003).

[146] *Id*, pp 43-5.

[147] R.A. Duff, *supra* note 144.

[148] Islamic Penal Code of Iran, Art 63-164, 1991[In Farsi].

[149] *Id*, Art 712, 1991[In Farsi].

Europe, on the other hand, has decriminalized or even legalized an increasing number of morals offenses, such as prostitution and drug offenses. Most of us are familiar with the liberal Dutch policies pertaining to cannabis and the legalization of prostitution.[152]

Different forms of punishment provisions threatening long prison terms for drug offenders and recidivists have led to an unprecedented growth in the prison population

Even though the desire for punitiveness in the United States and Iran may not be as diametrically different as current penal policies indicate, the types of discourse diverge dramatically. In the United States, arguments pertaining to the inherent dignity or human rights of individual offenders have fallen on deaf ears, and the law frequently affirms this attitude. In Iran even some particularly Islamic provisions have successfully asserted dignity rights, but not necessarily in Islamic criminal justice system.

In subsequent chapters it is obvious that social and political hierarchies have led to mild punishments while a weak state, violence in history or religion beliefs and egalitarianism have caused more degrading and harsh punishment in the United States and Iran.

2 Harshness and Penological Objectives

In order to determine whether a punishment is cruel and unusual, it is necessary to inquire into the extent the punishment deprives the offender of life, liberty, or property. Five objectives which may be achieved by the imposition of criminal sanctions: deterrence, retribution, rehabilitation, incapacitation and expression of society's condemnation. Moreover, are these goals observable in the harsh system of punishment or mild?

---

[150] *Id*, Art 165-175, 1991[In Farsi].

[151] Anti Narcotics Drug Act, Art 1, 16-19, 1988 [In Farsi].

[152] *Napier* v *Scottish Ministers* [2004] SLT 555.

Evolving standards of decency preclude inflictions of pain without penological justification because these would fall in the category of unnecessary and wanton inflictions of pain.[153] The severe pain resulting from the punishments can be justified as having a deterrent impact. Even small gains in deterrence can be defended as necessary to prevent serious crimes. Such claims are absurd. In Iran after the revolutionary restatement of Islamic punishments such criminal sanctions justified on precisely this ground. But a claim that cruel punishment such as corporal punishments deter considering high crime rates might be in error.

Accordingly the ordinary European view is that the role of retributivism must be strictly limited, and punishment professionals remain quite attached to rehabilitationist programs.[154] Of course there are no such limits in United States and Iran.

As Bentham indicates, "legislators and men in general are naturally inclined" to extreme harshness, since "antipathy, or a want of compassion for individuals who are represented as dangerous and vile, pushes them onward to an undue severity."[155] Criminal punishment does not only visit measured retribution on blameworthy offenders. Nor does it only deter. Nor does it only express considered condemnation.

The choice of rehabilitation for the criminal justice system is indeed the choice of a system that treat offenders as inferiors and also some measure of indulgence and even kindness. In practice, the choice for retributivism is turning out to be the choice, not for equality, but for degradation.[156]

Regarding incapacitation restricting the use of predictions of dangerousness in sentencing decisions itself safeguards against overly harsh punishment. We are less likely to endorse excessive criminal sanctions if we truly consider ourselves at risk of

---

[153] *Estelle*, 429 U.S. at 103.

[154] James Whiteman, *supra* note 145, p 3.

[155] Jeremy Bentham, **Principles of Penal Law**, in The Works of Jeremy Bentham, pp 365, 401, John Bowring ed.(1843).

[156] James Q. Whitman, **SYMPOSIUM: Model Penal Code: Sentencing: A Plea Against Retributivism**, 7 Buff. Crim. L. R. 85 (2003).

having the harsher sanctions apply to us. Conversely, the perception that only predictably dangerous persons are at risk of the harsher sentences, combined with a rare perception of ourselves as one of the predictably dangerous, will tend to render us more receptive to extending the higher end of the range of available sentences.[157]

An adequate definition of harsh punishment must focus on both punishment's objective effects and the punisher's culpability.[158] Imagine for a moment that the focus is solely on objective effects. On this view, a punishment is harsh if it does not promote a legitimate penological objective in point of fact. It does not matter that the punisher believes, even reasonably so, that the punishment has redeeming value.

The disqualifying problem with an exclusive focus on objective effects is that it does not give the punisher the required decision.[159] Sometimes explicitly and other times implicitly, it has required the punisher to possess culpability respecting a punishment's lack of redeeming value. As a general matter, the objective reasonableness standard the appropriate balance between respecting the decisional discretion of legislatures and other actors, on the one hand, and avoiding intrusive state-of-mind inquiries and imposing insurmountable evidentiary burdens, on the other.[160]

In short, we can define a harsh punishment as one that, first, does not promote a legitimate penological goal as a matter of objective reality, and second, is either not believed to have redeeming value by those authorizing or inflicting the punishment or is recklessly or negligently believed to have such value.

---

[157] Franklin E. Zimring & Gordon Hawkins, *Dangerousness and Criminal Justice*, 85 MICH. L. REV. 481 (1986).

[158] See Model Penal Code § 1.13(9) (1962). Mens rea elements concern the offender's degree of culpability, which most criminal offenses define in terms of the offender's subjective state of mind, such as intent. Id. 1.13(9) (b). Attendant circumstance elements require the existence of a specified state of affairs and do not depend on the offender's state of mind. Id. 1.13(9) (c-d).

[159] Richard S. Frase, *Excessive Prison Sentences, Punishment Goals, and the Eighth Amendment: "Proportionality" Relative to What?*, 89 Minn. L. Rev. 571, 574 (2005).

[160] Gregg v. Georgia, 428 U.S. 153, 183 (1976) (plurality opinion). See also Hudson v. McMillian, 503 U.S. 1, 5 (1992).

Chapter 2

Death Penalty

"Listen to the voice of justice and of reason. It tells us that human judgments are never so certain as to permit society to kill a human being judged by other human beings." [161]

Capital punishment, or the death penalty, is the execution of a convicted criminal by the State as punishment for crimes known as *capital crimes* or *capital offences*. The word "capital" is derived from the Latin "capitalis," which means "concerning the head"; therefore, to be subjected to capital punishment means to figuratively lose one's head. [162]

Throughout history, there have been three distinctly separate attacks on the death penalty. The first group believed in capital punishment but suggested that certain method of inflicting it were cruel and unusual. The second group objected to imposing the penalty for certain crimes, generally those other than murder. Members of third group have challenged the death penalty as being per se inhuman and barbarous.

I *History*

1   History of Death Penalty in the United States from Colonial Times to Twentieth Century

A   The Colonial Period (1597-1740)

For close to 400 years, capital punishment has been a transcendent feature of American criminal justice. According to the Body of Liberties, capital punishment was the sanction for idolatry, witchcraft, blasphemy, murder, manslaughter, poisoning,

---

[161] Francois Robespierre (quoted in Amnesty International, Statements Against the Death Penalty, at http://www.magnet.at/ai.dornbirn/state-dp.html. (Last modified September 7, 2000).

[162] See http://en.wikipedia.org/wiki/Capital_punishment.

bestiality, sodomy, adultery, kidnapping, and treason but not for property crimes.[163] The dissatisfaction of the Americans with the "Bloody Code" became immediately apparent as all the colonial systems abolished the death penalty for crimes against property.[164]

But other moral offenses became capital crimes in order to confirm with Mosaic law. While adultery was a capital offense in the Puritan colonies it was not so in Rhode Island and Plymouth. In addition, there were a whole host of other sexual offenses which were capital offenses in the Puritan colonies. Sodomy, homosexuality, even male masturbation in the presence of others could be punishable by death. The majority of the original capital laws of the Massachusetts Bay Colony reflect the religious focus of the colony. Capital laws of a more secular nature, such as prohibitions against rape and treason, were added later.[165] By the eighteenth century less moral offenses were capital crimes. Adultery was considered a capital crime in Massachusetts, although it was rarely carried out. In reality a shortage of population and other exigencies created a system in which statutes were rarely enforced to the letter of the law.[166]

In contrast to Puritan New England, executions were a common occurrence in Virginia, where hundred of crimes demanded the death penalty by the mid-1700s. According to one survey of the 164 people convicted of capital crimes between 1737 and 1772, 125 were executed without benefit of clergy.[167]

B   The Revolutionary times (1718-1797)

The eighteenth century is often referred to as the Age of Reason or the Enlightenment. During this era, great thinkers such as Beccaria, Bentham, Howard, and Penn had a great impact on the criminal justice system. Beccaria is considered one of the

---

[163] Mitchel P. Roth, *Crime and Punishment: A History of the Criminal Justice System*, p 65, Thomson Wadsworth, CA (2005).

[164] Bradley Chapin, *Criminal Justice in Colonial America 1606-1660*, p 8, Athens: University of Georgia Press (1983).

[165] *Id,* p 10.

[166] Mitchel P. Roth, *supra note* 163, p 66.

[167] *Id.*

first modern writers to publicly oppose capital punishment. Beccaria wrote, in his celebrated treatise *On Crimes and Punishments*: Capital punishment neither can nor be useful because of the example of barbarity it presents. If human passions or the necessities of war have taught men to shed one another's blood, the laws, which are intended to moderate human conduct ought not to extend the savage example, which in the case of the legal execution is all the more baneful in that it is carried out with studied formalities. To me it seems an absurdity that the laws, which are the expression of the public will, which abhor and which punish murder, should themselves commit one; and that, to deter citizens from private assassination, they should themselves order a public murder.[168]

Beccaria's ideas proved popular with some of the most prominent voices of revolutionary America. Thomas Jefferson cited this influence in his composition of a *Bill for Proportioning Crimes and Punishments in Cases heretofore Capital (1778)*, and in Pennsylvania Dr. Benjamin Rush claimed that Beccaria inspired his essay *Consideration of the Injustice and Impolicy of Punishing Murder by Death (1792)* and argued for the elimination of the death penalty altogether. But Rush remained in the minority. Jefferson's bill finally was approved in 1796, although it did not eliminate the death penalty in Virginia but rather limited it to the crimes of murder and treason and in Pennsylvania came the closest in 1794 by eliminating the death penalty for all crimes except first degree murder.[169]

C Death Penalty in the New Nation (1777-1857)

Following the Enlightenment and with a rise in public disorders, some states began to steer away from the inflammatory spectacle of public executions. Pennsylvania was the first state to hold private executions behind prison bard beginning in 1834. During the 1830s, New York and Massachusetts joined Pennsylvania in ending public executions.[170]

---

[168] Cesarre, Beccaria, ***On Crimes and Punishments***, Translated with an introduction by Henry Paolucci, Bobbs-Merrill, Indianapolis, U.S. (1963).

[169] Mitchel P. Roth, *supra* note 163, pp 87-88.

[170] *Id*, pp 110-111.

While the last public execution in America took place as late as 1936, there was a movement to end the death penalty in the antebellum period. The 1850s marked the climax of this crusade to abolish capital punishment. Michigan (1847), Rhode Island (1850s), and Wisconsin (1850s) abolished the death penalty, but opposition was barely existent in other states.[171]

D Civil War Era (1856-1876)

Abolitionist agitation against the capital punishment peaked in 1840s. Once executions in New York State were moved indoors and other states made the transition to private hangings, reformers began to direct their energies elsewhere. Others suggest that the bloodshed of the civil war ended the movement.[172]

During the civil war, soldiers were routinely executed for desertion and other crimes. 267 Union soldiers were executed between 1861-1867, more than the total of all other military executions in America's other wars.[173]

E Death Penalty in Victorian America (1870-1901)

Efforts to abolish the death penalty came to an abrupt halt as reformers diverted their attention toward slavery, the civil war, and reconstruction issues. Between 1865 and 1900, only Iowa, Maine, and Colorado abolished the death penalty, but all three would reinstate it within several years, and only Maine would once more than the abolitionist cloak for good beginning in 1887.[174]

---

[171] *Id*, p 133.

[172] *Id,* p 154.

[173] Robert Alotta, **Civil *War justice: Union Army Executions under Lincoln***, White Mane publishing, PA, U.S. (1989).

[174] Mitchel P. Roth, *supra note* 163, p 183.

Death Penalty 51

One development during this era was "delocalization of executions". This, along with discretion in death sentencing accrued after the civil war, when states began to require that execution be performed under state authority at one specific location. The movement toward state-mandated centralized execution began in Vermont and Maine. Between 1865 and 1900, twenty states made the transition from mandatory to discretionary capital punishment, permitting the jury to decide between death and alternative punishments. By the 1950s, however, there were still states that continued to conduct execution under local authority (Delaware and Montana).[175]

F Progressive era (1898-1938)

The twentieth century began with a recrudescence of abolitionist's activity against the death penalty. Through the progressive era, abolitionists such as lawyer Clarence Darrw (1857-1938) eloquently attacked capital punishment.[176]

During the first decades of the new century, studies by social scientists demonstrating the lack of deterrence value of death penalty convinced nine more states to abolish capital punishment. But this movement would end in the aftermath of the progressive era as concerns shifted to race riots, and raising crime rates. Four stated would in fact reinstate the death penalty in the early 1920s, while others would add new capital offenses.[177]

During the 1930s, America used the death penalty more than any pervious decade in American history. According to one study, 1676 execution took place in this decade, compared to an average of 1148 per decade between 1880 and 1920. However, this spate of executions considered with a raising population and murder rate.[178]

---

[175] William Bowers, *Executions in America*, Lexington Books, MA, U.S. (1974).

[176] Mitchel P. Roth, *supra note* 163, p 214.

[177] Roger Lane, *Capital Punishment: In Violence in America*, vol 1, ed. Ronald Gottesman, pp 198-203, Charles Scribner's Sons, New York, U.S. (1999).

[178] Victoria Schneider, and John Ortiz Smykla, *A Summary Analysis of Executions in the United States*, pp 6-7, Anderson Publishing, Cincinnati, U.S. (1991).

G Mid-century (1941-1959)

The number of capital crimes had been reduced since the eighteenth century. In fact American executions substantially decreased between the late 1940s and early 1950s. By the beginning of the 1950s, there were capital crimes for which no one had been executed in years, including kidnapping, treason, and, bombing. Since 1930s, the only capital crime that had regularly received the death penalty was murder.[179] Many allied nations either abolished or limited the death penalty, and in the U.S., the number of executions dropped dramatically. Whereas there were 1,289 executions in the 1940s, there were 715 in the 1950s, and the number fell even further, to only 191, from 1960 to 1976. In 1966, support for capital punishment reached an all-time low. A Gallup poll showed support for the death penalty at only 42%.[180]

H In to the Modern Era

Capital punishment has continued in the United States to the present despite repeated abolitionist movements. The first efforts in America originated in Pennsylvania towards the end of the eighteenth century. Dr. Benjamin Rush and William Bradford, early penal reformers, were major opponents of the death penalty. Rush would later be instrumental in developing the first modern prison in America. Abolitionist movements in the nineteenth and twentieth centuries have been somewhat successful as some states have permanently eliminated the death penalty while others have experimented with abolition only to reinstate it.[181]

The 1960s brought challenges to the fundamental legality of the death penalty. Before then, the Fifth, Eighth, and Fourteenth Amendments were interpreted as

---

[179] William Bowers, and Glenn Pierce, *Legal Homicide: Death as Punishment in America*, pp 25-26, Northeastern University press, Boston, U.S. (1984).

[180] R. Bohm, "*Deathquest:* **An Introduction to the Theory and Practice of Capital Punishment in the United States**," Anderson Publishing (1999).

[181] Steven A. Hatfield, **Criminal Punishment in America: From the Colonial to the Modern Era**, 1 USAFA J. Leg. Stud. 139 (1990).

permitting the death penalty. However, in the early 1960s, it was suggested that the death penalty was a "cruel and unusual" punishment, and therefore unconstitutional under the Eighth Amendment. In 1958, the Supreme Court had decided in *Trop v. Dulles*[182], that the Eighth Amendment contained an "evolving standard of decency that marked the progress of a maturing society." Although *Trop* was not a death penalty case, abolitionists applied the Court's logic to executions and maintained that the United States had, in fact, progressed to a point that its "standard of decency" should no longer tolerate the death penalty. [183]

The issue of arbitrariness of the death penalty was again being brought before the Supreme Court in 1972 in *Furman v. Georgia, Jackson v. Georgia,* and *Branch v. Texas* (known collectively as the landmark case *Furman v. Georgia)*. Furman argued that capital cases resulted in arbitrary and capricious sentencing. Furman, however, was a challenge brought under the Eighth Amendment. With the *Furman* decision the Supreme Court set the standard that a punishment would be "cruel and unusual" if it was too severe for the crime, if it was arbitrary, if it offended society's sense of justice, or it if was not more effective than a less severe penalty.

In 9 separate opinions, and by a vote of 5 to 4, the Court held that Georgia's death penalty statute, which gave the jury complete, sentencing discretion, could result in arbitrary sentencing. The Court held that the scheme of punishment under the statute was therefore "cruel and unusual" and violated the Eighth Amendment. Thus, on June 29, 1972, the Supreme Court effectively voided 40 death penalty statutes, thereby commuting the sentences of 629 death row inmates around the country and suspending the death penalty because existing statutes were no longer valid. [184]

Although the separate opinions by Justices Brennan and Marshall stated that the death penalty itself was unconstitutional, the overall holding in *Furman* was that the specific death penalty statutes were unconstitutional. With that holding, the Court essentially opened the door to states to rewrite their death penalty statutes to eliminate the problems cited in *Furman*. Advocates of capital punishment began proposing new

---

[182] *Trop v. Dulles* 356 U.S. 86 (1958).

[183] R. Bohm, *supra* note 180.

[184] *Furman v. Georgia 408 U.S. 238 (1972).*

statutes that they believed would end arbitrariness in capital sentencing. The states were led by Florida, which rewrote its death penalty statute only five months after *Furman*. Shortly after, 34 other states proceeded to enact new death penalty statutes. To address the unconstitutionality of unguided jury discretion, some states removed all of that discretion by mandating capital punishment for those convicted of capital crimes. However, this practice was held unconstitutional by the Supreme Court in *Woodson v. North Carolina*.[185]

Other states sought to limit that discretion by providing sentencing guidelines for the judge and jury when deciding whether to impose death. The guidelines allowed for the introduction of aggravating and mitigating factors in determining sentencing. These guided discretion statutes were approved in 1976 by the Supreme Court in *Gregg v. Georgia, Jurek v. Texas,* and *Proffitt v. Florida,* collectively referred to as the *Gregg* decision. This landmark decision held that the new death penalty statutes in Florida, Georgia, and Texas were constitutional, thus reinstating the death penalty in those states. The Court also held that the death penalty itself was constitutional under the Eighth Amendment.[186]

In addition to sentencing guidelines, three other procedural reforms were approved by the Court in *Gregg*. The first was bifurcated trials, in which there are separate deliberations for the guilt and penalty phases of the trial. Only after the jury has determined that the defendant is guilty of capital murder does it decide in a second trial whether the defendant should be sentenced to death or given a lesser sentence of prison time. Another reform was the practice of automatic appellate review of convictions and sentence. The final procedural reform from *Gregg* was proportionality review, a practice that helps the state to identify and eliminate sentencing disparities. Through this process, the state appellate court can compare the sentence in the case being reviewed with other cases within the state, to see if it is disproportionate.

Because these reforms were accepted by the Supreme Court, some states wishing to reinstate the death penalty included them in their new death penalty statutes. The Court, however, did not require that each of the reforms be present in the new statutes.

---

[185] *Woodson v. North Carolina* 428 U.S. 280 (1976).

[186] *Gregg v. Georgia* 428 U.S. 153 (1976), *Jurek v. Texas* 428 U.S. 262 (1976), and *Proffitt v. Florida* 428 U.S. 242 (1976).

Therefore, some of the resulting new statutes include variations on the procedural reforms found in *Gregg*. The ten-year moratorium on executions that had begun with the *Jackson* and *Witherspoon* decisions ended on January 17, 1977, with the execution of Gary Gilmore by firing squad in Utah.

At the beginning of 21 century, the position of United States on the law and practice of capital punishment is singular (Please refer to figure 2-1). Alone among the western democracies there is no clear indication of a willingness to stop execution in the United States. Alone among nations with strong traditions of due process in criminal procedure, criminal justice system in the United States attempt to merge a system of extensive procedures and review with execution as a legal outcome. Therefore the result has been a frustrating and lengthy process that combines all of the disadvantages of procedural regularity with unprincipled and arbitrary outcomes.[187]

Figure 2-1 States With Death Penalty (38) and the Number of Executions Since 1976

Source: American Civil Liberties Union, http://aclu.org/capital/facts.

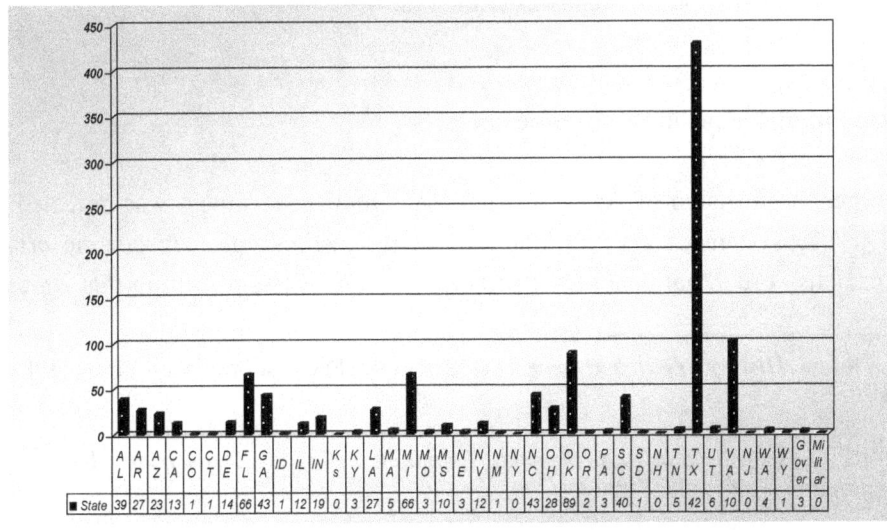

---

[187] Franklin Zimring, ***The Contradiction of American Capital Punishment***, p 5, Oxford University press, NY, U.S. (2003).

2 History of Death Penalty in Iran from the Ancient Times to Revolutionary Restatement of Capital Punishments

A Capital punishment in the ancient era

Iranian history starts in the beginnings of human life on earth, and yet the first Iranian ruling house was a dynasty of lawgivers.[188] Hence Iranian law began to take shape ever since humanity started forming itself society, and indeed that happened away in the past when we consider that man has been living on this globe for over ten million years, or probably for much more many ages than that huge period of time.

In ancient Persia punishments were harsh and in the majority of cases death penalty was applied. Capital punishment under Achaemenian (580-330 BC) and Sassanian (224-642 AD) dynasties was widely in practice. For instance punishment for third conviction of adultery was capital punishment or life imprisonment.[189] During Sassanian era death penalty became informed by Zoroastrian religion. Three convictions were punishable by death under Zoroastranism: blasphemy, rebellion against the king and, murder. For the first and second conviction death penalty was carried relentlessly, but for the third one the punishment was retaliation.[190]

B Capital punishment in the Islamic era

After the invasion of Arabs in Iran, the central government was defeated. The criminal justice system of ancient Iran collapsed. Muslims enforced Islamic criminal rules to establish order, national security and promotion of Islam. During this era capital

---

[188] Hassan Pirnia, *History of Ancient Iran*, Donyaye Ketab Publication, Tehran, Iran, (1982). [In Farsi].

[189] Aboulfazl Lesani, *Capital Punishment, Criminal Laws in Zoroastrian Religion*, Bar Association Journal, PP 54-55, Fifth year, 29.

[190] Mohammad bagher Karami, *Introduction on Criminal Justice System in Ancient Iran*, Khate sevvom (1380) in Farsi; Ava Vahedi, *Criminal Justice System in Sasanian Era*, Mizan publication (1380) [in Farsi].

punishment was practiced based on Islamic rules. Islamic punishments were administrated up to ratification of Penal Code in Iran. This occurred as the Pahlavi Dynasty replaced the Qajar Dynasty (1779-1925).

Iran has been ruled by monastic dynasties for over 2,500 years. Shiism became the official state religion under Safavid rule (1501-1722). The increasing influence of foreign powers in the region under the Qajars (1795-1925) began with a series of capitulations to Europeans, beginning with the Russians, in the 19th century. In 1906 the first Iranian Constitution was written. A series of laws were enacted, relating to criminal, civil, commercial, and family law.[191]

C   Capital Punishment under the Pahlavi Monarchy (1925-1979)

Iran's secular criminal justice system was formed under the Pahlavi Dynasty and its two monarchs, Reza Shah (1925-1941) and Mohammad Reza Shah (1941-1979). Modern criminal law was based on modern capitalist notions of crime and punishment. By 1936, Iranian legislation made secular education a requisite for serving judges. Major changes were introduced in the area of family law under Reza Shah. With the passage of the Family Protection Law of 1967 (significantly amended in 1975) extra-judicial divorce was abolished, required judicial permission for polygamy for limited circumstance. The Family Protection Law also established Family Courts for the application of the new personal status legislation.[192]

The first Penal Code of Iran was ratified in 1926. Based on Iran's Penal Code in addition to murder the death penalty was used to punish drug trafficking and offenses against public securities.

D   Capital Punishment Post -Islamic Revolution (1979)

The 1979 Islamic Revolution brought an end to Pahlavi dynasty (1925-1979). The Iranian Supreme Judicial Council issued a proclamation directing all courts that all

---

[191] Hassan Amin, *supra* note 96.

[192] *Id.*

non-Islamic legislation was suspended. The Council revised all laws to the Islamic legal system, with Ayatollah Khomeini's *fatawa* serving as transitional laws.

The punishment system in Iran is now based on the Twelve Imami Shii version of the Sharia Law. This system formed in the early 1980s during the tenure of the Ayatollah Ruhullah Mosavi Khomeini. In 1983 the first Islamic Penal Statute was ratified (Statute of Retaliation and Prescribed Punishments). Based on this Statute, capital punishment became applicable for crimes outlined in the Holy Quran and tradition. For other crimes jurists still refer to the modern Penal Code of Iran. In 1984 the Discretionary Punishment Statute was ratified. Chapter 2 and 3 of the Islamic Penal Code concern retaliation and prescribed punishments (It was ratified in 1992). Chapter 5 of Islamic Penal Code was ratified in 1997 (It was developed to deal with discretionary and preventive punishments).[193] The Islamic Penal Code provides death penalty for fifteen different crimes. (For more information please refer to chart 2-1). Furthermore, Article 729 of the Islamic Penal Code abolished all contrary statutes including modern Penal Code of Iran.[194]

---

[193] Iraj Goldouzian, ***Special Criminal Law,*** p 17, Tehran, Iran: Mizan Publication, (1999) [In Farsi].

[194] Islamic Penal Code of Iran, Art 729 (1991) [In Farsi].

Chart 2-1 Capital Crimes Based on Islamic Penal Code of Iran

- Incest
- Rape
- Adultery
- Sodomy
- Murder
- Defamation to sanctities
- Fornication of non Muslim with Muslim female
- Drug Trafficking In special amount
- Corruption on Earth

(Central node: Capital Crimes)

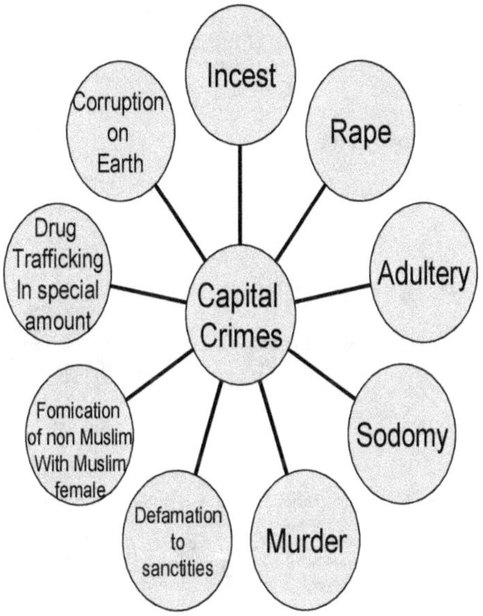

Corruption on Earth Crimes definition. under Islamic Penal Code of Iran is vague. Corruption on the Earth is not a crime, it can be attributed to crimes that include waging war against prophet and God, setting ablaze a mosque, destroying state during internal rebellion, and any criticism of state(crimes against public order).

The death penalty in Iran is applicable to an overly broad range of crimes in addition to murder: incest, rape, sex between a non-Muslim and a Muslim female; adultery, sodomy; other homosexual acts after fourth conviction, drinking liquor after three convictions, drawing arms to create fear, defamation to sanctities, drug trafficking in special amount, Corruption on Earth, Fornication (Fourth conviction), False accusation of unlawful intercourse (4th conviction), and Had Theft. (Please refer to chart 2-2).

Chart 2-2 Capital Crimes in Islamic Penal Code of Iran Based on Recidivism

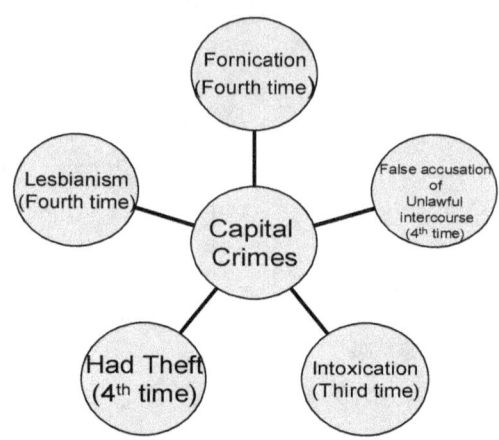

For this Haad *Theft* sixteen special conditions must be proven: puberty and sanity for thief, without threat and coercion on thief, intention, knowledge that property belongs to somebody else, knowledge that this act is unlawful, property should be located in the safe custody, breaking to the safe custody, the minimum value of property, lack of necessity, thief is not the father of the owner, safe custody had not belonged to thief previously, the act is for stealing, lack of famine, proportionate safe custody, and stolen goods are not government property of unknown ownership.

The Islamic Penal Code does not constrain the death penalty as punishment reserved for only a few crimes. In contrast, in United States capital punishment may be imposed only when the extinction of human life is brought about under circumstances society considers especially worthy of condemnation. Islamic law traditionally categorizes crimes according to the provenance of the authority to punish the offense. Islamic law recognizes four systems or category for punishment. Under Had or Hodoud, important crimes deemed to threaten the existence of Islam are punishable by penalties set by the Quran, or by the Sunna or Sunnah. Islamic jurists consider that these sanctions immutable. They conclude that the judge is left with no discretion.

The second system, Qisas, concerns intentional crimes against the person. Its fundamental premise is the lex talionis, "eye for eye, tooth for tooth." Lex talionis is set out in the Quran, verse 5.32 (further developed by verse 17.33). The lex talionis appeared first as the Code of Hammurabi. It was a progressive penal reform, at that time aimed at enhancing the principle of proportionality. It is now seen as a basis for retribution. According to the Quran, the victim or his or her heirs are to inflict the punishment, under

Death Penalty   61

the supervision of public authorities, the victims of such crimes may pardon the offender, in which case the death penalty set by Qisas will not be imposed.

In cases where the offender is pardoned by victims, two other systems of crime and punishment come to play. These are the Diyat, (prescribes restitution or compensation for the victim), and the Taazir (public authorities set their own punishment and in which the judge has wide discretion). Under the Taazir, public authorities may provide for capital punishment, but no religious text requires them to do so.

The rise in executions brought the number of executed in 2007 to about 150, compared to 177 in 2006. Iran is experiencing a dramatic increase in capital punishment (please refer to Figure 2-2). These executions come after the government launched a campaign targeting murderers, sex offenders, drug traffickers and others cast as a threat to 'national security'. It resulted in a wave of arrests, police raided working-class neighbourhoods in Tehran and other cities. Those arrested were paraded in public, often in humiliating poses.

Figure 2-2 Executions in Iran during 2005 & 2006

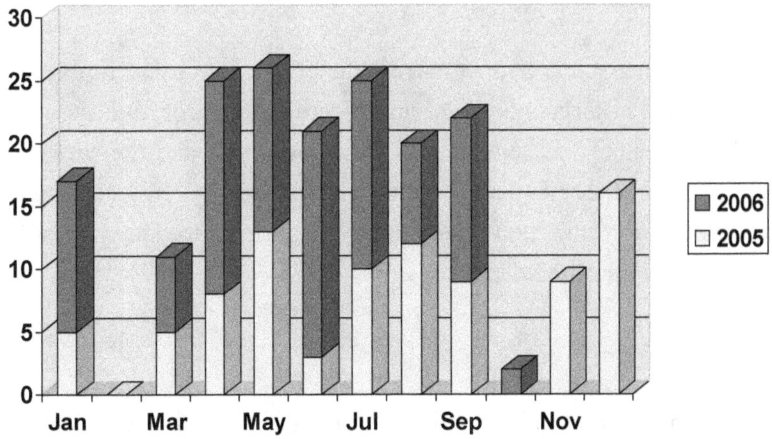

Source: http://www.richard.clark32.btinternet.co.uk/world.html.

II *Cruel and Unusual Per Se*

In this section we discuss how the members of third group have challenged the death penalty as being per se inhuman and barbarous. It is easy to claim that a punishment is barbaric. It is much more difficult to say why it is barbaric. If we call those bloody punishments of the past barbaric because they broke the body, what should we call those of today which constitute the abuse of individuals through the brutality of prison violence.[195] Although some scholars believe that capital punishment is not per se "cruel and unusual" under either original or modern understandings, but arbitrary and pain infliction of capital punishment are important factors that are against this hypothesis.

1   Arbitrary Infliction

In order not to inflict cruel and unusual punishment, must avoid arbitrary and capricious infliction of the death penalty, by considering rate and frequency of infliction must narrow the class of persons eligible for the penalty, as by a narrow definition of the capital offense, or a requirement that statutory aggravating factors be present.

The sentencing scheme must narrow the class of persons eligible for the penalty, by providing rational criteria and clear and objective standards, and specific and detailed guidance, which channel the sentencer's discretion and make the process rational and reviewable.[196] The absence of specific standards for weighing aggravating and mitigating factors are unnecessary, although a mandatory death penalty statute results in arbitrary and capricious infliction of the death sentence.[197]

---

[195] Graeme Newman, ***Just and Painful: A Case for the Corporal Punishment of Criminals***, p 83-94, Macmillan Publishing Company (1983).

[196] 24 C.J.S. Criminal Law § 2214.

[197] *Id.*

The "wanton" infliction of pain is prohibited. *Black's Law Dictionary* recognizes two forms of wanton behavior--malicious and reckless. Neither definition has been adapted specifically to methodology cases. As such, both are considered below. First, suppose the malice definition is adopted. In the context of legislatively decided punishments, malice appears to equate with sadism.

An examination of the reckless definition reveals that recklessness, unlike malice, does not stand as a separate intent element; rather, it is concerned with the degree of care exercised by a legislature in making the decision to impose a penalty. Therefore, the test for cruelty is whether there is a reckless infliction of unnecessary pain.

As a final test, What about treating the wanton and necessary terms not as two elements of one test, but as alternatives? This poses a problem because it is possible for a punishment to be the product of both legitimate and malicious motives, and it would be unjust for a criminal to go unpunished for this reason. Thus the suggested recklessness definition is the most workable and logical one. This definition prevents sadistic acts as well as those not based upon legitimate objectives. Also, it does not go so far that it abrogates the legislative prerogative. If a lesser standard were used, such as negligence, reviewing courts would be in a position to substitute their judgments for those of the legislatures. The reckless standard requires courts to treat legislative decisions with some deference. A punishment, therefore, would be wanton if there was reckless infliction of pain without sound penological justification.[198]

2   Pain Infliction

Question is that the offender experience pain in capital punishment. Some commentators and judges have defined cruelty in terms of great pain. This element is easily established because death penalty subjects the offender to both pain and indignity.

The critics argue that, since pain is a subjective phenomenon, we have never know whether a person really feels it or not, whether he in fact perceives it as pain or not, or whether all people experience pain in the same way.

---

[198] *Id.*

Does the scientific research back up such a claim? No, not really. Pain is certainly a subjective phenomenon, in that it is something that goes on inside a person and it is not directly observable to others. Perhaps the more important point is that some kinds of pain are more easily measurable than others. Mental pain is difficult to measure as are all others kinds of mental states. In contrast, physical pain is much easier to measure. It is clear then, that the claim that the capital punishment is perceived so subjectively that is can not be controlled does not hold water. The fact is that we can measure it quite precisely, and if we can measure it, we can control it.[199]

However, the point is that when punishments are ranked by their painfulness, they are not ranked against an absolute scale. Instead, society first decides which punishments are permissible. Then does society ranks punishments according to their painfulness; ranking always takes place in a context, and that context is not the universe of all possible punishments.[200] Therefore, the harshest punishment is not the one that causes the most pain. For when it comes to punishments that cause the offender to suffer, there is a least a vague sense of which punishments are really more painful than others. It is also possible to rule out punishments that do not cause pain as really punishments.[201]

But it is not still obvious how much pain is to be tolerated? How unique must a punishment be to rule it out? Considering above hypothesis it appears that a number of punishments still utilized today are extremely suspect. Capital Punishment is an obvious candidate for extinction. But will all scholars agree to rule out these penalties? Following legislative and judicial approval shows certainly not.

3   Legislative and Judicial Approval

Punishments are cruel when they involve torture or a lingering death; but the punishment of death is not cruel, within the meaning of that word as used in the Constitution. It implies there is something inhuman and barbarous, something more than

---

[199] H Merskey, *Pain: Psychological and Psychiatric Aspects*, London: Baillere (1967).

[200] Chad Flanders, *Shame and the Meanings of Punishment*, 54 Clev. St. L. Rev. 609 (2006).

[201] *Id.*

the mere extinguishments of life. The Supreme Court has firmly established that the death penalty, as punishment for certain homicides, does not violate the mandates of the Eighth Amendment to the Constitution of the United States.[202]

Since the death penalty was recognized as an available means of punishment at the time of the drafting of the U.S. Constitution and the Bill of Rights,[203] courts traditionally have assumed that capital punishment is not prohibited by either the Eighth Amendment[204] or the due process clauses of the Fifth and Fourteenth Amendments.[205] The Supreme Court never has held that capital punishment is per se unconstitutional. In fact, prior to 1968, the Supreme Court did not consider any cases where the validity of a death sentence was at issue, operating under the assumption that the death penalty was constitutional.[206]

Prior to 1968 the Court left the issue of death penalty legality to the states. In 1968, however, the Court reversed its traditional approach in *Witherspoon v. Illinois*, in which the Court reversed a death sentence after finding an integral procedure in the state's sentencing process to be invalid.[207] Although the particular issue addressed in this case involved the question of when a trial court is permitted to exclude jurors and for what reasons it may so exclude, this case opened the door to further Supreme Court review of closely related death sentencing procedures. As a practical matter, Witherspoon had a significant effect on states' criminal procedure, vacating approximately 150 capital sentences throughout the United States.[208]

---

[202] See Walter Berns, *For Capital Punishment,* pp 97-104, University Press of America (1979); Donald Hook & Lothar Kahn, *Death in the Balance* , pp 41-53, Lexington Books (1989); Igor Primoratez, *Justifying Legal Punishment,* pp 155-71, Prometheus Books (1990); Raymond Paternoster, *Capital Punishment in America,* pp 218-21, Jossey-Bass Inc., Publishers (1991).

[203] See Philip E. Mackey, *Voices Against Death*, Burt Franklin Books (1976).

[204] U.S. Const. amend. VIII.

[205] *Id,* amend. V & XIV.

[206] Welsh S. White, *The Death Penalty in the Nineties*, p 4, University of Michigan Press (1991).

[207] 391 U.S. 510 (1968). For the first time, the Supreme Court elevated the question of the procedural application of the death penalty to the constitutional level.

[208] *Id.*

In 1971, the Supreme Court granted certiorari for four death penalty cases in order to consider whether "the imposition and carrying out of the death penalty in [these cases] constitutes cruel and unusual punishment."[209] The states had no reason to believe that there were constitutional difficulties with such a sentencing scheme. For this reason, the Supreme Court's holding in *Furman v. Georgia*[210] came as an enormous surprise. In a per curium decision, the Court held that "the imposition and carrying out of the death penalty in these cases constitute[s] cruel and unusual punishment in violation of the Eighth and Fourteenth Amendments."[211] After Furman, if state legislatures wished to continue to use the death penalty they had to draft new legislation which more carefully channeled the judge or jury's sentencing discretion in order to avoid arbitrariness and inconsistent sentencing. This proved to be a difficult task as state legislatures were given little guidance.[212]

In Iran the legislature has approved capital punishment in three different categories:

1- **Prescribed Punishments (Hodoud)**:

The punishment of *fornication* (Fourth conviction) and the fornication of non Muslim with Muslim female is capital punishment as stated in the Holy Quran. Article 131 of Iran Penal Code provides that "if the act of lesbianism is repeated three times and punishment is enforced each time, death sentence will be issued the fourth time."[213]

Sodomy is punishable by death if both the active and passive persons are mature, of sound mind and have free will. Article 110 of the Islamic Penal Code provides that the "punishment for sodomy is death; the Sharia judge decides on how to carry out the killing." If an adult male of legal capacity commits sexual intercourse with an immature person, the doer will be killed and the passive one will be subject to Taazir (Discretionary punishment determined by the judge) of 74 lashes if not under duress.

---

[209] Aikens v. California, Furman v. Georgia, Jackson v. Georgia, and Branch v. Texas, 403 U.S. 952 (1971).

[210] 408 U.S. 238 at 248.

[211] *Id.*

[212] *Id.*

[213] Islamic Penal Code of Iran, Art 131 (1991). [In Farsi]

When active person is non-Muslim and passive person is Muslim punishment for passive person is the death penalty. If an immature person commits sexual intercourse with another immature person, both will be subject to Taazir[214] (For more information regarding sodomy laws in Iran refer to chart 2-3).

Chart 2-3 Criminal Statute Prohibiting Sodomy in Iran

Crime	Citation	Punishment	Explanations
Sodomy	Sections 108-120 Islamic Penal Code of Iran	Death Penalty	* Sodomy is sexual intercourse between two men. *If a mature man of sound mind commits sexual intercourse with an immature person, the doer will be killed and the passive one will be subject to 74 lashes if not under duress. If an immature person commits sexual intercourse with another immature person, both of them will be subject to 74 lashes unless one of them was under duress.
Tafhiz (rubbing thighs or buttocks)	Sections 121-122 Islamic Penal Code of Iran	Flogging (100 lashes)	*When active person is non-Muslim and passive person is Muslim punishment for passive person is death penalty. * If Tafhiz and the like are repeated three times without entry and punishment is enforced after each time, the punishment for the fourth time would be death.
Being naked under a cover	Section 123 Islamic Penal Code of Iran	Flogging (99 lashes)	*If two men not related by blood stand naked under one cover without any necessity.
Kissing	Section 124 Islamic Penal Code of Iran	Flogging (60 lashes)	*If one man kisses another man with lust.

-**Lesbianism** (Mosaheqeh) is female homosexuality. Punishment for lesbianism is one hundred (100) lashes for each party. Punishment for lesbianism established Vis-a -

---

[214] *Id*, Art 110-113, 121.

Vis someone who is mature, of sound mind, has free will and intention. In the Islamic Penal Code punishment for lesbianism there is no distinction between the doer and the subject as well as a Muslim or non-Muslim. If lesbianism is repeated three times and punishment is enforced each time, death sentence will be issued on the fourth conviction.[215] (For more information regarding lesbianism refer to chart 2-4).

Chart 2-4 Criminal Statute Prohibiting Lesbianism in Iran

Crime	Citation	Punishment	Explanations
Lesbianism	Sections 127-133 Islamic Penal Code of Iran	Flogging (100 lashes)	• **Lesbianism** (Mosaheqeh) is homosexuality of women by genitals. • In the punishment for lesbianism there will be no distinction between the doer and the subject as well as a Muslim or non-Muslim. • If the act of lesbianism is repeated three times and punishment is enforced each time, death sentence will be issued the fourth time.
Being naked under a cover	Section 134 Islamic Penal Code of Iran	Flogging (99 lashes)	*If two women not related by consanguinity stand naked under one cover without necessity, they will be punished to less than hundred (100) lashes. In case of its repetition as well as the repetition of punishment, hundred (100) lashes will be hit the third time.

-*False accusation of unlawful intercourse* is prohibited under Islamic Penal Code. Punishment for the fourth conviction is the death penalty. The rationale behind the Law of Qadhf or false accusation of unlawful intercourse is below:

---

[215] *Id,* Art. 127, 129, 130, 131.

1. It serves as a protection for the generality of the Muslims. The law of the Qadhf bans for publishing people's unlawful connections and illicit relationships to the society.

2. To serve as a deterrent for the accuser and his likes. When a person makes an allegation of adultery or fornication against someone and can not prove his case, he should be punished for slander, so that he might not slander in future.

Punishment for the fourth conviction of **Had Theft** is the death penalty. Theft is legally defined in Iran as the act of taking other people's property without any lawful claim to it.[216] Theft deprives a man of property. It is an encroachment upon the property of man without any justifiable society and is looked upon with terror. Therefore, strict measures have been ordered by Islamic Penal Code against thieves. The punishment for theft is in the Holy Quran: "As to the thief, male or female, cut of his or her hands as punishment by way of example from God for their crime. And God is exalted in power." According to a tradition of Prophet Mohammad, this punishment does not apply to petty larceny. However, the classical Islamic jurists differ as to the definition of petty larceny in terms of value of the stolen item. For this reason Islamic Penal Code regulates 16 different thefts[217] and just punishment of one category of theft is amputation.[218] (Punishment for nine categories of theft involves imprisonment and flogging.)

Punishment for **Wine drinking** during the time of Holy Prophet was beating with shoes, sticks, and hands without specifying the number of lashes. Under the Islamic Penal Code punishment of wine drinking is 80 lashes and for the third conviction the death penalty will be imposed.[219]

Moharebeh (*Resorting to arms to frighten people*) is defined as an act of robbery by a group of armed men within the territory of the Islamic state that creates anarchy under which the property, privacy, safety, dignity, and religious values of the people would be violated. The crime is regarded as a war against God and his messenger.

---

[216] *Id, Art.* 197.

[217] *Id, Art.* 651-667.

[218] *Id, Art.* 197-203.

[219] *Id, Art.* 165-182.

There are several alternative punishments, i.e. execution, crucifixion, amputation of hand and foot and exile. Therefore the judge has discretion to sentence which Moharebeh.[220]

Capital punishment based on the prescribed punishments is also imposed for *Adultery, Incest* and, *Rape.*

2- **Retaliation (Qisas)** is imposed for **Murder,** as explained in Article 205 of the Penal Code. Article 206 defines three types of intentional murder: (a) when the criminal intends to kill the specific person or non specific person, by the commission of a certain act whether that the acts results to inflict such a cut and/or injury; (b) when the criminal intentionally commits an act that results in killing although the intent was not to kill; and (c) when the criminal does not intend to kill, and his act does not result in killing, but, due to advanced age and/or infancy, the act result in death and it is known to the offender.

3- Discretionary punishments (Taazir) are the third category of punishments that provide for capital punishment. Islamic Penal Code uses capital punishment for the following offense: **Defamation to sanctities**[221], **Drug trafficking** [222] in special amount and for the **Corruption on Earth Crimes** (Corruption on Earth crimes is a vague definition. Under the Islamic Penal Code of Iran, Corruption on the Earth is not a crime, its definition can be attributed to crimes that include waging war against prophet and God, setting ablaze a mosque, destroying state property during internal rebellious, and any criticism of state (crimes against public order)).

Whether Taazir punishment may exceed the Had punishment, there is a Prophet tradition which says: "The man who shall inflict scourging, to the amount of punishment in case where Had is not established shall be counted an aggravator. (For information regarding executions based on capital crimes refer to figure 2-3).

---

[220] *Id,* Art 183-196.

[221] *Id,* Art 513.

[222] Anti Narcotics Drug Act, 1988 [In Farsi].

Figure 2-3 Executions in Iran Based by Capital Offenses Type during 2005 & 2006

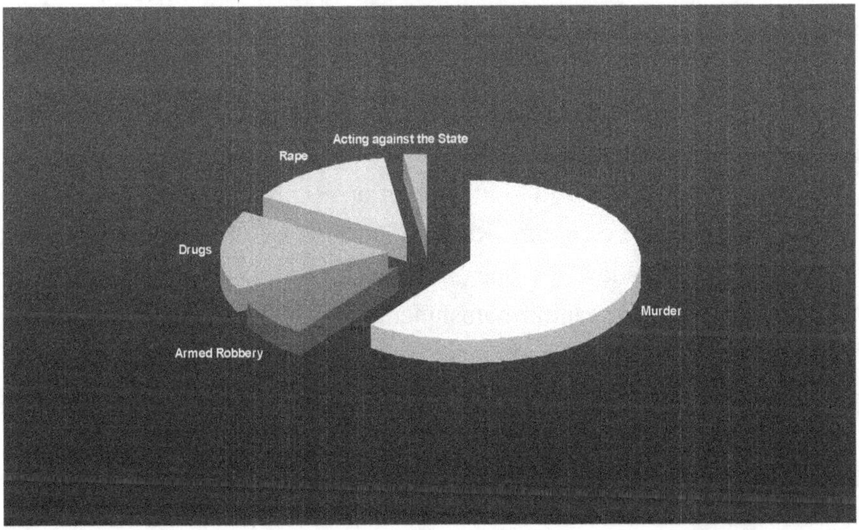

Source: http://www.richard.clark32.btinternet.co.uk/world.html.

III *International Aspect*

Although the death penalty has been used throughout the world for centuries, the concept of an international standard for the death penalty is relatively new. In the past, whether a country chose to resort to capital punishment was solely a domestic concern. International norms addressing the limitation and the abolition of the death penalty are essentially a post-Second World War phenomenon. The brutality of that war had a profound effect on those who were working towards building new international organizations designed to maintain peace among the nations of the world.[223]

---

[223] Ariane M. Schreiber, *States that Kill: Discretion and the Death Penalty– a Worldwide Perspective*, 29 Cornell Int'l L.J. 263 (1996).

1 The Right to Life under International Law

The right to life is the most sacrosanct of human rights. Although international law prohibits the arbitrary deprivation of human life, countries are increasingly prohibiting the taking of life under any circumstance.

A The Universal Declaration of Human Rights

On December 10, 1948, the United Nations (U.N.) General Assembly adopted the Universal Declaration of Human Rights ("UDHR").[224] Called "the cornerstone of contemporary human rights law" by one publicist,[225] the UDHR contains two provisions relevant to the imposition of capital punishment. Article 3 provides that "everyone has the right to life, liberty and security of person."[226] Article 5 states that "no one shall be subjected to torture or to cruel, inhuman or degrading treatment or punishment."[227] Although neither provision expressly prohibits the imposition of capital punishment, both are the result of a compromise reflecting a "common aspiration toward eventual abolition."[228]

The drafters of the Universal Declaration of Human Rights considered promoting abolition of the death penalty as a goal for civilized nations; however; the final declaration made no reference to capital punishment and only explicitly recognized the "right to life." During the drafting process, delegates from the United States and the United Kingdom submitted proposals urging that the death penalty should be viewed as an exception to the right to life, as it is in the United States with respect to the constitutionality of capital punishment. Nevertheless, these delegates, joined by others, including the Soviet delegate, argued that the United Nations should not signify any

---

[224] Universal Declaration of Human Rights, *supra* note 1.

[225] William A. Schabas, ***The International Sourcebook on Capital Punishment***, p 25, Northwestern University press (1997).

[226] UDHR, *supra* note 1, Art. 3

[227] *Id*. Art. 5.

[228] Joan Fitzpatrick & Alice Miller, ***International Standards on the Death Penalty: Shifting Discourse***, 19 BROOK. J. INT'L L. 273, 278 (1993).

approval of the use of capital punishment. Even though the drafters refrained from addressing capital punishment in this initial declaration, the notion of abolishing the death penalty was not abandoned.[229]

While the UDHR is not binding, it is frequently viewed as a codification of customary international law. Thus it is important to note that the compromise reached in the wording of Article 3, and its silence with respect to the death penalty, has been characterized as "reflecting an overwhelming acceptance of abolition as a goal." Although at the time the death penalty was widely regarded as an exception to the right to life, the failure to incorporate this view in the UDHR supports the notion that abolition of the death penalty was seen as a goal of the international community and an emerging norm of international law. For the most part, the few explicit dissents to that notion during the debate over the UDHR were based entirely upon grounds that capital punishment was a matter of domestic and not international concern.[230]

B The International Covenant on Civil and Political Rights

The twenty-year drafting period of the International Covenant on Civil and Political Rights ("ICCPR"),[231] which was adopted by the U.N. General Assembly in 1966, reflected the realization that the death penalty was indeed a human rights issue and within the scope of international concern.[232]

Article 6 of the ICCPR provide:
(1) Every human being has the inherent right to life. This right shall be protected by law. No one shall be arbitrarily deprived of his life.
(2) In countries which have not abolished the death penalty, sentence of death may be imposed only for the most serious crimes in accordance with the law in force at the time of the commission of the crime and not contrary to the provisions of the present

---

[229] William A. Schabas, *Supra* note 225, pp 25-34.

[230] James H. Wyman, *Vengeance is Whose?: The Death Penalty and Cultural Relativism in International Law*, Journal of Transnational Law and Policy Summer, (1997).

[231] International Covenant on Civil and Political Rights, *supra* note 139.

[232] James H. Wyman, *supra* note 230.

Covenant.... . This penalty can only be carried out pursuant to a final judgment rendered by a competent court.

(4) Anyone sentenced to death shall have the right to seek pardon or commutation of the sentence. Amnesty, pardon or commutation of the sentence of death may be granted in all cases.

(5) Sentence of death shall not be imposed for crimes committed by persons below eighteen years of age and shall not be carried out on pregnant women.

(6) Nothing in this article shall be invoked to delay or to prevent the abolition of capital punishment by any State Party to the present Covenant.[233]

Throughout the drafting period, Sweden and several Latin American countries, most notably Uruguay and Colombia, urged immediate abolition of capital punishment.[234] In 1957, Uruguay and Colombia introduced an abolitionist proposal: "Every human being has the inherent right to life. The death penalty shall not be imposed upon any person."[235] Oddly enough, much of the opposition to the proposal came from states such as the United Kingdom, New Zealand, Australia, and Canada, all of which have since abolished capital punishment. In addition, several Islamic states, including Morocco, Afghanistan, Saudi Arabia, and Indonesia, voiced opposition to the proposal while at the same time expressing hopes for eventual abolition.[236]

Unlike the Universal Declaration, the International Covenant on Civil and Political Rights is binding on all nations which become party to it.[237] This Covenant is the first affirmative indication that the United Nations approves of, if not advocates, an abolitionist position regarding the death penalty.[238] The proposal was defeated by a roll-call vote of fifty-one to nine, with twelve members abstaining. However, the proposal did

---

[233] ICCPR, *supra* note 139, Art. 6, 999 U.N.T.S. at 174-75.

[234] James H. Wyman, *supra* note 230.

[235] U.N. GAOR 3d Comm., 12th Sess., Agenda Item 33, U.N. Doc. A/C.3/L.644 (1957).

[236] William A. Schabas, *supra note* 225.

[237] Sonia Rosen & Stephen Journey, **Abolition of the Death Penalty: An Emerging Norm of International Law**, 14 Hamline J. Pub. L. & Policy 163, 164 (1993).

[238] Ariane M. Schreiber, *supra* note 223.

lead to the adoption of abolitionist language in paragraphs 2 and 6 of Article 6, adopted by the General Assembly in 1966. The ICCPR entered into force on March 23, 1976, following the thirty-fifth ratification.[239] The United States, which in 1968 expressed the view that no justification existed for the death penalty,[240] finally ratified the ICCPR in 1992 with extensive reservations to the death penalty provisions in Article 6. [241]

C The Second Optional Protocol to the International Covenant on Civil and Political Rights

At the close of 1989, the U.N. General Assembly took affirmative steps towards establishing an international standard advocating the world-wide abolition of the death penalty by adopting the Second Optional Protocol to the International Covenant on Civil and Political Rights Aimed at the Abolition of the Death Penalty.[242]

Article 1 of the draft Protocol, which was presented by the Federal Republic of Germany, provided that:
(1) Each State party shall abolish the death penalty in its territory and shall no longer foresee the use of it against any individual subject to its jurisdiction nor impose nor execute it.
(2) The death penalty shall not be re-established in States that have abolished it.[243]

As the draft Protocol was debated by different U.N. committees throughout the 1980s, comments from various states were submitted to the Secretary-General. These comments were divided almost equally between abolitionist and retentionist states. The bulk of the opposition to the Protocol came from Islamic states, of which Egypt expressed the most typical sentiment: " The death penalty cannot be abolished in the

---

[239] William A. Schabas, *supra note* 225.

[240] U.N. GAOR 3d Comm., 23d Sess., 1557th mtg. 20, U.N. Doc. A/C.3/SR.1557 (1968).

[241] 138 CONG. REC. S4783 (daily ed. Apr. 2, 1992).

[242] Second Optional Protocol to the International Covenant on Civil and Political Rights Aiming at the Abolition of the Death Penalty, G.A. Res. 44/128, U.N. GAOR, 44th Sess., Supp. No. 98, U.N. Doc. A/RES/44/128 (1990).

[243] Crime Prevention and Control, U.N. GAOR 3d Comm., 35th Sess., Agenda Item 65, U.N. Doc. A/35/742 (1980).

cases where it is laid down as Had (prescribed castigation decreed by God or the Prophet) or Qisas (equal retribution) but ... may be commuted in those cases where it is laid down as Taazir (deterrent)."[244] In addition, Saudi Arabia, observing that abolition of the death penalty was "incompatible with Islamic principle," insisted upon a recorded vote.[245] Almost all of the states[246] that spoke in opposition to the draft were those with significant Muslim populations; references to Islamic law and the Quran were made repeatedly with the exception of the United States, China, and Japan.[247]

After the debate over the draft, Islamic states repeatedly objected to its provisions and cast dissenting votes. The draft finally emerged and was presented to the Third Committee of the General Assembly with the following language:

(1) No one within the jurisdiction of a State Party to the present Protocol shall be executed.

(2) Each State Party shall take all necessary measures to abolish the death penalty within its jurisdiction.[248]

On December 29, 1989, the General Assembly adopted the Protocol by a vote of fifty-nine to twenty-six, with forty-eight abstentions. Following its tenth ratification, the Protocol entered into force on July 11, 1991.[249] As of 1996, twenty-nine states had ratified it.[250]

Even though this protocol is optional, it unequivocally voices its opposition to the continued use of capital punishment. In addition, unlike other international

---

[244] William A. Schabas, *supra note* 225, p 164.

[245] U.N. GAOR 3d Comm., 39th Sess., 60th mtg. 22, U.N. Doc. A/C.3/39/SR.60 (1984).

[246] The states voting against the protocol were: Afghanistan, Bahrain, Bangladesh, Cameroon, China, Djibouti, Egypt, Indonesia, Islamic Republic of Iran, Iraq, Japan, Jordan, Kuwait, Malaysia, Maldives, Morocco, Nigeria, Oman, Pakistan, Qatar, Saudi Arabia, Sierra Leone, Somalia, Syrian Arab Republic, Sudan, United Republic of Tanzania, United States of America, and Yemen. See William A. Schabas *Supra* note 225.

[247] William A. Schabas, *supra note* 225, p 169.

[248] Second Optional Protocol to the International Covenant on Civil and Political Rights Aiming at the Abolition of the Death Penalty, *supra* note 242.

[249] William A. Schabas, *supra note* 225, p 170.

[250] See Amnesty International, **Abolition of the Death Penalty Worldwide: Developments in 1995** (AI Index ACT 50/07/96).

agreements, the Second Optional Protocol explicitly states that, as a general rule, signatory parties may not ratify the treaty or become signatory parties while also making reservations to it. This international instrument is open to any member of the United Nations who previously signed the International Covenant on Civil and Political Rights.[251]

D Convention Against Torture

The Convention Against Torture, on the other hand, forbids physical and psychological abuse or any act by which severe pain or suffering is intentionally inflicted on a person by a public official.[252] The Torture Convention also prohibits the infliction of pain and suffering based on discrimination of any kind.[253] While the Torture Convention arguably could be used as a tool to challenge capital punishment generally, it is more effective in challenging the manner of execution, the prolonged length of time between sentencing and execution, and the discriminatory manner in which the death penalty is sought and applied.[254]

E The American Convention on Human Rights

During the years following World War II, in 1978, the American Convention on Human Rights became the first international treaty to take an unequivocal abolitionist stand on the use of the death penalty.[255] Article 4 of the treaty, entitled "Right to Life," specifically addresses capital punishment and delineates the international standards to which the parties agreed to adhere:

---

[251] Second Optional Protocol to the International Covenant on Civil and Political Rights Aiming at the Abolition of the Death Penalty, *supra note* 242.

[252] Convention Against Torture, *supra* note 9, Art. 1.

[253] *Id.*

[254] William A. Schabas, *supra* note 225, pp 126-127.

[255] The American Convention on Human Rights, Nov. 22, 1969, 1144 U.N.T.S. 123, O.A.S.T.S. No. 36, at 1 (entered into force July 18, 1978).

1."[e]very person has the right to have his life respected. This right shall be protected by law and, in general, from the moment of conception. No one shall be arbitrarily deprived of his life."

2. In countries that have not abolished the death penalty, it may be imposed only for the most serious crimes and pursuant to a final judgment rendered by a competent court and in accordance with a law establishing such punishment, enacted prior to the commission of the crime. The application of such punishment shall not be extended to crimes to which it does not presently apply.

3. The death penalty shall not be reestablished in states that have abolished it.

Unlike other U.N. treaties, this treaty established restrictive rules on the use of the death penalty instead of merely advocating heightened respect for life and suggesting eventual abolition of the death penalty. It was particularly innovative in forbidding capital punishment for political offenses or related common crimes and forbidding the execution of individuals under the age of eighteen, individuals over the age of seventy, and pregnant women.[256] This treaty was also the first to limit the exercise of the death penalty to only "the most serious crimes," in those countries that have not abolished its use and to forbid the extension of capital punishment to new crimes.[257]

During the debates for adoption of the American Convention, the United States initially proposed omitting language prohibiting execution of those who committed their crimes while younger than eighteen years of age because it set an arbitrary age limit that "presents various difficulties in law." The United States delegate also noted that the provision weakened the text of article 4 as a whole because there already was a general trend toward abolishing the death penalty for juveniles, thereby making the text unnecessary. The United States later withdrew its proposal and signed the treaty on June 1, 1977, after twelve states had already signed it on November 22, 1969. As of today, twenty-five states have ratified the American Convention. The United States has not.[258]

---

[256] *Id*, Art 4.

[257] *Id.*

[258] Anthony N. Bishop, ***The Death Penalty in the Unites States: An International Human Rights Perspective***, 43 S. Tex. L. Rev. 1115 (2002).

F The European Convention for the Protection of Human Rights

The European Convention specifically protects the "right to life," but only implicitly protects individuals from arbitrary imposition of the death penalty. The Council of Europe interprets Article 2 not "to protect unconditionally life itself or to guarantee a certain quality of life. Instead, these provisions [Article 2 and Protocol No. 6] [259] aim to protect the individual against any arbitrary deprivation of life by the State."[260]

The European Convention on Human Rights, which Protocol No. 6 supplements, was signed on November 4, 1950, and entered into force on September 3, 1953.[261] Article 2 of the European Convention recognizes capital punishment as an exception to the right to life, and it does not include the limitations and safeguards governing the use of capital punishment in retentionist nations that are found in subsequent international treaties.[262]

In February 1985, European nations took an even greater step towards an international standard promoting the abolition of the death penalty when they became parties to Protocol No. 6 to the European Convention for the Protection of Human Rights and Fundamental Freedoms Concerning the Abolition of the Death Penalty.[263] Article 1 explicitly states that "[t]he death penalty shall be abolished. No one shall be condemned to such penalty or executed."[264] Because nearly all of Western Europe had become, at least in practice, abolitionist for ordinary crimes including murder, the Council of Europe recognized the need to take a more affirmative stance against the continued use of capital punishment.[265]

---

[259] Council of Europe, *Short Guide to the European Convention on Human Rights*, p 17 (1991).

[260] *Id.*

[261] Convention for the Protection of Human Rights and Fundamental Freedoms, 1955, 213 U.N.T.S. 221, E.T.S. 5.

[262] William A. Schabas, *supra* note 225, pp 61-104.

[263] Protocol No. 6 of the Convention for the Protection of Human Rights and Fundamental Freedoms Concerning the Abolition of the Death Penalty, Nov. 4, 1950, E.T.S. 114.

[264] *Id.* Art. 1.

As of February 1, 1993, nineteen nations had ratified Protocol No. 6.[266] Some scholars have gone so far as to say that "for all intents and purposes, we can speak of Europe as being an abolitionist continent."[267]

The Council of Europe's Committee of Ministers adopted Protocol 13 to the European Convention on Human Rights. Protocol 13 is the first legally binding international treaty to abolish the death penalty in all circumstances with no exceptions. When it was opened for signature in May 2002, 36 countries signed it.

G The Universal Islamic Declaration of Rights

In 1981, the Islamic Council adopted a Universal Islamic Declaration of Rights, which states: "(a) Human life is sacred and inviolable and every effort shall be made to protect it. In particular no one shall be exposed to injury or death, except under the authority of the law."[268] The final phrase appears to permit capital punishment and is in any case consistent with the practice of all Islamic states. The Islamic Conference has prepared a document on human rights and Islam, in which Article 2 guarantees the right to life to "every human being" adding: "It is the duty of individuals, societies and states to protect this right from any violation, and it is prohibited to take away life except for a Sharia-prescribed reason."[269]

---

[265] William A. Schabas, *supra* note 225, pp 211-212.

[266] *Id,* p 323.

[267] *Id, pp* 2-3.

[268] Universal Islamic Declaration of Rights, 4 EUROPEAN HUMAN RIGHTS REPORTS 433 (1982).

[269] Organization of the Islamic Conference, Secretary General, doc. OIC/POL/MD/82-83/7, Djeddah, Apr. 25, 1982. Article 2 indicates: "a) Life is a God-given gift and the right to life is guaranteed to every human being. It is the duty of individuals, societies and states to protect this right from any violation, and it is prohibited to take away life except for a Sharia-prescribed reason. (b) It is forbidden to resort to such means as may result in the genocidal annihilation of mankind. (c) The preservation of human life throughout the term of time willed by God is a duty prescribed by Sharia." (d) Safety from bodily harm is a guaranteed right. It is the duty of the state to safeguard it, and it is prohibited to breach it without a Sharia-prescribed reason.

H United Nations Resolutions

In December 1984, the General Assembly, building upon the Covenant on Civil and Political Rights, passed a resolution which established further measures, designed to protect the rights of those facing capital punishment around the world. The "**Safeguards Guaranteeing Protection of the Rights of Those Facing the Death Penalty**" enumerates the essential restrictions and safeguards on the exercise of capital punishment.[270] Even though the United Nations still has not adopted an abolitionist posture towards world-wide use of the death penalty, the new safeguards send an unambiguous message to retentionist nations that international organizations recognize capital punishment as a ripe area for human rights abuses and the need for it to be regulated and monitored. These safeguards are more specific and provide greater protection to those subject to capital punishment under the CCPR,[271] but Amnesty

---

[270] G.A. Res. 39/118, U.N. GAOR, 39th Sess., Supp. No. 12, at 19, U.N. Doc. A/RES/39/119 (1984).

[271] The resolution states in relevant Art:
1. In countries which have not yet abolished the death penalty, capital punishment may be imposed only for the most serious crimes, it being understood that their scope should not go beyond intentional crimes, with lethal or extremely grave consequences.
2. Capital punishment may be imposed only for a crime for which the death penalty is prescribed by law at the time of its commission, it being understood that if, subsequent to the commission of the crime, provision is made by law for the imposition of a lighter penalty, the offender shall benefit thereby.
3. Persons below 18 years of age at the time of the commission of the crime shall not be sentenced to death, nor shall the death penalty be carried out on pregnant women, or on new mothers or persons who have become insane.
4. Capital punishment may be imposed only when the guilt of the person charged is based upon clear and convincing evidence leaving no room for an alternative explanation of the facts.
5. Capital punishment may only be carried out pursuant to a final judgment rendered by a competent court after legal process which gives all possible safeguards to ensure a fair trial ... including the right of anyone suspected of or charged with a crime for which capital punishment may be imposed to adequate legal assistance at all stages of the proceeding.
6. Anyone sentenced to death shall have the right to an appeal to a court of highest jurisdiction, and steps shall be taken to ensure that such appeals shall become mandatory.
7. Anyone sentenced to death shall have the right to seek pardon, or commutation of sentence; pardon or commutation of sentence may be granted in all cases of capital punishment.
8. Capital punishment shall not be carried out pending any appeal or other recourse procedure or other proceeding relating to pardon or commutation of the sentence.
9. Where capital punishment occurs, it shall be carried out so as to inflict the minimum possible suffering.

International scholars believe that the provisions of this resolution represent restatements of the protections guaranteed under the Covenant on Civil and Political Rights.[272]

In 1994, *Italy proposed a draft resolution* in the United Nations General Assembly on the issue of the death penalty. The proposed draft resolution attempted to place a world-wide moratorium on executions.[273] To give effect to this resolution, the draft invited all nations which had not signed existing human rights treaties directed at the abolition of the death penalty to do so.[274] After active debates, several proposed drafts, no-action motions, and amendments, the General Assembly's Social, Humanitarian and Cultural Committee ultimately rejected the resolution. States who spoke opposing the resolution included Malaysia, Bangladesh, Sudan, Saudi Arabia, Libya, Egypt, Iran, and Jordan. During the debate, Sudan described capital punishment as "a divine right according to some religions, in particular Islam." Earlier that year, during the 1994 session of the United Nations Commission on Human Rights, the Special Reporter on the Sudan, Gaspar Biro, said that so-called Islamic punishments such as stoning to death for the crime of adultery, run contrary to the prohibition of torture or cruel, inhuman and degrading treatment of punishment found in Article 7 of the International Covenant on Civil and Political Rights.[275] He was vehemently denounced by the Sudanese representative, Abdelaziz Shiddo, who accused him of insulting religious values in a "Satanic paragraph" of his report, adding that "he must assume the responsibility" for his comments. The report, continued Ambassador Shiddo, was "flagrant blasphemy and a deliberate insult to the Islamic religion."[276]

---

[272] Amnesty International, *When the State Kills: The Death Penalty: A Human Rights Issue,* p 13 (1989).

[273] Weekend Edition*: U.N. Resolution Calls for Abolition of Death Penalty*, National Public Radio broadcast (Nov. 27, 1994).

[274] *U.N. Rejects Move to End Death Penalty*, UPI, Dec. 9, 1994, available in LEXISNexis Library, UPI file.

[275] U.N. Doc. A/49/234, Add.1, Add.2 (1994), later revised by U.N. Doc. A/C.3/49/L.32-71/Rev.1 (1994). And U.N. Doc. E/CN.4/1994/48.

[276] U.N. Doc. E/CN.4/1994/122, <section> 58-64.

The draft resolution opponents second major objection was embodied in an amendment introduced by Singapore.[277] This amendment, which a majority of the Committee members voted to include in the draft resolution,[278] explicitly, recognized the "sovereign rights of states to determine the legal measures and penalties which are appropriate in their societies to combat serious crimes effectively."[279] Singapore's Permanent Representative to the United Nations, Chew Tai Soo, explained that "what works in other countries need not work in Singapore, and vice-versa."[280] The draft resolution lost substantial support once Singapore's amendment was adopted. All of the resolution's original sponsors withdrew their sponsorship, and several of them abstained from the final vote, as they were unwilling to support the amendment. The Social, Humanitarian and Cultural Committee defeated the draft resolution by a vote of forty-four to thirty-six, with seventy-four nations abstaining.[281]

More recently, on April 3, 1998, the UN Commission on Human Rights passed a ***resolution specifically on the death penalty***.[282] This resolution urges those States that have not yet become parties to the ICCPR or the Optional Protocol to do so. Additionally, the resolution reinforces the limitations of the ICCPR and the Convention on the Rights of the Child by restating five regulations on the use of the death penalty. Most significantly, the resolution calls for both the restriction of the number of offenses that are death penalty-eligible and the imposition of a moratorium on all executions, "with a view to completely abolishing the death penalty."[283]

---

[277] U.N. Rejects Move to End Death Penalty, *supra* note 274.

[278] Evelyn Leopold, ***U.N. Panel Defeats Resolution on Capital Punishment***, Reuters Word Service, Dec. 10, 1994, available in LEXIS, Nexis Library, Reuters File.

[279] Weekend Edition: U.N. Resolution Calls for Abolition of Death Penalty, *supra* note 273.

[280] *Id.*

[281] Evelyn Leopold, *supra* note 278.

[282] This resolution passed by a vote of 26 to 13, with 12 abstentions. New Human Rights Declaration Approved in Geneva, DEUTSCHE PRESS-AGENTUR, Apr. 3, 1998, available in LEXIS, Europe Library, DPA File. Among those States voting against the resolution were the United States, China, Pakistan, and Rwanda. Mark Tran, ***U.S. Singled Out as Death Penalty is Condemned***, GUARDIAN, London (Apr. 4, 1998).

[283] *Id.*

In 2005 the United Nation Commission on Human Rights (UNCHR) approved Human Rights Resolution 2005/59 on the question of the death penalty, which called for all states that still maintain the death penalty to abolish the death penalty completely and, in the meantime, to establish a moratorium on executions.

Finally in 2007 the UN General Assembly (UNGA) approved Resolution 62/149 which called for all states that still maintain the death penalty to establish a moratorium on executions with a view to abolishing the death penalty.

2 Death Penalty and International Law in U.S. Courts

According to the Declaration, if the death penalty is a form of cruel, inhuman, or degrading punishment, then the abolition of the death penalty may indeed be customary international law.[284] But the United States has not accepted the international definition of "cruel, inhuman, or degrading punishment;" rather, the United States uses the interpretations of, and the law surrounding, the Fifth, Eighth, and Fourteenth Amendments to limit the scope of this phrase.[285] Furthermore, the U.S. Supreme Court's most recent holding concerning the constitutionality of the death penalty is that it is not cruel and unusual punishment or arbitrary per se.

Unlike the Fifth and Fourteenth Amendments to the United States Constitution, article 3 is not subject to due process limitations. Article 3 guarantees an absolute right to life, and the United States recognized this absolute right when it signed the Universal Declaration on December 10, 1948.[286]

The Court resolves disputes submitted to it in accordance with international law, applying the following:

---

[284] Thomas Butergenthal, *International Human Rights in a Nutshell*, pp 29-32 (1988).

[285] United Nations, *Multilateral Treaties Deposited with the Secretary-General: Status as of Dec. 31 1997*, p 121 (1998).

[286] Anthony N. Bishop, *supra* note 258.

(a) International conventions, whether general or particular, establishing rules expressly recognized by the contesting states;

(b) International custom, as evidence of a general practice accepted as law;

(c) The general principles of law recognized by civilized nations;

(d) ... judicial decisions and the teachings of the most highly qualified publicists of various nations, as subsidiary means for the determinations of rules of law.[287] The decisions of international tribunals, however, seem to be the least respected sources of international law by the United States government and the fifty states For example; the United States has consistently argued that the ICJ does not have jurisdiction over it in lawsuits brought against it by foreign governments.[288]

The United States ratified the International Covenant on June 8, 1992, to be effective September 8, 1992.[289] The United States, however, ratified the International Covenant with broad reservations, effectively excluding itself from almost all the provisions regulating capital punishment: "The United States reserves the right, subject to its Constitutional constraints, to impose capital punishment on any person (other than pregnant women) duly convicted under existing or future laws permitting the imposition of capital punishment, including such punishment for crimes committed by persons below eighteen years of age."[290]

The United States ratified the Torture Convention. However, recognizing that the Torture Convention could possibly be construed to prohibit capital punishment, the United States entered the following reservation:

> The United States understands that international law does not prohibit the death penalty, and does not consider this Convention to restrict or prohibit the United

---

[287] Statute of the International Court of Justice Art. 38(1) (1945), reprinted in Leland M. Goodrich et al., Charter of the United Nations: Commentary and Documents 707 (3d & rev. ed. 1969).

[288] Ironically, the United States has sought relief against other countries in the ICJ on several occasions, implying that it views the court and its decisions as having legal authority over the United States and other member states only when the United States seeks relief. When the ICJ has ruled against the United States, the United States frequently treated the decisions as not binding, even though they are binding under international law. See Anthony N. Bishop, *The Death Penalty in the United States: An International Human Rights Perspective*, 43 S. Tex. L. Rev. 1115 (2002).

[289] Office of the United Nations High Commissioner for Human Rights, Status of Ratification of the Principal International Human Rights Treaties, at http://www.unhchr.ch/pdf/report.pdf.

[290] Senate Committee on Foreign Relations, Report on the International Covenant on Civil and Political Rights, S. Exec. Rep. No. 102-23 (2d Sess. 1992) reprinted in 31 I.L.M. 645, 643 (1992).

States from applying the death penalty consistent with the Fifth, Eighth and/or Fourteenth Amendments to the Constitution of the United States, including any constitutional period of confinement prior to the imposition of the death penalty.[291] The reservation was also intended to avoid challenges based on the "death row phenomena."

Along the lines outlined above, the Sixth Circuit ruled that the death penalty is illegal neither by treaty law nor by CIL. Richard Buell was convicted and sentenced to death in Ohio for sexually assaulting and killing eleven-year-old Kristen Lee Harrison. In a habeas appeal to the Sixth Circuit, he argued, inter alia, that the Ohio death penalty was illegal under the American Declaration, the ICCPR, and CIL, in particular as a jus cogens norm. The court stated, "Buell's argument is wholly meritless."[292]

First, because both the American Declaration and the ICCPR do not outlaw capital punishment, and the United States made reservations to these agreements that foreclose any reliance on them to the extent that they deviate from Supreme Court interpretations of the Constitution, also, in any event, both are non-self-executing and therefore "neither is binding on federal courts."[293]

Second, the court held that CIL does not ban capital punishment, stating that "[t]he prohibition of the death penalty [in domestic law] is not so extensive and virtually uniform among the nations of the world that it is a customary international norm" and that "[t]here is no indication that the countries that have abolished the death penalty have done so out of a sense of legal obligation, rather than for moral, political, or other reasons." The court added that since capital punishment is not banned by CIL, it cannot be a violation of a jus cogens norm.[294]

Third, the court stated that even if CIL banned capital punishment, it would not strike down the Ohio death penalty. The court stated that U.S. courts have rejected claims

---

[291] See Multilateral Treaties Deposited with the Secretary-General: Status as at 31 December 1994 at 175, U.N. Doc. ST/LEG/SER.E/13, U.N. Sales No. E. 95. V. 5 (1995).

[292] Buell v. Mitchell, 274 F.3d 337 (6th Cir. 2001).

[293] *Id.*

[294] *Id.*

of private civil rights of action against state officials by U.S. citizens based on CIL, and Buell "is attempting to interpose customary international law as a defense against acts committed by government officials against a citizen of the United States."[295]

Thus, the death penalty provides an illuminating case study of the importance of maintaining American sovereignty in the face of organized campaigns by the human rights movement to impose foreign moods, fads, or fashions on Americans.[296] As demonstrated in this section, because various human rights instruments do not prohibit the death penalty, are non-binding as matters of international law, and do not apply internally as a matter of U.S. law. Likewise CIL does not prohibit the death penalty, and if a CIL norm existed, it would not apply directly in U.S. courts. Therefore, the U.S. death penalty survives scrutiny under international law.

3 Fundamental Conflict between Theocracy and Principles of Human Rights

The suggestion from some Islamic states that religious law forbids abolition of the death penalty constitutes an important obstacle to universal abolition. International human rights standards, as embodied in the U.N. treaties, represent the opposite end of the political spectrum from conservative religious fundamentalism.

With the advent of Islamic fundamentalism in the 1970s, more and more Islamic states began objecting to international norms for human rights and abolition of the death penalty, as being contrary to Sharia[297], the historically formulated traditional law of Islam.[298]

---

[295] *Id.*

[296] Laurence E. Rothenberg, ***International Law, U.S. Sovereignty, and the Death Penalty***, 35 Geo. J. Int'l L. 547 (2004).

[297] Sharia was developed in the centuries following the Prophet Mohammed's death in 632, and its formulation was essentially complete by the thirteenth century.

[298] Joan Fitzpatrick & Alice Miller, *supra* note 228.

To justify the conflict between Theocracy and principle of human rights we can apply cultural relativism notion to conclude that current International human rights norms do not necessary apply to Islamic states or by considering evolution of Islamic law we can say, Islamic laws need to be updated and meet demands of the modern time.

A Cultural Relativism in International Law

Cultural relativism is used in international law to describe a "'cultural chasm' in which irreconcilable cultural differences preclude the pervasive realization of substantive international law and morality." Because all cultures are equal, according to this view, the human rights practices of different cultures must be equally tolerated.[299] The theory of cultural relativism thus supports the view that different regions, cultures and, traditions should have different, norms.

Based on Samuel P. Huntington's controversial Foreign Affairs article, it is possible to carve the world into several civilizational regions, including, in addition to the West, an "Islamic civilization" and a "Confucian civilization." [300]

By considering this theory Iran as an Islamic government, stung by criticism of their human rights practices, can adopt cultural relativism as rationale for not fully implementing international human rights norms.

Based on the Islamic Declaration of Human Rights: "All the rights and freedoms stipulated in this Declaration are subject to the Islamic Sharia."[301] Clarifying things even

---

[299] Christopher C. Joyner & John C. *Dettling, Bridging the Cultural Chasm: Cultural Relativism and the Future of International Law,* 20 CAL. W. INT'L L.J. 275, 275 (1990).

[300] Samuel P. Huntington, *The Clash of Civilizations?,* p 22-25, FOREIGN AFF., Summer (1993).

[301] Cairo Declaration, Art. XXIV, U.N. GAOR, *World Conf. on Human Rights*, 4th Sess., Agenda Item 5, at 10, U.N. Doc. A/CONF.157/PC/62/Add.18 (1993).

further is Article 25, which provides that the "Sharia is the only source of reference for the explanation or clarification of any of the articles of this Declaration."[302]

The question is whether classical Islamic law envisions the implementation of any specific criminal justice system as a matter of religious concern. Islamic law arose out of various sources, but more specifically from the teachings of the prophet Muhammad. It developed in a formal sense during the seventh and eighth centuries (670-720 AD). Its two most important elements are the Sharia and the Fiqh. Sharia refers to the sacred laws and ways of life proscribed by God. The Quran and the Sunna or Sunnah comprises the Sharia. These are considered the most important sources of Islamic law. The Quran is considered to be the primary source of guidance because it is regarded as the spoken word of God[303] and the Sunnah refers to the words and actions of the Prophet. The Sharia is said to deal with ideology and faith, behavior and manners, and practical daily matters. It is a comprehensive body of norms covering "every aspect of life including international, constitutional, administrative, criminal, civil, family, and religion" The Fiqh[304], or Islamic jurisprudence, on the other hand, refers to "the legal rulings of the Muslim scholars derived from the Sharia."[305]

The problem is how the Islamic Declaration of Human Rights purports to interpret Sharia as a working legal code in a twentieth-century world Leaving interpretations of the eight-hundred-year-old Sharia to individual states is what Sinha, an advocate of civilizational norms, calls "extreme relativism run amok, wherein a state becomes its own normative arbiter."[306]

In addition, there is a fatal flaw in the notion that civilizational norms based upon the primacy of communal over individual rights can even have their own standards of human rights. Groups are not human; individuals are. Without the individual, there is no group, yet the converse cannot be said. Thus human rights are, of their very essence, a

---

[302] *Id, Art.* XXV.

[303] J.N.D. Anderson, ***Law as a Social Force in Islamic Culture and History***, 20 BULLETIN OF SOAS 13-40 (1957).

[304] The Fiqh is a second important source of guidance for Islamic law.

[305] J.N.D. Anderson, *supra* note 303.

[306] Surya Prakash Sinah, ***Legal Polycentricity and International Law***, pp146-47, California academic Press (1996).

recognition that individuals are human and possessed of certain rights and freedoms that the community cannot take away.[307] Thus the act of the state in executing a citizen is the ultimate denial of individuality; it says that the state is stronger than the individual. The source of an individual's human rights is the state rather than the individual's humanity. The state wields its power to extinguish the lives of humans who, in the view of the state, cross the line and encroach upon what the state believes is necessary to hold on to that power.[308]

Iran and United States by executing criminals, both deny what is arguably an emerging international law norm. In Iran this approach means execution for transgressions against a religion that the regime invokes as the basis for its authority. And in the United States, it means execution for committing a crime whose portrayal in the news media arouses the vengeful instincts of a majority of the government's political constituents.[309] Both countries consider retribution as one of the main justifications for the death penalty. In the United States Retribution is justified, because a majority of state legislatures say it is justified say in Iran, because Sharia says it is.

It seems Iran and United States invoke this justification as an excuse to legitimate their undemocratic regimes and human rights policies outside of international law norms. Therefore, capital punishment is political, rather than cultural, in nature.[310]

B Can Islamic Law Evolve?

The primary religion in each country molds the individual country's ideology regarding the death penalty. Although, there are some basis for the claim that capital punishment is part of Islamic law. Its scope, however, is considerably but capital punishment is a mandatory penalty under the Sharia for only a small category of crimes.

---

[307] William A. Schabas, ***Symposium: Religion's Role in the Administration of the Death Penalty Islam and the Death Penalty***, 9 Wm. & Mary Bill Rts. J. 223.

[308] James H. Wyman, *supra* note 230.

[309] *Id.*

[310] *Id.*

The fact is, there can be no question that the Sharia was developed within a clear historical context. Like the Quran, the tradition, the second most important source of Islamic law, is also a response to specific historical circumstances. Indeed, countless traditions strive to explain the historical context in which a certain revelation was revealed.[311]

Islam professes the basic principle that everyone has the right to life. However, this principle, stated in the Quran, allows for an exception. Killing is only allowed when a court of law demands it: "Do not kill a Soul which God has made sacred except through the due process of law." Therefore, this exception authorizes the administration of capital punishment when Islamic law dictates. Intriguingly, the Islamic law position would seem to be the same as that found in the Fifth Amendment to the United States Constitution and such international instruments as the European Convention on Human Rights.[312]

Iran has ratified the International Covenant on Civil and Political Rights concerning Article 6(2) it seems Iran has accepted international norms. Therefore, in accordance with Article 6(2) of the International Covenant on Civil the imposition of the death penalty for crimes that do not result in loss of human life is contrary to the Covenant.[313] And, crimes for which Islamic Penal Code mandates the death penalty cannot by any effort at interpretation be deemed to be the "most serious crimes" for which the death penalty may be imposed.

Reynaldo Galindo Pohl, formerly Special Rapporteur of the Commission on Human Rights on Iran, observed that "there are groups of Islamic legal scholars and practitioners who recommend the abolition of the death penalty for political crimes on the ground that it is contrary to Islamic law. They state that the number of crimes punishable by death is limited." [314]

---

[311] *Id.*

[312] William A. Schabas, *supra note* 225, p 147.

[313] U.N. Doc. CCPR/C/79/Add.25, <section> 8.

[314] Report on the Human Rights Situation in the Islamic Republic of Iran by the Special Representative of the Comm'n on Human Rights, Mr. Reynoldo Galindo Pohl, pursuant to Commission Resolution 1988/69, U.N. ESCOR, Hum. Rts.Comm'n, 45th Sess., 26th mtg. <section>36, at 12, U.N. Doc. E/CN.4/1989/26 (1989).

Islamic law has an ability to demonstrate some degree of flexibility in the interpretation of capital punishment. Although, it appears that religion is little more than a pretext to justify a resort to harsh penalties that is driven by backward and repressive attitudes in the area of criminal law.

As we discussed, the Sharia specifically permits the imposition of capital punishment only for four Hodoud offenses and murder (Qisas) committed with deliberate intent. Even then, the evidentiary requirements for the conviction of Hodoud crimes ensure that punishment will be rare, while the Quran pointedly admonishes that it is more meritorious to pardon a murderer than to seek retaliation. While it has been argued that Islamic law governs the social order of Islamic societies, this has not prevented the Shari's from being amended or ignored when the environment dictated. This has been referred to as the doctrine of necessity. The doctrine of necessity dispenses Muslims from observing religious laws when the situation or environment dictates otherwise.[315]

Enforcing capital punishment for different crimes appears more a political slogan than a return to past realities, in which the Muslim state was able to escape 'the restrictions of the jurists' bureaucracy to enforce its own decrees.' Mandating capital punishment are, in the area of Taazir (Discretionary punishment) and preventive punishments characterized as manifestations of the will of Muslim States, not the commands of Islamic law, we should determine their application by the demands of a specific culture and time.

It is unlikely at any rate that any contemporary laws mandating capital punishment coincide with the values of classical Islamic law. For offenses and punishments that were both defined and imposed according to the discretion of the judge or ruler and for the small number of Hodoud offenses, equally orthodox scholars differed as to each Had's scope and application, often in significant details we can restrict the use of the death penalty, as did the Quranic exhortation to pardon those who commit a Qisas offense. Upon Ijma[316] on the details of these offenses becomes solidified, one may argue

---

[315] Joseph Schacht, **Problems of Modern Islamic Legislation**, p 101, 12 STUDIA ISLAMICA 99 (1960).

[316] Consensus of Opinions among Muslim Jurists.

that God's meaning has finally been understood: the Hadith[317] promises that 'My community shall never agree upon an error.'[318]

If we seek to justify capital punishment in the Islamic Penal Code by claiming authorization from God betrays willful disavowal of Islam's legal history. In my view capital punishment constitutes a perversion of the values of Islamic faith. Conservative Islamic states fighting to retain capital punishment use religious arguments in order to force the debate into one of cultural or religious norms. The Bible also contemplates capital punishment for such crimes as magic, violation of the sabbath, blasphemy, adultery, homosexuality, relations with animals, incest and rape.[319] Although Judeo and Christian jurists will rarely argue that this ancient text dictates contemporary legal practice.

Islamic punishments originated in the Arabs tribal system of punishment. Imam Bukhari narrated a Hadith (tradition) on the authority of Ibn Abbas that the law of retaliation was originally prescribed to the Israelites.[320] It shows these punishments belong to many ancient cultures. If a poll were conducted tomorrow in Iran and other Islamic countries, we would find considerable support for these punishments? Why cruel and unusual punishments that are not deeply rooted in Iran's cultural and background continually be applied. In determining the possibility of moratorium or abolition of these punishments we should contemplate that the application of Hodoud (prescribed punishments) to be conditional upon the society, which must be just before this punishment, can be effectively and consistently applied. Thus, Islamic laws need to be reformed comply demands of modernity. The Bible reminds us that **"*religions are for human being not human being for religions*"**.

---

[317] Saying: Tradition of the Prophet or the Imams.

[318] Mohammed Hashim Kamali, **Principles of Islamic Jurisprudence**, p 179, Paul & Co Pub Consortium (1989).

[319] Exodus 21:14, 22:18; Leviticus 20:15, 24:13; Deuteronomy 21:21, 22:11, 22:25, 29:13; Numbers 13:5, 17:7, 19:19, 22:23, 33:14, 33:37.

[320] Mohammad Ibn Esmaeil Bukhari; **Sahih Bokhari**, *vol.* 6, Hadith No. 25, pp 22-23, Lebanon: Dar 'Fekr Publication (1401 Lunar Hejiri) [In Arabic].

Chapter 3

Execution Methods

The method of execution has no bearing on this position as, in Amnesty International's view, the problem lies not with the method of execution but with the punishment itself.[321]

I *Biblical Times to Modern Era*

Literally dozens of methods of inflicting the death penalty have been invented by man. Most have not been utilized in the United States and Iran. This section will examine execution methods from a historical perspective to demonstrate that our ancestors have used a wide variety of execution methods throughout history but no execution is painless, and all executions are certainly cruel. Trends in most of the world have long been to move to less painful, or more "humane", executions. France developed the guillotine for this reason in the final years of the 18th century while Britain banned drawing and quartering in the early 19th century. Hanging by turning the victim off a ladder or by dangling him from the back of a moving cart, which causes death by suffocation, was replaced by "hanging" where the subject is dropped a longer distance to dislocate the neck and sever the spinal cord. In the United States, electrocution and the gas chamber, which were introduced as more humane alternatives to hanging, have been almost entirely superseded by lethal injection, which in turn has been criticized as being too painful. Nevertheless, some countries still employ slow hanging methods, beheading by sword and even stoning, although the latter is rarely employed. (Please see Chart 3-1).

---

[321] Amnesty International, http://asiapacific.amnesty.org/apro/APROweb.nsf/pages/ACT500072007_brief.

Country	Shooting	Hanging	Beheading	Injection
United States				60
Bangladesh		4		
China				77+
Indonesia	3			
Iran		88		
Iraq		3		
Japan		1		
Jordan		10		
Kuwait		11		
Libya	15			
North Korea	5			
Pakistan		23		
Palestine	1	4		
Saudi Arabia			90	
Singapore		2+		
Taiwan				3
Vietnam	9			
Uzbekistan	1			
Yemen	7			
Total	41	146+	90	140+

Chart 2-3   Source: http://www.richard.clark32.btinternet.co.uk/world.html.

1 History of Execution Methods

The death penalty and some methods used to inflict it have existed for thousands of years. Though no one is certain, some legal scholars have maintained that the oldest reference to the death penalty is located in the Code of Hammurabi.[322] In biblical times, the primary methods used in executions were stoning,[323] burning,[324] and hanging.[325] Crucifixion was also a common form of the death penalty, and was first used by the Phoenicians approximately 1000 BCE. Later it was imported by the Greeks, Assyrians, Egyptians, Persians and Romans, and also used in Japan.[326] Persians used crucifixion to punish treason in ancient era.[327] In Iran, during the ancient era, punishments were harsh and in the majority of cases the death penalty was applied. In addition to hanging, execution methods such as beheading and poisoning were practiced.[328]

During the reign of the emperor Nero, many Romans were sentenced to death. They suffered execution by impalement, a practice not fully abandoned until the nineteenth century. The Romans inflicted the death penalty by various means, including drowning, burial while alive, and severe beating. Generally, beheading was seen as an

---

[322] Hammurabi's Code is estimated to be nearly 4000 years old. Its development took place nearly 1000 years prior to the time of Moses.

[323] For more information please refer to Stoning section.

[324] Burning was one the most common execution methods used by the Romans to kill Christians. See Lewis Lyons, The History of Punishment, The Lyons press, Guilford, CT (2003).

[325] Hanging was used not only as a means of execution, but also as a frighteningly blatant means of deterrence. This occurred since the body of the condemned man or woman was often allowed to hang until nightfall before it was cut down.

[326] Lewis Lyons, **The History of Punishment**, p 162, The Lyons press, Guilford, CT (2003).

[327] Mohammad bagher Karami; *supra* note 190; Ava Vahedi; *supra* note 94.

[328] *Id.*

honorable way to execute Romans sentence only to nobility and enemies, not common criminals.[329]

By the middle Ages, the number of crimes punishable by death increased. The modes of execution took on more devilish ingenuity than they had before. In most instances, the execution method varied a lot based on the crime, the gender of the criminal, and the criminal's status in society.[330]

By the late seventeenth century, the hanging procedure had changed. In 1871 executioner Thomas Marwood perfected the science of hanging. Marwood was dedicated to the task of perfecting a human and reliable method of hanging. He calculated the length of the noose, taking in to account the victim's weight and muscular neck strength. Marwood concluded that a drop of eight feet was effective quick execution without decapitation. Dr. Joseph Guillotin, a French physician, proposed beheadings to France's Constituent Assembly to best carry out all capital sentences. After controversy and a lengthy assembly period, a mechanism was developed to behead in a "mechanical" manner. The new method, which became known as the guillotine, was popular with the government but unpopular with many of the people who witnessed its use. [331]

2   Legislative Endorsement of the Execution Methods in the United States and Iran

Punishments involving the intentional infliction of physical pain by the state have gradually disappeared in modern legal systems. Among the most significant remaining examples of such practices are hanging, electrocution, shooting, and lethal injection in the United States and hanging in Iran. Although the execution method is hanging in Iran, the execution of retaliation or other forms of capital punishment may be carried out by hanging, shooting, electrocution or any method that has been indicated in

---

[329] Robert J. Sech, *A Proposal for Thoroughly Evaluating The Constitutionality Of Execution Methods*, 30 Val. U. L. Rev. 381 (1995).

[330] *Id.*

[331] Lewis Lyons, *supra* note 326, pp163-168.

the sentence. In the case that execution method is not been mentioned in the sentence, the hanging will be carried out.[332]

A Hanging

Hanging is the oldest of the currently legal forms of execution. It is an ancient practice obscure origin invented probably for its "advertisement value" as other methods of execution were probably more effective.[333] According to the United Kingdom's Royal Commission on Capital Punishment, "[h]anging inflicted a signal indignity on the victim in a uniquely conspicuous fashion. It displayed [the victim] to the onlookers in a most ignominious and abject of postures and would thus be likely to enhance the deterrent effect of his punishment on anyone who might be tempted to do what he had done." [334] United Kingdom's Royal Commission indicates "hanging is a practice of great antiquity and obscure origin." The Commission observed that hanging was probably invented for its advertisement value rather than as a method that was more effective than other forms of capital punishment, such as beheading, drowning, stoning, impaling, and precipitation from a height.[335]

Based on remarkable findings of the United Kingdom's Royal Commission hanging is alleged to offer some form of inherent dignity. The Commission referred to striking and unanimous testimony on the stoicism with which condemned men or women almost always face death on the hanging scaffold. The Commission concluded that hanging was clearly the preferable execution method when assessed with respect to the criteria of humanity and certainty, although it conceded that electrocution, asphyxiation, and lethal injection rated higher on the decency scale. The Royal Commission also

---

[332] Regulation regarding the execution method of retaliation sentences of general and revolutionary courts, Art 14, 1999 [In Farsi].

[333] Michael A. Cokley, *Whatever Happened to that Old Saying "Thou Shall Not Kill?" A Plea for the Abolition of the Death Penalty*, 2Loy. J. Pub. Int. L. 67 (2001).

[334] *Id.* (citing UNITED KINGDOM, Royal Commission on Capital Punishment, 1949-1953, Report, London: Her Majesty's Stationery Office, 1953 at p. 246).

[335] *Id.*

admitted that if capital punishment were now being introduced for the first time, hanging would likely not be chosen.[336]

In Iran, Hanging originated as a method of execution in Persia (now Iran) about 2500 years ago. Trough the history of Persia hanging was widely practiced. As one of the means of capital punishment in Iran, hangings are violently carried out using an automotive telescoping crane to hoist the condemned aloft.[337]

Though many methods were available, most capital crimes in early America were punished by hanging. Hanging remained the most popular form of execution throughout the eighteenth and early nineteenth centuries. Hanging became an official method of execution in 1778 when the State of New York passed legislation providing for its preferred method of execution.[338] It has been estimated that nearly sixteen thousand people have been legally hanged in the United States prior to and subsequent to New York ushering in this method of execution.[339]

By the 1840s, various reform movements and humanitarian campaigns pushed for the abolition of hanging through anti-gallows campaigns.[340] Though these crusades declined as the United States entered the Civil War, many were rejuvenated after the war's conclusion.[341] The campaigns' efforts prompted many states to abolish all methods

---

[336] *Id.*

[337] Mohammad Bagher Karami, *supra* note 190.

[338] 1886 N.Y. LAWS 19.

[339] Robert J. Sech, *Note, supra* note 329.

[340] Deborah W. Denno, ***Is Electrocution An Unconstitutional Method of Execution? The Engineering of Death over the Century***, 35 WM. & MARY L. REV. 551, 554 (1994).

[341] Philip English Mackey, ***Hanging in the Balance: the Anti Capital Punishment Movement in New York State***, 1776-1861, at 267-70 (1982).

of the death penalty.[342] However, in New York, the movements prompted the landmark move from hanging to electrocution, an allegedly more humane method of execution.[343]

Until the 1890s, hanging was the primary method of execution used in the United States. Hanging is still used in Delaware and Washington, although both have lethal injection as an alternative method of execution. Despite, this United States Supreme Court has never been called upon directly to decide whether hanging is a cruel and unusual punishment.[344] In the controversial case of *Campbell v. Wood*,[345] the majority ruled that hanging, as a method of execution, does not involve the infliction of unnecessary pain. Consequently, the Court held that hanging did not violate the Eighth Amendment. Inexplicably, though, the majority ignored several other crucial factors which would have offered a more comprehensive analysis of the constitutionality of hanging. The majority's refusal to utilize factors other than pain in their evaluation has serious repercussions. Technically, under the Court's analysis, any form of egregiously savage execution would be constitutional provided it inflicted no more pain than necessary. An angry dissent reasoned that the scope of the Cruel and Unusual Punishments Clause was drastically curtailed by the ruling.[346]

It is also hard to argue that execution by hanging is not painful. When the execution is botched one of two things occur, - asphyxiation or decapitation. In a study done on the "hangman's fracture," victims in an English prison hanged in the late nineteenth and early twentieth century were examined to determine the accuracy of hanging.[347] The study found that out of the thirty-four victims, the "hangman's fracture"

---

[342] John F. Galliher et al., *Abolition and Reinstatement of Capital Punishment During the Progressive Era and Early 20th Century*, 83 J. CRIM. L. & CRIMINOLOGY 538, 541 (1992)

[343] Deborah W. Denno, *supra* note 340.

[344] Larry Charles Berkson, *supra* note 42, p 21.

[345] 18 F.3d 662 (9th Cir.1994).

[346] *Id.*

[347] Ryk James & Rachel Nasmyth-Jones, *The Occurrence of Cervical Fractures in Victims of Judicial Hangings*, 54 FORENSIC SCI INT'L 81, 90 (1992).

occurred in only nineteen percent of the cases, and that forty-eight percent of the prisoners died from asphyxiation.[348]

History shows that performing a "perfect" hanging is not an exact science; however, the common denominator in each is that the victim undoubtedly experienced pain beyond comprehension.[349] Commentators have stated that a hanging does not violate a person's dignity. Almost all instances of hanging, however, involve some instance of the condemned losing control of their body, whether it is through violent episodes, or flailing, or losing control of their bodily functions.[350] It is hard to imagine how hanging can comport with the Eighth Amendment, when, as a result of its impreciseness, there is no guarantee that the condemned would not face a very painful, lingering death that could entail some measure of mutilation to the body. Various eyewitness testimonials and other evidence substantiate claims that hanging is a method which causes a lingering death in many instances. In addition, hanging is a form of punishment which involves a visible degree of pain.[351]

Because of the risk involved in possible decapitations or strangulations, a valid case can be made for hanging's meager reliability.[352] Despite precautions, every hanging entails more than a nominal risk that some bodily mutilation will occur. Moreover, prisoner undergo degrading preparations prior to the execution, the method is endorsed by only two states in the United States.[353]

---

[348] *Id.*

[349] Michael A. Cokley, *supra* note 333.

[350] Negley K. Teeters, ***Hang by the Neck***, p 135, Charles C. Thomas, Springfield, IL (1967).

[351] *Id.*

[352] Campbell v. Wood, 18 F.3d 662, 687 (9th Cir.1994).

[353] Negley K. Teeters, *supra* note 350, pp 4-5.

B Crucifixion

Around the time of Jesus Christ, crucifixion was a popular form of execution.[354] This method of execution was used primarily as a form of torture. Crucifixion eventually challenged in as being cruel and unusual. Crucifixion is an extremely slow method of execution. It is written that Christ hung on the cross for nearly three hours before expiring.[355]

It is also, doubtlessly, a painful way to be executed. In addition to the pain of being nailed to pieces of wood, the prisoner often died from suffocation. Crucifixion, however, is reliable. It guaranteed that the prisoner would die a slow, painful death each time it was used. Crucifixion also involves bodily mutilation. Historical references suggest that large amounts of blood emanated from the prisoner's body. Normally, the prisoner did not have to undergo any special preparations prior to death; Finally, Crucifixion is an extremely brutal form of punishment. In addition to being painful, it is a slow and gruesome spectacle in which torture played a large part.[356]

C Stoning

Stoning is one of the ancient execution methods that still in practice.
There is a serious legal challenge regarding cruelty of this punishment. The vigorous Islamic dialogue over the proper interpretation and application of these laws in the Sharia, will be discussed in a separate section.

D Shooting

Shooting as a form of execution, the firing squad has been around since 1852 (was a method traditionally used under military law). There is no exact procedure for

---

[354] Martin Hengel, *Crucifixition in the Ancient World and the Folly of the Message of the Cross*, pp 86-87, Augsburg Fortress Publishers (1977).

[355] *Id.*

[356] *Id,* pp 25-31.

carrying out an execution by firing squad.[357] Death by firing squad, however, is not insulated from indignity. The most obvious indignity is mutilation to the body when the individual is shot. In the cases where the execution is botched, suffering a slow, painful death is a further form of indignity.

Following the 1979 revolution, Iran shot hundreds if not thousands of criminals, reaching a peak in the early 1980's. Their crimes allegedly included murder, drug trafficking, adultery, prostitution, armed robbery, political violence and religious offences. Typically those who were to be shot were lined up in groups seated on the ground along a wall and blindfolded. They were shot by Revolutionary Guard using an automatic rifle. Since the 1980s, Iranian executions have been mostly conducted by hanging.[358]

In the United States shooting remains a method of execution in Idaho, although lethal injection as an alternative method is allowed. The most recent execution by this method involved John Albert Taylor. By his own choosing, Taylor was executed by firing squad in Utah on January 26, 1996.[359]

Under "historical interpretation test," [360] the court looked at the reasons why the firing squad had been used historically, and compared the use of the firing squad to other methods of execution in effect at the time the Bill of Rights was adopted in 1791. At the time of the decision, the firing squad was a method of execution still used in military law in cases of desertion or mutiny. The Court upheld the constitutionality of the firing squad, distinguishing it from other methods such as disembowelment, drawing and quartering, which the Court considered cruel and unusual under the Eighth Amendment.[361]

---

[357] Michael A. Cokley, *supra* note 333.

[358] See: http://www.richard.clark32.btinternet.co.uk/world.html.

[359] Mitchel P. Roth, *supra* note 163.

[360] Roberta M. Harding, **The Gallows to the Gurney: Analyzing the (Un) Constitutionality of the Methods of Execution**, 6 B. U. PUB. INT. L. J. 153, p 135-136 (1996).

[361] Michael A. Cokley, *supra* note 333.

E Electrocution

In 1890, William Kemmler, a fruit peddler sentenced to die in the electric chair for the murder of his mistress, brought the first constitutional challenge to the new electrocution method. Deferring to the judgments of the New York legislature and the New York courts, the Supreme Court of the United States denied Kemmler's plea. The state executed Kemmler on June 27, 1893. Despite questions about the cruelty of electrocution, more than half of the states which authorized the death penalty were using electrocution as their method of execution by the end of the 1920s.[362] Today, electrocution is used as the sole method of execution only in Nebraska.

Evidence and testimony support the contention that electrocution is a slow method of punishment[363]. Several experts have claimed that electrocution is a method which borders on torture.[364] Additionally, eyewitness accounts of electrocutions state that the prisoners' deaths are not immediate but delayed. Although some people claim that the prisoner feels no pain after the onset of electrical surges, medical experts state that the prisoner is able to feel extreme pain through a substantial portion of the execution.[365] The pain that the condemned is subject to is unfathomable. Understanding that the brain has four parts is the start to understanding that the individual experiences pain.[366] Some courts have upheld electrocution based analyses which involve only a cursory consideration of pain.[367] Such analyses, in addition to being wholly inadequate, rest on the unfounded and false premise that the Eighth Amendment requires only that a method of execution not inflict pain unnecessarily.[368] The recent set of "botched" electrocutions

---

[362] Robert J. Sech, *supra note* 329.

[363] *Id.*

[364] Chales Duff, ***A Handbook on Hanging***, p 118, New York Review of Book (1974).

[365] *Id.*

[366] Philip R. Nugent, Note, ***Pulling the Plug on the Electric Chair: The Unconstitutionality of Electrocution***, 2 WM. & MARY BILL RTS. J. 185 (1993).

[367] Jackson v. State, 516 So. 2d 726, 738 (Ala. Crim. App. 1985).

[368] Campbell v. Wood, 18 F.3d 662, 687 (9th Cir.1994).

in several states has shown that electrocution is a highly unreliable form of execution.[369] In addition, electrocution requires the prisoner to undergo degrading preparations prior to the execution.[370] Finally, by looking at electrocution, it is a punishment which is painful, slow, and perhaps most strikingly, very unreliable.

In *State v. Black*, the petitioner challenged electrocution as a cruel and unusual method of punishment. The Tennessee Supreme Court dismissed the claim because a previous case held that electrocution was constitutional.[371] By dismissing the claim in this manner, the court overlooked a litany of evidence which suggested that electrocution might constitute cruel and unusual punishment.[372]

Although it has some legislative support in the United States, under the "modern interpretation" test, electrocution violates the Eighth Amendment. Many opinions have been offered as to whether death is instantaneous. Proponents argue that even if death is not instantaneous, the condemned is rendered unconscious with the first jolt.[373]

F   Lethal gas

In 1931, Nevada became the first state to use lethal gas as a method of execution. The gaseous asphyxiation method has an intriguing origin which is demonstrated by the fact that prison officials attempted to be as humane as possible when executing a prisoner. Modern gas chambers operate in a similar manner. As in Kemmler, a quick challenge was made to the new method but was rejected by the Nevada Supreme Court. Eventually, seven other states set up gas chambers during the 1930s, and from 1955 to 1960, three more states chose lethal gas as their method of inflicting the death penalty.[374]

---

[369] Deborah W. Denno, *supra* note 340.

[370] Robert J. Sech, *supra* note 329.

[371] 815 S.W.2d 166 (Tenn. 1991).

[372] Black, 815 S.W.2d at 199 (Reid, J., dissenting).

[373] Philip R. Nugent, *supra note 366*.

[374] Robert J. Sech, *supra* note 329.

The evidence also shows that the effects of the gas chamber are cruel. Lethal gas kills a person by cutting off the supply of oxygen to the body's cells. Eyewitnesses to lethal gas executions assert that prisoners are conscious and suffering several minutes after the execution has begun.[375]

The proscription against a lingering death is also violated. The condemned is subject to a slow death with death occurring as long as ten to twelve minutes after the gas is released. The brain remains alive upwards of two to five minutes after the gas is released and that the heart beats for five to seven minutes longer.[376]

As Judge Patel's extensive factual findings in *Fierro v. Gomez* (865 F. Supp. 1387, 1391 (N.D. Cal. 1994) show, generally accepted medical teachings regarding cyanide conclude that death by cyanide is quite painful, lasting several minutes and involving suffocation at the cellular level, intense buildup of lactic acid in the muscles (including the heart), and tetany, spasms of the muscles so intense that the surrounding bones sometimes break.

The most disturbing part of an execution by lethal gas is that the pain suffered is immeasurable. What transpires is an indictment as to the method's unconstitutionality. The cyanide gas prevents the utilization of the oxygen in the body's cells.[377] In *Hunt v. Smith*,[378] the petitioner claimed that execution by lethal gas violated the Eighth Amendment and constituted cruel and unusual punishment. Without analyzing whether the punishment resulted in a quick death or was consistently reliable, the court held that the evidence was insufficient to show that a lethal gas execution involved the unnecessary infliction of pain. Based solely on a consideration of pain, the court held that death by lethal gas was constitutional.[379]

---

[375] *Id.*

[376] Roberta M. Harding, *supra* note 360, pp 165-172.

[377] *Id.*

[378] Hunt v. Smith, 856 F.Supp. 251 (D.Md.1994).

[379] *Id.*

G   Lethal injection

Compared to electrocution, lethal gas, or hanging, death by lethal injection appears humane, perhaps because it mimics a medical procedure. More palatable to the general public, lethal injection has become the most prevalent form of execution in the United States.[380]

Subsequent to the reinstatement of the death penalty, states faced the expensive task of repairing or replacing the equipment used to end a person's life. That, coupled with the problems of botched executions states had experienced, resulted in a movement for a more humane method of execution. In 1977, Oklahoma became the first state to adopt lethal injection as a means of execution, though it would be five more years until Charles Brooks would become the first person executed by lethal injection in Texas on December 2, 1982. Today, 37 of the 38 states that have the death penalty use this method. After being strapped to a gurney, the condemned person is usually given a sedative, followed by a combination of lethal drugs administered intravenously. Though many point to the coforting, hospital-like aura of lethal injection as an indication of its humane nature, this method has drawn sharp criticism from several physicians who claim the procedure is ethically wrong.[381]

Lethal injection seemed to provide the answer to the issue whether death penalty was a form of cruel and unusual punishment. Since the reinstatement of the death penalty, 537 individuals have been executed by lethal injection.[382]

For the same reason just stated, lethal injection also violates the requirement the individual not be subjected to a lingering death. But there have been at least forty-one cases before state and federal courts challenging the constitutionality of lethal injection protocols. No court has ever ruled lethal injection executions unconstitutional. In two

---

[380] Human Right Watch, *so Long as They Die Lethal Injection in the United States*, Human Rights Watch Vol. 18, NO. 1(G).

[381] Robert J. Sech, *supra* note 329.

[382] Death Penalty Information Center, *Executions Since 1976*, at http://www.deathpenaltyinfo.org/dpicexec.html. (Last modified March 14, 2001).

recent cases in California and North Carolina, federal courts have been sufficiently troubled by new evidence of possible problems with lethal injection executions that they ordered corrections officials to change their lethal injection procedures in particular ways, or the executions would be stayed. In both cases, the courts proposed the presence throughout the execution of someone trained in anesthesia. In the California case, the court also suggested the option of injecting the condemned prisoner, Michael Morales, with a single massive dose of a barbiturate. The California Department of Corrections rejected the use of a single barbiturate and was not able to find anesthesiologists willing to monitor the prisoner's level of anesthesia and to make adjustments as necessary for the three-drug protocol execution. The court stayed the prisoner's execution and scheduled an evidentiary hearing on California's lethal injection protocols for May 2 to 3, 2006. As of April 10, 2006, North Carolina has not responded to the court order in its case. On April 26, the U.S. Supreme Court will hear oral arguments about the procedures a prisoner must use to challenge the constitutionality of a lethal injection protocol.[383]

Even the characteristic that is lethal injection's selling point, that it is painless, is not one-hundred percent settled, because much is unknown about what the individual undergoes when injected with the drugs. Although supporters of lethal injection believe the prisoner dies painlessly, there is mounting evidence that prisoners may have experienced excruciating pain during their executions. This should not be surprising given that corrections agencies have not taken the steps necessary to ensure a painless execution. They use a sequence of drugs and a method of administration that were created with minimal expertise and little deliberation three decades ago, and that were then adopted unquestioningly by state officials with no medical or scientific background. Little has changed since then. As a result, prisoners in the United States are executed by means that the American Veterinary Medical Association regards as too cruel to use on dogs and cats.[384]

Adding to the troubling trend is the fact that several courts rely exclusively on case law when analyzing a method's constitutionality. In doing so, these courts exclude relevant scientific and eyewitness evidence which is vital in ascertaining whether a method constitutes cruel and unusual punishment. In light of the fact that the Supreme Court has not addressed the constitutionality of any execution method in over a century,

---

[383] Human Right Watch, *supra* note 380.

[384] *Id.*

such evidence will contain the necessary medical and technical information that case law alone is unable to supply.[385]

Since executions had been on hold for almost eight months from September 2007 to April 2008 as the Supreme Court considered the lethal injection issues, it was expected there could be a move forward of executions in 2008, depending on the Court's decision in *Baze v. Rees*. When the Court upheld Kentucky's lethal injection process in *Baze*, many execution dates were set. However only 9 states carried out executions in 2008, and only one of those was outside of the south-Ohio.

II *Stoning, Harshness and Abolition*

In some Muslim countries, governed by Sharia law stoning is still practiced. These countries include Nigeria, Saudi Arabia, Sudan, and the United Arab Emirates. At the beginning of 2002, four stoning verdicts against women in Islamic states were announced: two in Nigeria, one in Sudan and one in Pakistan. All of these were charged with adultery. Stoning punishments have been handed down recently in Nigeria for the crimes of adultery and sodomy.[386]

In Iran stoning is not in practice currently and even before 2002, stoning was rare in Iran, (Although hanging is a common punishment for serious offenses, such as drug-smuggling and murder).

This section argues that the only means of affecting permanent change in Islamic adultery laws is through a vigorous Islamic dialogue over the proper interpretation and application of these laws in the Sharia. For a close analysis of the complexities and contradictions of these laws, when combined with a proper reform methodology of the Sharia, necessarily demands an end to what is an archaic and grossly misapplied practice.

Stoning is a form of capital punishment in which the convicted criminal is put to death by having stones thrown at them, generally by a crowd. In some cultures, this was seen as allowing the larger community to participate in the administration of justice.

---

[385] Robert J. Sech, *supra* note 329.

[386] Extracts from Kitab Al-Hudud: Book 017, Number 4192, 4218.

Stoning has been used since ancient times to punish people judged as criminals; these included prostitutes, adulterers, and murderers. Stoning became criticized as cruel and its use in most places was abandoned for methods believed to be more humane, such as hanging and decapitation.[387]

Stoning as a form of punishment is provided in the criminal codes of at least the following Muslim countries[388]: Iran, one province in Indonesia (Aceh), two federal states of Malaysia (Terengganu, Kelantan), twelve federal states in Northern Nigeria (Bauchi, Borno, Gombe, Jigawa, Kaduna, Kano, Katsina, Kebbi, Niger, Sokoto, Yobe, Zamfara), Pakistan, Saudi Arabia, Sudan and the United Arab Emirates. However, provisions providing for stoning in the Penal Codes do not necessarily entail its application.

1 Definition

A Definition of stoning in Islam

To understand stoning as a punishment in Islamic criminal law, one must consider that Islamic criminal law does not constitute an integrated whole. Rather, it deals with relatively few individual questions, since the Quran itself gives only very insufficient details on crime and appropriate punishment for a comprehensive code of criminal law. Most Muslim countries possess a statute law, orientated towards various European, e.g. French or Italian, codes of law. These statutes regulate details the Quran or the Hadith did not regulate. Only Saudi Arabia and Oman do not have a general Penal

---

[387] Theoretical analysis about crimes or the history of crime and punishment is a subject covered by Western literature. Some like Michel Foucault in *Discipline and punishment* have argued about the inhumanity and hypocrisy of hidden human state-punishment as a sanitized form of state-hegemony.

[388] The criminal codes of these Islamic countries are based on Sunnah or Shiite school of Islam. Sunni Islam acknowledges four schools of law, which developed during the course of the 8th century AD in the large centers of Islamic learning. Each of them is named after its founder or one of his students: Hanifite, Maliki, Shafi'ite and Hanbali schools. They differ in dogmatic and the interpretation of Quran regulations, i.e. the practical rules in the life of the individual. In addition there is one Shiite school of law.

Code. In Iran after ratification of Islamic Penal Code in 1983 the modern Penal Code of Iran that was regulated in accordance with novel concepts of crime and punishment was abolished. The present criminal law in Iran based on the 12 Imami Shii version[389] of Sharia law (Islamic law).[390]

In Iran there are 5 different punishments based on Article 12 of Islamic Penal Code: 1-Prescribed punishment (Hodoud) 2-Retaliation (Qisas)[391] 3-Taazir (Discretionary punishment)[392] 4- Preventive punishments[393] 5- Blood money (Diyat).[394]

---

[389] The most important Shiite school of law is the school of the Jafarites or Imamites. According to Shiite belief it goes back to the Sixth Imam Hazrat Jafar As-Sadiq (700 - 765). Written records have exited since the 11th century.Shiite Islam differs from Sunni Islam that it believes in the system of the "Imamate". This means that, after the prophet, the only true leader of the Muslims, at a given time, is an Imam, who, like the prophets, is directly appointed by god. The Imam must be a direct descendent of the family of the last prophet. Like the prophets, the Imam is sinless (Masum) and his rulings should therefore be obeyed under any circumstances. Unlike in Sunni Islam, where the Caliph is the political but not the religious leader of the community, Shiite Islam believes in both the political and the religious authority of the Imam. Shiite Islam regards the Imam to be an autonomous source of religious behavior with the same standing as the Quran and the Hadith and must therefore be obeyed the same way. This means that any behavior contradicting the instructions of the Imam is just as sinful and punishable as behavior contradicting the Quran and the Hadith. Today the Twelve Shia can be found mainly in Iraq, Iran and the Indo-Pakistani area, as well as minority groups in Afghanistan, Lebanon, Central Asia, Turkey, Bahrain and in the Persian Gulf States.

[390] The present punishment system in Iran based on the Twelve Imami Shii version of the Sharia law. This system formed in the early 1980s during the tenure of the Ayatollah Ruhullah Mosavi Khomeini. In 1983 the first specific Islamic Penal Statute was ratified (Statute of retaliation and prescribed punishments). Based on this statute flogging, mutilation and stoning were applicable for crimes with fixed punishment in the Holy Quran and tradition. Therefore for other crimes jurists still refer to the modern Penal Code of Iran. In 1984 discretionary punishment statute was ratified. Subsequently and now chapter 2 and 3 of the Islamic penal code is about retaliation and prescribed punishments (ratified in 1992). And, immediately after, chapter 5 of Islamic Penal Code was ratified in 1997 (discretionary and preventive punishments). Furthermore, Article 729 of this statute abolished all contrary statutes including modern Penal Code of Iran.

[391] It is prescribed in the Holy Quran thus:" We ordained therein for them, life for life, eye for eye, nose for nose, ear for ear, tooth for tooth and wounds equal to equal.

[392] Meaning to prevent, to respect, and to reform. In the Islamic legal context, Taazir is defined thus: discretionary punishment to be delivered for transgression against Allah, or against individual for which there is neither fixed punishment nor penance.Taazir denotes a punishment aimed at the prevention of crime and reformation of the criminal. It is stated by a scholar that the aim of Taazir punishment is thus: disciplinary, reformative and deterrent.... Taazir punishments

Execution Methods

The word Hodoud is the plural form of Had (prescribed punishment) meaning restraint, obstruction, hindrance or prohibition. Stoning is included in Had or Hodoud crimes which are crimes with fixed punishment in the Holy Quran and Sunnah. The punishment in Hodoud is not subject to any amendment, alteration or commutation, substation, change or waiver by the judge, ruler or any person in authority. The infliction of the Had punishment is restricted when the accused person repent. For instance, if a thief repented and returned the stolen property before being prosecuted then the Had lapse. The sanction for prescribed punishment in many cases is corporal punishment from flogging to death penalty and because it is the principle punishment there is no alternative sanction for that under Islamic law.

The punishment of stoning to death (Rajm) has a long tradition in Islam. When it comes to the practice of stoning adulterers, however, the traditions indicate that Talmudic law primarily influenced Mohammad. The Hadith present Mohammad as first prescribing stoning explicitly for Jews who had been found guilty of adultery and then later referring to the Jewish law whenever was passing similar sentences on members of his own community. Mohammad even criticized the Jews for relaxing their adultery laws by replacing the punishment of stoning with the smearing of coal on the face.[395]

---

are not textually specified either in the Holy Quran or Sunnah of the Holy Prophet. But they mentioned some crimes for which there is no fixed punishment and concerning which it is left for the judge or the ruler to decide what sort of punishment to impose the manner of inflicting it (such as imprisonment, fine and flogging less than prescribed punishments).

[393] Preventive punishments are prescribed by government in order to protect order and regard of public interests in violation of governmental regulations. Such as imprisonment, fine... .

[394] Blood money (Diyat) is defined as compensation that is prescribed by holy Quran and tradition.

[395] A Hadith recorded by al-Bukhari, on the authority of ibn Umar states: A Jew and a Jewess were brought to Allah's Apostle (S) on a charge of committing illegal sexual intercourse. The Prophet asked them: 'What is the legal punishment (for this sin) in your Book (Torah)?' They replied: 'Our priests have innovated the blackening of faces with charcoal and Tajbiya' (being mounted on a donkey, with their faces in opposite directions, and then mortified in public). Abdullah bin Salaam said: 'O Allah's Apostle, tell them to bring the Torah.' The Torah was brought, and then one of the Jews put his hand over the Divine Verse of the Rajm (stoning to death) and started reading what preceded and what followed it. On that, Ibn Salaam said to the Jew: 'Lift up your hand.' The Divine Verse of the Rajm was under his hand. So Allah's Apostle (S) ordered that the two (sinners) be stoned to death, and so they were stoned."

The **Quran** (24:2 Surah a Nur) only stipulates 100 lashes for the adultery. When, Prophet Mohammad stoned a number of men and women, and so this punishment is Sharia, Islamic Law. But there is no historical evidence that this ever happened and there are to specific stories that are repeated and in each the prophet required not only confession but the culprits actually asked for their punishments.[396]

Based on the following **Hadiths**[397] (sayings and actions of Prophet Mohammad or tradition) stoning is the punishment for adultery:

- The Prophet said: "When unmarried couples fornicate they should receive one hundred lashes and banishment for one year. In the cases of a married male committing adultery with a married female, they shall receive one hundred lashes and be stoned to death. If one of the pair is unmarried, one hundred lashes and exile for a year.[398]

- The Prophet said: "Do not stone the adulteress who is pregnant until she has had her child." After the birth she was put into a ditch up to her chest and the Prophet commanded them to stone her. Khalid came forward with a stone which he threw at her head, and there spurted blood on the face of Khalid and he cursed her. The gentle Prophet prayed over her and she was buried.[399]

- Malik came to Abu Bakr and said: "I am a base fellow for I have committed adultery."Abu Bakr replied: "Repent before the Lord and tell no one else." The man still felt guilty and went to Umar who gave him the same reply. Still feeling guilty he went to the Prophet who asked if he was ill or mad, married or single. On hearing that Ma'iz was healthy and married, the Prophet ordered him to be stoned to death.[400]

---

[396] Eesa Ebrahimi., *Philosophy of Punishment in Islam,* p 36, 38, Bar Association Journal, Tehran (1333 Solar Hejira) [In Farsi].

[397] Some of the Hadith no doubt have a claim top authenticity, but many, perhaps most, do not.

[398] Alnoovi; *Sahihe Moslem*, Lebanon: Dar 'Ketab Arabi Publication (1407 Lunar Hejira) [In Arabic].

[399] *Id.*

[400] Emam Malek, *Motan*, Lebanon: Dar 'ehyae Torase Arabi Publication (1985) [In Arabic].

- The Prophet was told: "My son was employed with this man; he committed adultery with his wife. I gave 100 sheep and a slave girl in compensation." The Prophet said: "Take back your sheep and your slave girl. Your son will receive 100 lashes and a year in exile. As the adulteress has confessed she will be stoned."[401]

After Mohammad's death, the first generation of Muslim legal scholars included adultery, as one of the six major offenses (Hodoud) in Islamic law for which the penalty is fixed by God in the Quran and whose application is the right of God (Haqq Allah). This made adultery an unalterable and unpardonable component of the Islamic Penal Code. Unlike the other five major offenses (Had) clearly laid out in the Quran, both the application and the definition of adultery have been sources of confusion and controversy in the Islamic legal tradition for centuries. The inconsistencies between the Quran and the Hadith with regard to the punishment for adultery were ultimately explained by the Caliph Umar[402] based on following Hadiths:

- A man went on a journey with the slave-girl of his wife and went into her. The envious wife reported it to Umar who said the husband would be stoned unless the slave girl was owned by him. The wife spoke out to save him: "I had given her as a gift."[403]

- Umar said, I am afraid that after a long time has passed, people may say, We do not find the Verses of the Rajm in the Holy Book and consequently they may go astray by leaving an obligation that Allah has revealed "Surely Allah's Apostle carried out the penalty of Rajm, and so did we after him." [404]

Umar's claim has only furthered the stoning controversy among Sharia scholars, most of whom question the tradition's ability to abrogate the Quran in the first place. Because Umar was the only source to report the inclusion of the "verse of stoning," it cannot be considered reliable for determining Sharia.[405] In any case, it is highly unlikely

---

[401] *Id.*

[402] Caliph 'Umar is the second Caliph based on Sunnah school of Islam; therefore his indication is not a source for Shitte school.

[403] Emam Malek, *supra* note 400.

[404] Mohammad Ibn Esmaeil Bokhari; ***Sahihe Bokhari***, Lebanon: Dar 'Fekr Publication, 1401 Lunar Hejira [In Arabic].

that Umar's "verse of stoning" is genuine. If it were, it would be an extremely embarrassing problem for Muslim jurists to explain, for how could a revelation originally be part of the Quran but fail to be included in the sacred text. Punishment for adultery relies, according to Umar, solely on the Sunnah and not on the Quran violates the very definition of Hodoud as "punishments mandated by God." Indeed, this fact alone should be enough to put an immediate end to the practice of stoning adulterers.[406]

Mohammad tradition occasionally orders stoning however, the most reliable Hadith are not free from controversy. Because tradition demonstrates that Mohammad may have confirmed stoning and not lashes for adulterers, there was a great deal of confusion as to whether he had done so before after Surah al Nur, which unmistakably prescribes 100 lashes for adultery.

B   Definition of stoning in Judaism

To understand the biblical death penalties, one must consider not only the written Torah, the first five books of the Bible, but also the Jewish Oral Law, that is, the Talmud, a sixty-tractate, 5000 folio page masterpiece, whose two parts are the Mishnah and the Gemara. The Mishnah, which generally states terse, black-letter law, was redacted circa 200 C.E.; the far lengthier Gemara, which is an extraordinary commentary consisting largely of rabbinic debates invoking biblical, mishnaic, and midrashic sources, was redacted some three centuries later. Indeed, at least from the perspective of traditional Judaism, to divine original intent with respect to any law, one must view the Bible and the Talmud as an indivisible partnership in which it is often difficult to discern who the senior partner is.[407]

---

[405] In other decisions regarding actions by Umar, e.g. a raped slave-woman who asked foe compensation from her rapist and Umar asked that he pay it to her, a story which has also been reported as the woman being a free woman raped by a man and Umar asking her if she would marry him, at her refusal he asked the rapist to pay her the dowry expected of her equals.

[406] Reza Aslan, *The Problem of Stoning in the Islamic Penal Code: AN Argument for reform*, UCLA J. Islamic & Near E. L. 91, (Fall/Winter 2003-2004).

[407] Irene Maker Rosenberg, *Of God's Mercy and the Four Biblical Methods of Capital Punishment: Stoning, Burning, Beheading, and Strangulation*, 78 Tul. L. Rev. 1169 (March, 2004).

Execution Methods

Capital punishment is a penalty prescribed by Biblical law for the commission of offenses that violate ritual prohibitions (such as deliberate desecration of the Sabbath) as well as laws regarding interpersonal relationships (murder, kidnapping, incest).[408] The Mishnah mentions four modes of execution for a capital crime (stoning, burning, strangulation and beheading.[409]

In the Old Testament of the Bible, stoning is specifically prescribed as the method of execution for crimes such as murder, blasphemy or apostasy. However, the Talmud seriously limits the use of the death penalty to those criminals who were warned not to commit the crime in the presence of two witnesses, and persisted in committing the crime also in front of two witnesses. It was said about the death penalty that if a court killed one person in seventy years, it was a barbarous court and should be condemned as such.(Extracts from Deuteronomy 13:6 to 13:10).

If thy brother, the son of thy mother, or thy son, or thy daughter, or the wife of thy bosom, or thy friend, which is as thine own soul, entice thee secretly, saying, Let us go and serve other gods, which thou hast not known, thou, nor thy fathers; (13:6) But thou shalt surely kill him; thine hand shall be first upon him to put him to death, and afterwards the hand of all the people. (13:9)And thou shalt stone him with stones, that he die; because he hath sought to thrust thee away from the LORD thy God, which brought thee out of the land of Egypt, from the house of bondage (13:10).

Palestine being a very rocky country, the abundance of stones made it natural to use them as missiles. Stone throwing might be merely a mark of hatred and contempt[410], or the means of carrying out murderous intentions against which provision had to be made in the Law.[411] Death by stoning was first an expression of popular fury analogous to "lynching", later came to be a socially acceptable and legally recognized method of execution. Stoning was this regulated by law as an appointed means of capital

---

[408] Mosaic Law defines 36 capital crimes, including murder, sexual offences, idolatry, blasphemy and desecration of Sabbath.

[409] *Mishnah*, Sanhedrin 49b-50b. But the Bible lists three methods of execution.

[410] *Bible*, 2 Samuel 16:6-13.

[411] *Id,* Exodus 21:18, Numbers 35:17.

punishment.⁴¹² Stoning is also mentioned in Acts 7:57-58, as the means by which Stephen the first Christian martyr was put to death: "And casting him forth without the city, they stoned him."

2 Stoning crimes

A In Islam

Stoning as the punishment of adultery applies to an illicit sexual liaison where at least one of the parties is married to a third party. Article 63 of Iran Penal Code indicates: "Adultery is the act of intercourse, including anal intercourse, between a man and a woman who are forbidden to each other, unless the act is committed unwittingly." It does not include premarital sex, although that too is forbidden. Both adultery and fornication, although the penalties differ, are classified together in Islamic law as Zina. Adultery is punishable by death by stoning.[413]

The definition of adultery can become complicated in the different interpretation of Muslim sexual ethics. Some Muslim jurists argue that adultery should not be applied to instances in which a married person is unable to consort with their spouse due to legally acceptable conditions, such as prolonged travel or life imprisonment. Shiite schools of law contend that adultery can be eluded by using a temporary marriage (Muta)[414] while sodomy certainly falls in the category of Zina; it is supposed to connote homosexual behavior. As such, it is more often deviation, not adultery, because sodomy challenges the harmony of the sexes and upsets God's will for creation.[415]

If adultery is committed by a legally married man with a permanent wife or by a legally married woman with a permanent husband, then the punishment is stoning to

---

[412] *Id,* Deuteronomy 17:5-7; Acts 7:58.

[413] Shahid avval, ***Lomeh Demeshghieh***, p 221-225, translation by Ali Shyravani, Qom: Dar 'Fekr Qom publication (1376 Solar Hejira) [In Farsi].

[414] *Id.*

[415] Aslan; *supra* note 406.

death.⁴¹⁶ A man who commits pedophilia is stoned to death, a woman guilty of the same crime may receive only lashes; this is because the fact that Islamic law commonly recognizes the age of puberty to be nine for girls and fifteen for boys.⁴¹⁷

B In Judaism

Mishna, Sanhedrin 7.4 is about offenders sentenced to stoning: [1] one who has intercourse with his mother or his father's wife, his daughter-in-law, a male or a beast. [2] a woman who copulates with a beast. [3] the blasphemer and the idol-worshipper. [4] one who curses his father or his mother. [5] one who has intercourse with a girl who is betrothed. [6] the instigator (to apostasy) [mesith] and the imposter [maddich; cf. Deut 13]. [7] the sorcerer, and [8] the disobedient or rebellious son.

In addition to stoning crimes such as adultery or rape with a girl who is betrothed⁴¹⁸, idolatry⁴¹⁹, blasphemy⁴²⁰, sorcery⁴²¹, cursing parents⁴²², bestiality⁴²³,

---

⁴¹⁶ Shahid Avval, *supra* note 413.

⁴¹⁷ Article 83.of Iran Penal Code:" Adultery in the following cases shall be punishable by stoning: (1) Adultery by a married man who is wedded to a permanent wife with whom he has had intercourse and may have intercourse when he so desires; (2) Adultery of a married woman with an adult man provided the woman is permanently married and has had intercourse with her husband and is able to do so again." Note. Adultery of a married woman with a minor is punishable by flogging.

⁴¹⁸ Bible, Deuteronomy, 22:23-26:"If a man happens to meet in a town a virgin pledged to be married and he sleeps with her, you shall take both of them to the gate of that town and stone them to death—the girl because she was in a town and did not scream for help, and the man because he violated another man's wife. You must purge the evil from among you. But if out in the country a man happens to meet a girl pledged to be married and rapes her, only the man who has done this shall die. "

⁴¹⁹ *Id*, Deuteronomy, 17:2-6: "If a man or woman living among you in one of the towns the LORD gives you is found doing evil in the eyes of the LORD your God in violation of his covenant, 3 and contrary to my command has worshiped other gods, bowing down to them or to the sun or the moon or the stars of the sky, 4 and this has been brought to your attention, then you must investigate it thoroughly. If it is true and it has been proved that this detestable thing has been done in Israel, 5 take the man or woman who has done this evil deed to your city gate and stone that person to death."

adultery[424] and insect[425] Old Testament prescribed stoning as the penalty for other different crimes:

- "If, however, the charge is true and no proof of the girl's virginity can be found, she shall be brought to the door of her father's house and there the men of her town shall stone her to death. She has done a disgraceful thing in Israel by being promiscuous while still in her father's house. You must purge the evil from among you".[426] Contrary to this approach in Islam even regency of woman dose not indicate her guilt as an adulterer.

- "For six days, work is to be done, but the seventh day shall be your holy day, a Sabbath of rest to the LORD. Whoever does any work on it must be put to death."[427] Although the stoning as a punishment for Sabbath breaking has not been indicated in Bible, Talmud has prescribed stoning for Sabbath breaking.

---

[420] *Id*, Leviticus, 24:16: "anyone who blasphemes the name of the LORD must be put to death. The entire assembly must stone him. Whether an alien or native-born, when he blasphemes the Name, he must be put to death".

[421] *Id*, Leviticus, 20:27: "A man or woman who is a medium or spiritist among you must be put to death. You are to stone them; their blood will be on their own heads".

[422] *Id*, Leviticus, 20:9: "If anyone curses his father or mother, he must be put to death. He has cursed his father or his mother, and his blood will be on his own head".

[423] *Id*, Leviticus, 20:16: "If a woman approaches an animal to have sexual relations with it, kill both the woman and the animal. They must be put to death; their blood will be on their own heads".

[424] *Id*, Leviticus, 24:16: "If a man commits adultery with another man's wife—with the wife of his neighbor—both the adulterer and the adulteress must be put to death".

[425] *Id*, Leviticus, 20:12: "If a man sleeps with his daughter-in-law, both of them must be put to death. What they have done is a perversion; their blood will be on their own heads".

[426] *Id*, Deuteronomy 22:20-21.

[427] *Id*, Exodus, 35:2.

- "If, however, the bull has had the habit of goring and the owner has been warned but has not kept it penned up and it kills a man or woman, the bull must be stoned and the owner also must be put to death".[428]

- "If a man lies with a man as one lies with a woman, both of them have done what is detestable. They must be put to death; their blood will be on their own heads"[429].

3   Evidentiary & Execution Procedure

A   In Islam

The number of confessions necessary for an adultery conviction is derived from Iran Penal Code[430] in the following manner: The accused was forced to confess four times before his conviction was accepted and sentencing was occurred[431], if both perpetrator and victim admit the "crime". Otherwise, four independent male witnesses have to be found. These four witnesses must all profess to be direct eyewitnesses to the crime. If four men are not available, three men and two women will suffice. In cases of fornication sharia prescribes that a condemned is to be punished with 100 lashes, if unmarried or with death by stoning, if married, since this would then constitute adultery.[432]

---

[428] *Id*, Exodus, 21:29.

[429] *Id*, Leviticus, 20:13.

[430] In regards to evidentiary law, this is a profound subject and is applied differently in different Muslim countries. For instance in Egypt, except for confession, there has to be four witnesses to the actual act of fornication. Legists have described that as witness that no string could be passed between the two bodies, i.e. that copulation was in fact taking place. i.e. they were caught in the actual act of copulation. Jordanian law however indicates the adultery can be determined when a man and the woman are found in the same solitude together and so on.

[431] Bokhari, *supra* note 320.

[432] Islamic Penal Code of Iran, Art 68, 74, 75 (1991) [In Farsi].

The convicted person is wrapped in a shroud and placed into a pit and buried either to the waist (if a man) or the chest (if a woman).[433] "If the individual is sentenced to flogging and stoning, flogging is carried out first and stoning is carried out consequently."[434] If the adultery was proven in court by confession, the judge has the responsibility of throwing the first stone. If the case was proven through witnesses, they start first, followed by the judge and then by any others who are present, numbering no less than three. The lack of presence of the religious judge or not throwing the first stones by the religious leader or the lack of witnesses would not prevent the sentence; it should be carried out under any circumstances.[435] The stones are then hurled one by one until the accused is killed.[436] The Iran Penal Code explicitly outlines proper stones usage. Article 104 states, with reference to the penalty for adultery: "the stones should not be too large so that the person dies on being hit by one or two of them; they should not be so small either that they could not be defined as stones". Under the law, the stones must be big enough to injure but not kill with just a few blows.

B In Judaism

A court of at least 23 judges would have to be satisfied, to a legal certainty, that the capital offense had been committed by the accused before the court could impose a death sentence. Since the testimony of two eye-witnesses was required, and the witnesses were subjected to searching and detailed interrogation by the court, there was rarely an instance when the evidence met the prescribed legal standard.[437]

---

[433] Abolhassan Mohammadi, *Islamic Criminal Law*, p 23, Tehran: University publication (1374 Solar Hejira) And see Article 102 of Iran Penal Code stipulates that "for stoning, men should be buried up to their waist and women must be buried up to their chest."

[434] Islamic Penal Code of Iran, Art 89 (1991) [In Farsi].

[435] *Id,* Art 99.

[436] Arefeh Madani, *Execution of Criminal Sanctions*, p 60, Tehran: Majd publication (1374 Hejira). [In Farsi].

[437] See Maimonides, *Mishneh Torah*, Book of Judges, Sanhedrin, chapter XII.

Execution Methods

The execution of the criminal usually took place outside the city walls, and according to Deuteronomy 17:7, the witnesses in the case were to cast the first stone: "Thou shalt bring forth the man or the woman, who have committed that most wicked thing, to the gates of thy city, and they shall be stoned. By the mouth of two or three witnesses shall he die who is to be slain. The hands of the witnesses shall be first upon him to kill him, and afterwards the hands of the rest of the people".[438]

Death by "stoning" is carried out by hurling stones at the condemned individual until they die from the force of the objects thrown at them. The Talmud describes the stoning punishment (called Skila in Hebrew) in different terms than the stereotypical notion of hurling rocks at an immobile defendant/victim. Rather, the defendant is brought to the top of a large scaffold, and thrown off. After that (if the defendant was not already dead) very large rocks were dropped on top of the defendant.

The Mishna in tractate Sanhedrin (45a) describes execution by stoning. The condemned defendant was pushed from a platform set high enough above a stone floor that his fall would probably result in instantaneous death. The place of stoning was the height of two men. One of the witnesses knocked (the convict) down on his back. If he turned over on his chest, the witness turned him on his back. If he died right away, that was enough; but if not, the second (witness) took a stone and dropped it on his chest. If he died right away, that was enough; but if not he was stoned by all Israelites present.[439]

According to the Talmud the height from which the accused was pushed was substantial enough that death was virtually certain. An immediate death (Leviticus 19:18), "You shall love your fellow as yourself." This commandment requires a court to select for a condemned man a humane (i.e., painless) death. Rashi, the leading medieval commentator on the Talmud, explained that when the Talmud says a "humane death" it means a "quick death."[440]

The Gemara discusses why the Mishnah chose the height it did when it is clear from other sources that a fall from a lesser height is sufficient to cause death. The answer is, because the Sages wished to bring about a "favorable death," one that would not

---

[438] Bible, Deuteronomy 17:5-7.

[439] Mishna, Sanhedrin 6.4.

[440] Talmud, Sanhedrin 45a.

prolong his death agony. A fall from greater height would cause death sooner and with less pain. Raising the stoning ground smashed the defendant/victim body to become "grotesque," "adding markedly to the indignity of his execution."[441]

A Mishnaic source states that the second stone was so heavy it had to be lifted by two men, but then it goes on to say that he would take it and throw it on the chest of the condemned. The Gemara disagrees, concluding that the stone will have a greater velocity if thrown by one person. If the two were to throw the stone, it would be difficult to coordinate the exact moment of release, and thus one witness might lift the stone while the other was released it. In contrast to the Mishnah rule that if the defendant does not die as a result of the stone hurled at him, then all Israel must stone him. Another Mishnaic era source says that it never happened that a person repeated the stoning procedure.

The Gemara Sages resolve the seeming contradiction, asserting that the Mishnah is only giving the law if the stone does not kill the defendant. If that is not the case, however, that is, the condemned man dies, and then no additional stoning by the congregation is required. The Gemara challenges this premise and brings forth various proofs which it then refutes. Finally, the Gemara finds a Mishnaic era source supporting the view that generally biblical verses must be followed literally.[442]

Considering the stones size and execution conditions the rabbis' ultimate concern was that the mode of execution be as quick and as painless as possible, with minimal disfigurement. When one rabbi suggested that the height of the platform should be increased so that death from the fall would be certain, another rabbi responded that raising the platform is unacceptable because a fall from too high a platform would result in disfigurement.

When a male condemned is a few feet from the stoning grounds, court officials remove all his clothing, save for a piece of material to cover the man's genitals. Rabbi Yehudah argues that the only difference between a condemned man and woman is that "both in the front and in the back" she is covered, but otherwise disrobed. The Sages

---

[441] Irene Rosenberg, *supra* note 407.

[442] Talmud, Sanhedrin 45a (3).

argue, however, that only a man is stoned unclothed.[443] The Gemara contends that a redundancy in the biblical text, "and they shall stone him," establishes that only male condemned are to be stoned naked. Rabbi Yehudah, on the other hand, explains the extra word as implying that each condemned be stoned without clothing, and that gender is irrelevant.[444]

The Mishnah begins with the words *Nigmar Ha-Din* (when the judgment has been concluded). The procedure begins with one foot in the court, the decision and the language of the court. The bulk of the Mishnah is focused on procedures in the stoning house for the execution. The last two Mishnahs Five and Six, the stoning punishment returns to the court: Executioners would not bury the condemned in the graves of his fathers, separate gravesites were prepared fort hose executed by decapitation and strangulation, and one for those executed by stoning and burning. When the flesh is consumed, they gather the bones. And the relatives come and ask after the welfare of the judges and the welfare of the witnesses, that is to say, that we have nothing in our hearts against you, that you judged a judgment of truth. And they would not mourn with full ceremonies, but they would mourn the day of the death, since mourning the day of the death is only in the heart.[445]

Thus the execution begins and ends with the court house, after a long detour through the stoning house. Through this sequence, the Mishnah emphasizes the link between the court and the execution. The stoning punishment ends with the relatives making reconciliation with the court. Separate burial is prescribed for the criminal, not in the gravesite of his fathers but in "gravesites prepared for the court." The criminal, now as a corpse, makes his way back to the court, so to speak, which, in a final act of appropriation, refuses to hand the body over to the family.[446]

---

[443] Art Scroll Mishnah, Sanhedrin 6:3, at 97.

[444] Talmud bavil, Sanhedrin 45a (1).

[445] *Id.*

[446] *Id.*

4   Stoning Location

When the judgment has been concluded, executioners take the condemned out to stone him. The stoning house was outside the court house, as it is said, "Take out the blasphemer" [Lev. 24:14]. One stands at the entrance of the court, and the scarf is in his hand, and one person rides the horse far enough away from him so that he can still see him. One says, "I have to argue for his innocence," that person waves the scarf, and the horse runs and stops him. And even if he says, "I have to argue for my own innocence," they bring him back, even four or five times, only provided that there be substance in his words. [447]

The Biblical text first establishes that the execution site (the "stoning house") must be far from the court house, citing Leviticus 24:14 and it then stages a rescue effort on behalf of the convicted criminal. As he is processed from the court to the execution site, exonerating evidence is sought in a last-ditch attempt to reverse the verdict. The exegesis provided in this Mishnah is peculiar. In Leviticus 24:14, God delivers to Moses a command for the community to stone a blasphemer. God directs the people to perform their stoning "outside the camp": "Take the blasphemer outside the camp; and let all who were within hearing lay their hands upon his head, and let the whole community stone him." While the verse quoted requires that the criminal be taken outside the camp, the Mishnah requires that the criminal be taken outside the court.[448]

In Islam it is not possible to execute the stoning in territory of Islam's enemies. In addition it should be executed in public. Article 101 of the Iran Penal Code stipulates: "It is adequate that the religious leader should notify people about the time of carrying out stoning and it is required that a number of believers, no less than three, be present at the time of carrying out the sentence." Article 107 stipulates: The presence of witnesses is necessary at the time of carrying out the stoning but their absence would not make it

---

[447] Mishnah Sanhedrin Chapter Six is about the Court House and the Stoning House, Talmud, p 318-322.

[448] Beth Berkowitz, *Symposium: Rethinking Robert Cover's Nomos and Narrative: Negotiating Violence and the Word in the Rabbanic Law,* 17 Yale J. L. & Human 125 (Winter 2005).

null and void. In Judaism also based on Deuteronomy17:7 stoning should be executed in public.

5 Reversal of Punishment

A In Islam

Victims who can dig themselves out are acquitted. If the Condemned escape from the hole during the stoning and if his guilt is proved by his own confession, it will result in pardon. If the crime has been proved by confession escape indicates his withdrawal.

Men who are stoned to death are buried to the waist, while women are buried deeper, to stop the stones from hitting their breasts; as for women the possibility of escaping is much fewer than men. That is why in Islamic countries fewer men have been stoned than women. This apparent regard actually has a negative impact for women: If a condemned manages to pull free during a stoning, he or she can be acquitted.[449] In addition, the escape of witness, the denial after confession and repentance of sin will also result in avoiding the punishment.

It should also be noted that the law usually provides a stay of execution for a pregnant or nursing woman if there is no one to care for the child, though. In some cases the capital punishment would merely be postponed until the child is old enough to no longer need nursing.[450]

---

[449] Mohhaghegh Helli, *Sharaye 'Islam*, p 307, translation by Abdo 'Ghani Ebn Abi Taleb [InFarsi].

[450] Article 91 of Islamic Penal Code Indicates:" An adulteress shall not be punished while pregnant or in menstruation or when, following birth and in the absence of a guardian, the newborn's life is in danger. If, however, the newborn becomes the ward of a guardian the punishment shall be carried out."

B In Judaism

There are also conditions about avoiding this punishment in Judaism. Witnesses push the condemned by the hips so that he will fall to the ground sideways. If the condemned fell on their chests, they turned onto his hips. If the fall kills the defendant, no stones were cast. If they survive, then the other witness casts a stone on their chests. If they died from no further stones were cast. If they survived, "all of Israel," that is, all those present at the execution, stone them to death. [451]

Despite the Gemara grapples with yet another statement of the law, this is that if the witnesses' hands are severed before they can carry out the execution, then the defendant must not be killed.[452] This practice is based on Deuteronomy 17:7, which states that "the hand of the witnesses shall be upon him first to put him to death."

6 Stoning and contemporary standards of societies

The evolving standards of decency that mark the progress of a maturing society are final resort for challenging the stoning punishment. Why does stoning appear so revolting to us? It is because we are civilized and we do not do that sort of things any more. As Emile Durkheim, believed society's punishments are a window through which society's "true nature" can be viewed.[453] And an important reason why this punishment is thought of with such repugnance is that they have been historically linked to the process of torture.

In many cases two terms are synonymous, often what one individual would call a just form of punishment another would term torture. In many cases the actual punishment which society imposed was preceded by torture.

---

[451] Art Scroll Misnah, Sanhedrin 6:4.

[452] Talmud, Sanhedrin 45b (1)-(2).

[453] Emile Durkheim, ***TheDivision of Labor in Society,*** p 109, George Simpson trans., The Free Press (1933).

The debate over the application of the cruel and unusual punishment to the practice of stoning includes that the words "cruel," "unusual," and "punishment" have changed their meanings. The debate surrounds whether the application of the cruel and unusual punishments should be tied to perceptions of values and customs contemporaneous with its enactment, or whether that the principle must ever reflect current, evolving, presumably progressive, values.

The punishment, the harshest one in Talmudic law, was intended to be as quick and painless as possible given the nature of the punishment. (That is, there are quicker and more painless punishments, but the Talmud specifically condemns long, drawn out, and torturous punishments).

The harsh Biblical penalties may have been carried out to the letter at one time, but certainly by Mishnaic times courts favored a lenient interpretation of the law. Stoning was replaced by the quicker method of simply pushing the convicted off a ledge. Stone hitting a person's body was the same as a person's body hitting stone ran the argument. Stoning horses were constructed using a ledge placed at twice the height of a man, as it was determined that this height would kill the man but not do him the indignity of mutilating the body. If the condemned was not killed, a heavy stone was dropped on his chest to kill him quickly.[454]

Contemporary Jewish Law coincides with the Jewish Law doctrines that governed two millennia ago. It is not permissible to execute a condemned man or woman by means that cause unnecessary pain, delay or disfigurement. Even in the rare case when the State has determined that the accused must be put to death because a heinous offense was committed, the condemned is legally entitled to consideration and dignity.

This brief does not address the question of whether all capital punishment should today be rejected as "cruel and unusual" punishment. But almost two millennia ago, the rabbis of the Talmud in prescribing methods for imposition of the death penalty were concerned about the same factors that have emerged from this Court's Eighth Amendment jurisprudence. Primary concerns under Talmudic law are (1) the prevention of unnecessary pain and (2) avoidance of mutilation or dismemberment of the body. Therefore, the four means of execution described in the Talmud were designed to minimize the pain of the person who was being put to death, and to avoid mutilation of

---

[454] Talmud, Sanhedrin 45a.

his or her body. The methods described in the Talmud, therefore, differ significantly from what is assumed from a reading of the Biblical text.

Therefore contemporary Jewish law considers the standard of decency for this reason they do not execute stoning and this is possible for Muslim jurists to adopt this approach, "most Muslim policymakers in offending countries want to make changes in certain aspects of their strict penal codes and they are looking for the language and justifications that would make it palatable to do so. Regardless, change, if it is to be both compelling and permanent, must always come from within" [455]

The more the situation of the Muslim community changed, the more the Revelation altered to match the community's needs. To coordinate with the contemporary standards of Islamic societies Islamic scholars developed a vital exegetical tool called *Naskh*, which can best be understood as the purposeful abrogation (not cancellation) of one verse with another. For the vast majority of Muslims in the world, *Naskh* signifies that the Quran is a living, evolving scripture that developed alongside the Muslim community. More than anything else, however, *Naskh* demonstrates the importance of historical context in Quranic interpretation. At the very least, according to Abdullahi An-Na'im, *N*askh exposes the possibility that modern situations can allow the later Medinan texts of the Quran to be superseded by the more universal Meccan verses because, to quote the great Sudanese legal reformer Mahmoud Mohamed Taha: "the Meccan and Medinese texts [of the Quran] differ, not because of the time and place of revelation, but essentially because of the audience to which they are addressed." And while it is true that, with the Prophet Mohammad's death, the Revelation ceased evolving, it would be ludicrous to think that the Muslim community has also ceased evolving over the past fifteen hundred years. Quite the contrary, in fact there can be no question that the Sharia was developed within a clear historical context. Like the Quran, the tradition, the second most important source of Islamic law, is also a response to specific historical circumstances. Indeed, countless traditions strive to explain the historical context in which a certain revelation was revealed.[456]

Thus, because personal dignity and humanity are highly valued in current societies, Muslim jurists by adapting these tools can avoid punishments that violate these

---

[455] Aslan, *supra* note 406.

[456] *Id.*

values and would have to be deemed problematic and in contrast to the idealism embodied in the ban on cruel and unusual punishment.

7 Abolition of stoning or moratorium[457]

Although stoning is exist in the Islamic and Jewish textual references without substantial abolition, we can consider various evidentiary, procedural, and barriers to imposition of the stoning. These barriers such as lack of just and ideal religious criminal justice system, prevention of stoning in case of doubt, evidentiary requirement and considering 21 century conditions served to make stoning a rarity.

The judges of the rabbinic courts were deemed to be agents of God, and indeed the word used for such judges in the Bible is often the same as one of the names of God - a name that denotes His aspect of strict justice.[458]

In the Talmud the claim is made that the power of criminal punishment was withdrawn from the Jews forty years prior or at the time of the destruction of the Second Temple, before the rabbinic period had even begun. Based on the Talmudic evidence as well as historiography of Roman Palestine in this period, it remains a matter of more than some doubt whether the Mishnah's procedure for capital punishment was ever implemented, indeed, whether much of the Mishnah's entire set of legislations was ever implemented in its own time. If the legislators who authored the Mishnah assumed a set of political conditions in which they were unable to carry out the death penalty, surely that would alter our reading of the role that violence plays.[459]

Although the Biblical text appears to contemplate frequent imposition of capital punishment, the weight of authority among rabbis of the Mishnaic period (1st-3rd centuries of the Common Era), who first committed to writing what had theretofore been

---

[457] "Moratorium" generally means "a temporary cessation" usually for tactical reasons.

[458] Rosenberg, *supra* note 407.

[459] Berkowitz, *supra note* 448.

transmitted from generation to generation as the Oral Law, clearly condemned frequent executions. The Mishna in the tractate *Makkoth* (7a) declared:

The Sanhedrin that executes one person in seven years is called "murderous." Rabbi Elazar ben Azariah says that this extends to one execution in seventy years. Rabbi Tarfon and Rabbi Akiva say, "If we had been among the Sanhedrin, no one would ever have been executed." Rabbi Simon ben Gamliel responds, "Such an attitude would increase bloodshed in Israel."

This exchange among rabbis living in the first and second centuries reflects differences over the deterrent value of capital punishment that continues among legal scholars to this day. Some rabbis of the Mishnaic period (such as Rabbis Tarfon and Akiva) were unwilling to participate in a process that would take human life, while other rabbis (like Rabbi Simon ben Gamliel) believed that capital punishment had a deterrent effect that permitted it to be employed.

In Jewish law stoning used mainly for crimes that affected the wellbeing of the whole community and was carried out collectively, but the prosecuting witnesses were required to cast the first stones. It was thought that the heavy responsibility of carrying out the execution would deter witnesses from making false accusations.[460]

Several currents of thought exist in the Islamic world today. Disagreements are numerous, deep and recurring. Among these, a small minority demands the immediate and strict application of Hodoud, assessing this as an essential prerequisite to truly defining a "Muslim majority society" as "Islamic". Others, while accepting the fact that the Hodoud are indeed found in the textual references (the Quran and the tradition), consider the application of Hodoud to be conditional upon the state of the society which must be just and, for some, has to be "ideal" before these injunctions could be applied. Thus, the priority is the promotion of social justice, fighting against poverty and illiteracy etc. Finally, there are others, also a minority, who consider the texts relating to Hodoud as obsolete and argue that these references have no place in contemporary Muslim societies.[461]

---

[460] Lyons, *supra* note 326, p35.

[461] Tariq Ramadan Calls for a Moratorium on Stoning in the Islamic World, http://www.jihadwatch.org/dhimmiwatch/archives/005577.php, (April 02, 2005).

All the Muslim jurists, of yesterday and of today and in all the currents of thought, recognize the existence of scriptural sources that refer to corporal punishment (Quran and Sunna), stoning of adulterous men and women (tradition). The divergences between the Muslim jurists are primarily rooted in the interpretation of a certain number of these texts, as well as its degree of relevance to the contemporary era.

The majority of the Muslim jurists, historically and today, are of the opinion that these penalties are on the whole Islamic but that the conditions under which they should be implemented are nearly impossible to reestablish. These penalties, therefore, are "almost never applicable". The Hodoud would, therefore, serve as a "deterrent," the objective of which would be to stir the conscience of the believer to the gravity of an action warranting such a punishment. Therefore it isn't that the penalties themselves are un-Islamic. The penalties are Islamic. But conditions are not appropriate for their implementation.[462]

In Islam, "Hodoud punishments are to be prevented in case of doubt". This based on the prophetic tradition which says thus: "Prevent the application of Had punishment as much as you can whenever any doubt exists." The standard of proof in Hodoud punishment is very high and difficult to attain. It is even recommended by the Sharia that a judge suggest the possibility of withdrawal of confession to an accused who has confessed to the commission of crime.[463]

Because of the severity of punishment there are very strict evidentiary requirements for proving adultery. For instance there must be four male witnesses instead of normal two, or the accused must confessed to the crime. Some jurists have been considered that it is meritorious for the witnesses not to testify, leaving the offender to atone for the offence privately with God. Witnesses are also constrained by the more practical consideration that it the accusation is dismissed then they are subject to the punishment for false accusation of adultery.

Considering the above approaches, Iran has imposed a moratorium on stoning. Prior to 1983 stoning as a punishment did not exist in Iran. In ancient Iran punishments

---

[462] *Id.*

[463] Mohammad Bahrami, *Islamic Jurisprudence and Legal Analysis of Hodoud punishments are to be prevented in case of doubt*, 5 Legal viewpoints Journal, (1376 Solar Hejira) [In Farsi].

were harsh but we can not find precedence of stoning as a punishment during this era. After the invasion of Arabs to Iran, the central government was defeated and criminal justice system of ancient Iran was collapsed. Muslims enforced Islamic criminal rules to establish order, social security and promotion of Islam. Although Islamic punishments were administrated up to ratification of Penal Code in Iran; When Pahlavi Dynasty[464] replaced the Qajar Dynasty (1779-1925) stoning was not practiced in Iran. The present punishment system in Iran is based on the Twelve Imami Shii version of the sharia law. This system formed in the early 1980s. In 1983 the first specific Islamic penal Statute was ratified (Statute of retaliation and prescribed punishments). Based on this statute stoning were applicable for the adultery. Subsequently and now chapter 2 of the Islamic Penal Code is about prescribed punishments (ratified in 1992). Although stoning was imposed in the early years after the 1983, stoning was rarely applied (Before 2002).

Finally in Iran moratorium on stoning was first announced in December 2002, the head of the judiciary had sent a directive to judges instructing them to stop issuing death verdicts by stoning, Ayatollah Mahmud Hashemi-Shahrudi, head of Iran's judiciary, indicated that execution by stoning would be replaced with other means of punishment. He did not say whether this was a temporary or permanent move, but some Islamic jurists have defended stoning as part of Islamic law and thus impossible to abolish it per se.

Shii Islam, which follows a line of succession from the family of the Prophet rather than Sunni acceptance of the authority of the Caliphs, is better suited for flexibility in deciding legal issues. The main branch, Twelve Shiism, believed there were 12 imams who were the direct descendants of Mohammed and succeeded him as the true Caliph. The last disappeared while a child and is known as the "hidden Imam" who will eventually return to rule the Islamic world. During the occultation of the Twelfth Imam, the people are to be guided by mullahs who are empowered to interpret the laws. If they chose to engage in modern individual legal reasoning by a Muslim jurist (Ejtehad) to resolve conflicts between traditional Islamic law and international human rights, the prominent Shii clerics in Iran may be a positive force for safeguarding human rights in that country and an example to other Muslim governments. For instance former Iranian

---

[464] Iran's secular criminal justice system was formed under the Pahlavi Dynasty and its two monarchs, Reza Shah (1925-1941) and Mohammad Reza Shah (1941-1979). Modern criminal law was based on modern capitalist notions of crime and punishment. First Penal Code of Iran was ratified in 1926.

President Rafsanjani declared that stoning is not an appropriate punishment and is generally only imposed by tasteless judges. This could be an isolated remark; it could also be a first step toward a revival of Shii Ejtehad in this area. Based on above interpretation other jurists in Iran also challenging the stoning punishment:

Grand Ayatollah Naser Makarem Shirazi said in a written fatwa, or religious ruling "In certain circumstances, death by stoning can be replaced by other methods of punishment,"Shirazi is a highly influential cleric in the city of Qom — Iran's religious center. Abiding by the ruling of senior clerics is considered a religious obligation for the country's Shiite-dominated Muslim population: Ayatollah Hussein Mousavi Tabrizi, another senior cleric in Qom, about 80 miles south of the capital Tehran, said stopping stoning was a response to the demands of modern age. "Any punishment, including stoning, that defames Islam or depicts a bad picture of the religion in the world is harmful to Islam and it is fully Islamic to stop it."

Modern application of Jewish law implements the principle of humanity and consideration for this issue too. The State of Israel has abolished capital punishment for all offenses other than genocide, war crimes, and crimes against humanity, crimes against the Jewish people, and treason in wartime. The only execution that has taken place in Israel was the execution of Adolf Eichmann, in which the condemned man was hanged.[465]

In an important prisoners'-rights case, however, Deputy President of the Supreme Court Menachem Elon wrote an opinion in which he said (*State of Israel v. Tamir*, 37(iii) P.D. 201 (1983)): Jewish Law was particularly insistent on the preservation of even a criminal's rights and dignity during the course of punishment. Maimonides, after dealing with the types of punishment a court may impose, including imprisonment, concludes: "All these matters apply to the extent that the judge deems appropriate and necessary for the needs of the time. In all matters, he shall act for the sake of Heaven and not regard human dignity lightly. He must be careful not to destroy their dignity." According to Jewish law, a death sentence must be carried out with the minimum of suffering and without offense to human dignity. This is based on the

---

[465] The Jerusalem Post Newspaper, Online news from Israel.

Biblical verse, "Love your fellow as yourself," and the rule is, "Choose for him a humane death." From this we declare that even a condemned felon is your "fellow."[466]

Yet, despite the fact that the stoning of adulterers is a problematic and inconsistently applied punishment in Islamic law, the practice continues unabated in a number of conservative Muslim countries, particularly within their poor, rural regions.[467]

Considering that the opinion of most Islamic scholars regarding the comprehension of the texts and the application of stoning are neither explicit nor unanimous, accepting the fact that the Quran mentions adultery in some twenty-seven verses, it never mentions stoning as a possible punishment. Instead, it calls for lashes in one verse, ignoring for a moment the rather absurd incongruity of finding four blameless men who have simultaneously witnessed the very private act of sexual intercourse between two people, it must also be noted that one of the six Hodoud in the Sharia is the false accusation of adultery, a crime punishable by eighty lashes, bearing in mind that under Jewish law, even in the case of stoning, which is the most severe form of capital punishment and is presumably reserved for the worst offenses, being necessary for expiation of the particular sin, the Rabbis sought in the first instance to prevent conviction (e.g., by reopening the case as often as necessary), and, if that failed, to prevent execution (by requiring that the biblical verse be followed literally), and, at the very least, to minimize suffering and indignity and bring about a favorable death, and finally taking in to account all various evidentiary and procedural barriers to imposition of stoning can lead to Muslims through the world to place an immediate moratorium on the application of stoning.

I am not discussing the question of whether stoning should be abolished per se but Islamic countries which still apply stoning can learn Jewish and shiism approaches. Furthermore in according to the contrast of these punishment with human rights, while particular countries may treat people arbitrary and severely curtail their human rights, this is in spite of, rather than in keeping with, Islamic law. Therefore, Our Islamic laws need to be updated and meet demands of the modern time.

---

[466] Justice Elon's opinion in the *Tamir* case, translated into English, is reprinted in full in Elon, *et al.*, *Jewish Law (Mishpat Ivri): Cases and Materials*, pp. 567-572 , Matthew Bender & Co, Inc., New York (1999).

[467] Reza Aslan, *supra* note 406.

III Challenging the Various Methods of Inflicting the Death Penalty

In recent years, the study of the execution process has become increasingly scientific. Therefore several factors have been identified in efforts to address the compatibility of various methods of execution with the norm prohibiting cruel and unusual punishment. Modern technology may develop new and innovative methods of execution but the results from scientific and eyewitness evidence, suggest that certain methods of execution fail to end a person's life in a humane manner. Further, such evidence reveals that several execution methods are slow, painful, and unreliable.

Today, most scholars agree that the clause in the United States, when adopted in America, was intended to apply to the methods of punishment, including modes of inflicting the death penalty.[468] One Supreme Court Justice has written that prevention of both torture and other cruel punishments was clearly part of the Founding Fathers' intentions when the clause was placed in the Eighth Amendment.[469]

In Iran cruel and unusual execution method is prohibited, Article 263 of Iran Penal Code indicates "Retaliation with the blunt and non-sharp tool that tortures the condemned is prohibited and mutilation of him/her is a crime."[470] In addition based on the Article 16 of Regulation regarding the execution method of retaliation sentences of general and revolutionary courts "The executioners of capital punishment should precisely examine the execution tools and instruments before the execution and they should be certain about their stability. The mentioned tools should not be excessive, considering the necessity of sentence, also all the procedures should be executed tranquility, without violence, torture and mutilation by experts."[471]

Although for me arguments about the humanity of any method are absurd. The physical and psychological pain associated with the death penalty are barbaric, such pain

---

[468] Anthony F. Granucci, *supra* note 44.

[469] See Furman v. Georgia, 408 U.S. 238, 377 (1972) (Burger, C.J., dissenting).

[470] Islamic Penal Code of Iran, Art 263 (1991) [In Farsi].

[471] Regulation regarding the execution method of retaliation sentences of general and revolutionary courts, Art 16, 1999 [In Farsi].

exists whether the death penalty is carried out by stoning, hanging or lethal injection. United Kingdom after a through analysis of execution methods rejected the newer techniques in favor of hanging, but then abolished the death penalty altogether because the horror of entire discussion must surely have influenced members of Parliament. Once we admit that the means of capital punishment may be suspect, it seems impossible to find a method of killing that is human certain, and decent.[472]

1   Considerable Factors

A Duration of Procedure

This consideration involves number of possible approaches. Some have considered that the laps of time between infliction of punishment and the moment when the death is formally pronounced by a medical practitioner. Hanging is rapid if it causes the neck to break, but it is more drawn out when the strangulation is the cause of death. Electrocution often requires more than a single jolt of current, in one reported case[473] the condemned man survived, only to be submitted to the same procedure somewhat later, this time successfully. The Human rights Committee studied evidence indicating that death in the gas chamber may take more than ten minutes after the condemned person begins to inhale cyanide. It viewed this as a cruel, inhuman, and degrading punishment, running afoul of article 7 of the International Covenant on Civil and Political Rights.[474]

B The Pain Involved in the Execution Method

The element of pain is an integral part of the cruel and unusual execution method. Therefore, the element of pain should be considered "first and foremost" when reviewing challenges to a method of punishment. If we just determine a method's based on the fact that, in legislator's opinion, no unnecessary pain was involved in the method.

---

[472] William Schabas, *supra* note 225, p 201.

[473] Louisiana ex rel.Francis v. Resweber, 329 U.S. 459, 463, 67 S.Ct. 2159, 2163 (1985).

[474] William Schabas, *supra* note 117, p 160.

Despite their importance, physical and mental pains are only one indication of inhumane punishment. Further, they are only one of several reasons why many forms of corporal punishment have been discontinued.

In modern system of criminal justice the method should attempt to avoid undue suffering. But there is an evidence to support that all execution methods are likely to cause some degree of pain. In analyzing a particular method to see if it complies with the "cruel and unusual punishments" clause, one must keep in mind that cruelty encompasses more than the amount of pain involved. Punishments can be cruel without being painful--pain is merely a form of cruelty.[475] Cruelty is any act that diminishes human dignity.[476]

C The Reliability & mutilation caused by Execution Method

One of the features of human execution is certainty. United Kingdom's Royal Commission said in its final report that during the present century there is no record of failure or misshape in connection with an execution and, execution by hanging can be regarded as speedy and certain but there are many documented cases of botched hangings in various countries. There are also a few cases in which hangings have been messed up and the prison guards have had to pull on the prisoner's legs to speed up his death or use a hammer to hit his head.[477]

Human dignity also entails respect for one's bodily integrity. Thus, a method of execution which unnecessarily disfigures or mutilates a prisoner's body should be discouraged.

---

[475] Peter S. Adolf, *Killing Me Softly: Is the Gas Chamber, or any Other Method of Execution, "Cruel and Unusual Punishment?"* 22 HASTINGS CONST. L.Q. 815, 842 (1995).

[476] *Id.*

[477] William Schabas, *supra* note 117, pp 169-177.

D The Degrading Preparation Involved in the Method

Some methods of execution involve preparations which may unnecessarily heighten a prisoner's anxiety beyond the actual execution. The preparations involved in hanging and electrocution are two examples. The day before a hanging, a prisoner must endure the harrowing experience of being weighed and measured for a proper drop length. Electrocution requires a prisoner to have his head and the calf of one of his legs shaved in order to facilitate contact with the electrodes.[478]

Death is a fearful and frightening experience. The agony felt by the condemned prisoner after he is sentenced to death is profound regardless of the method involved. Consequently, courts must consider whether a method involves preparations which heighten an already distressful experience.[479]

2 Socio-Humanity Perspective

A Unacceptable to Society

Like other aspects of the norm prohibiting cruel punishments, a society conception of what methods of execution are acceptable will evolve over the time, and some methods which had once been widely employed would become unacceptable to society. Therefore "evolving standards of decency" concept is a subjective element that compels abounding one form of punishment because society deems it unacceptable.

The evolving standards of decency and the infliction of cruel and unusual analyses constitute a two-part inquiry to determine whether an execution methods.[480] The first question is whether execution methods involve "the unnecessary and wanton

---

[478] Robert J. Sech, *supra* note 329.

[479] *Id.*

[480] Hudson v. McMillian, 503 U.S. 1, 10-11 (1992) ("Punishments 'incompatible with the evolving standards of decency that mark the progress of a maturing society' or 'involv[ing] the unnecessary and wanton infliction of pain' are 'repugnant to the Eighth Amendment.'"

infliction of pain." Although considering our above discussion pain has integral role in all different execution methods through the history.[481]

An older and more established second inquiry addresses societal standards and their evolution: the "evolving standards of decency" analysis. Punishments reflect shared public standards of morality under a consensus of social orders through shared norms and values, mutual cooperation, and compromise to maintain stability.[482] Thus by utilizing legislative analysis in determining whether punishments conform with evolving standards of decency we conclude that legislative trends toward or away from a certain punishment can indicate societal acceptance or rejection, and according to this analysis, punishments that violate our evolving standards of decency are cruel and unusual and, thus, unconstitutional. But sever execution methods are not simply a reflection of public standards of decency. The use of hanging in Iran may serve numerous functions at different times, but it dose not necessarily reflect acceptance of public view about its appropriateness.

B Public Executions

Publicly held of capital punishment has evolved over time, no doubt because of changing perception about decency. Public execution at first blush seems to be in keeping with some objectives of capital punishment, particularly deterrence.[483] "Public execution" is a legal phrase, means that anyone who wants to attend the execution may do so. Also it means that all the public has access. Research shows that there is no relationship between deterrence, in the form of lowered homicide rates, and the public executions.[484]

---

[481] For more information please see pervious sections.

[482] Terance Miethe and Hong Lu, **Punishment: A Comparative Historical Perspective**, pp 194-200, Cambridge University Press (2005).

[483] William Schabas, *supra* note 117, p 167.

[484] Steven stack, **Publicized Executions and Homicide**, *Am. Soc. Rev. 532 (1987).*

Under Islamic law, execution should be public conducted in to enhance its alleged effect of general deterrence. There is no open indication regarding public execution in penal system of Iran. Public hangings are normally carried out sparingly in Iran and reserved for cases that have provoked public outrage, such as serial murders or child killings. Based on Regulation regarding the execution methods of retaliation... sentences "if the presence of viewers or other people during the execution is not advisable with district attorney instruction, police may prevent the public from the execution scene"[485] (Please see Figure 3-1).

Figure 3-1 Public v. Private Executions in Iran

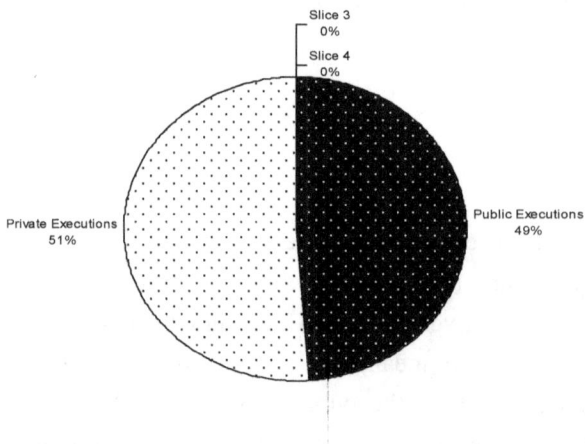

Figure 2-1 Source: http://www.richard.clark32.btinternet.co.uk/contents.html.

---

[485] Regulation regarding the execution method of retaliation, stoning, Crucifixion and body mutilation sentences of general and revolutionary courts, Art 22 (1991).

Public executions were, in fact, legal in many jurisdictions in United States, with the last documented instance occurring as recently as the late 1930s.[486] But Gary Gilmore[487] was publicly executed, in accordance with his express wishes, by the State of Utah. Gilmore waived his personal due process rights and refused to appeal his case. Under the present analysis of the cruel and Unusual Punishments Clause, the result was inappropriate. One may not consent to cruel and unusual punishment. For example, even if given the choice of punishments between torture and death, the prisoner could not choose torture.[488]

Moreover, "Eighth Amendment not only protects the right of individuals not to be victims of cruel and unusual punishment, but that it also expresses a fundamental interest of society in ensuring that state authority is not used to administer barbaric punishments."[489] And also "protections of the Eighth Amendment are not waivable.[490]

Today, there are always witnesses to executions--sometimes numerous witnesses, for example, Fred Adams was legally hanged in Kennett, Missouri, on April 2, 1937, within a 10-foot wooden stockade. Roscoe "Red" Jackson was hanged within a stockade in Galena, Missouri, on May 26, 1937. Two Kentucky hangings were conducted after Galena in which numerous persons were present within a wooden stockade, that of John "Peter" Montjoy in Covington, Kentucky on December 17, 1937, and that of Harold Van Venison in Covington on June 3, 1938. An estimated 400 witnesses were present for the hanging of Lee Simpson in Ryegate, Montana, on December 30, 1939. The execution of Timothy McVeigh on June 11, 2001, was

---

[486] John D. Bessler, *Televised Executions and the Constitution: Recognizing a First Amendment Right of Access to State Executions*, 45 Fed. Comm. L.J. 355, 441 n.53 (1993).

[487] 429 U.S. 1012 (1976).

[488] Seth F. Kreimer, *Allocational Sanctions: The Problem of Negative Rights in a Positive State*, 132 U.PA.L.REV. 1293, 1387 (1984)

[489] *Supra* note 469 at 1019 (Marshall, J., dissenting).

[490] *Id*, Justice White, dissenting.

witnessed by some 300 people (some by closed circuit television), so some might call it a "public execution," even though federal law does not permit public executions.[491]

Florida, Texas[492] and Utah are the states with serious advocates of public execution. Officials in these states can thus carry out public executions; that is, executions that members of the general public may voluntarily attend.[493] In recent years, Florida[494] executions proceed regularly and there is a waiting list of citizens asking to see condemned men die.[495]

C   International Human Rights Perspective

International human rights bodies have also examined methods of capital punishment within the scope of the norm prohibiting torture and cruel treatment. The United Nations Human rights committee, in its general comment on article 7 of the International convent on civil and political rights[496] noted that when the death penalty is applied by a state party for the most serous crimes, it must not only be limited in accordance with article 6 it must be carried out in a such a way as to cause the least

---

[491] See 18 U.S.C.A. § 3596 and the federal administrative regulation implementing it, 28 CFR § 26.4. A.

[492] In Texas, Roger "Animal" DeGarmo announced that he would auction seats for witnesses to his planned 1986 execution, and he claimed to receive two $1,500 bids and five $1,000 bids. Texas Department of Correction officials refused to allow the sales. The State's Attorney General, however, subsequently agreed that "cameras should be allowed in the death chamber so the public could see how a criminal is put to death."

[493] Steven A. Blum, *Public Executions: Understanding Cruel and Unusual Punishments Clause,* 19 Hastings Const. L.Q. 413 (Winter 1992).

[494] The Department of Corrections selects twelve witnesses from a volunteer list to watch each execution alongside clergy, medical personnel, the prisoner's attorneys, and state officials. Currently, there are no policies or guidelines for witness selection, and declared motives for wanting to see an execution vary.

[495] *Id.*

[496] International Convention on Civil and Political Rights, *supra* note 139.

possible physical and mental suffering.[497] The committee against torture has also expressed some mild interest in the subject.[498]

        Human Rights Watch opposes capital punishment in all circumstances. But until the thirty-eight death penalty states and the federal government abolish the death penalty, international human rights law requires them to use execution methods that will produce the least possible physical and mental suffering. It is not enough for public officials to believe that lethal injection is inherently more humane than the electric chair. States must choose carefully among possible drugs and administration procedures to be sure they have developed the specific protocol that will reduce, to the greatest extent possible, them prisoner's risk of mental or physical agony.[499]

---

[497] General Comment 20/44, U.N. Doc. CCPR/C/21/Rev.1Add.3, 6.

[498] Initial Report of China, U.N. Doc. CAT/C/7/Add.14, 126.

[499] Human Right Watch, *supra* note 380.

Chapter 4

Cruel and Unusual due to the Doctrine of Proportionality

The third challenge to the death penalty as a cruel and unusual punishment is imposing the penalty for certain crimes, generally those other than murder. Provisions against cruel and unusual punishment are aimed primarily at the kind of punishment imposed, not its degree. Nevertheless, where the degree of a sentence imposed on one convicted of crime is so disproportionate to the offense committed as to shock the moral sense of the community, the punishment is prohibited. The Proportionality doctrine states that in criminal cases the Cruel and Unusual Punishment Clause requires some measure of proportionality between the punishment imposed and the offense committed. This proportionality principle is not symmetric. The proportionality doctrine forbids only those punishments that are disproportionately severe, not those that are disproportionately lenient.[500]

I *When the Death Penalty is Appropriate?*

1   The Death Penalty as Excessive

Following the Mosaic principle of an eye for an eye, a tooth for a tooth, the Quran also stipulates that weaker members of society can not be used as substitutes for the punishment of the stronger social members. That is why the text advises the proportionality principle in the following formula: a free man for a free man, a woman for a woman, and a slave for a slave. Under Islamic law if someone is charged with a crime, he/she should be subjected to a proper punishment that fits the crime.

Under Iranian law the infliction of any punishment should be just and commensurate with the crime committed. Justice is achieved when the offender is

---

[500] Stephen Parr, *A New Perspective on the Cruel and Unusual Punishment Clause*, 68 Tenn. L. Rev. 41 (2000).

appropriately punished without any excess. An important aspect of the Islamic law of crimes is that whatever punishment for crime should be proportionate to the harm inflicted without any excess.

Iranian law does not construe the death penalty as a unique and ultimate punishment reserved for the most serious crimes. In contrast, United States capital punishment may be imposed only when the extinction of human life is brought about under circumstances society considers especially worthy of condemnation.[501]

> In Iran legislature has approved capital punishment in three different categories:
> 1- Prescribed punishments (Hodoud) such as: adultery, sodomy, Moharebeh, rape, incest and ... .
> 2- Retaliation or Lex Talionis (Qisas)

The statement of *Lex Talionis* "an eye for an eye, a tooth for a tooth" can be fount in the Old Testament. In Genesis, it states: "whose sheddeth man's blood , by man shall his blood be shed: for the image of God made he man,"[502] Yet Cain, the son of Adam and Eve, was not punished in this way, but only condemned to exile, bearing a distinctive brand on his forehead. The principle also appears in several places in Exodus, in which Moses receives the laws from Yahweh[503] (the Jewish God) and is expressed more amply in Leviticus: "If a man injures his neighbor, what he has done must be done to him: broken limb for broken limb, eye for eye, tooth for tooth. As the injury inflicted, so must be the injury suffered."

The *lex talionis* is now generally viewed as a mandate to vengeance and retribution. During its early development it was a progressive principle towards a rule of proportionality in the determination of criminal sanctions. It should also be considered as a limitation on abusive or excessive punishment. The Latin *talio* means "equivalent to" and the *lex talionis* imposes a limit on punishment by prescribing that it may be exceed

---

[501] Tex Penal Code § 19.03 (1994) (defining murder as capital if it is committed, inter alia, during the course of a kidnapping, burglary, or aggravated sexual assault; for remuneration; or on the person of an on-duty peace officer or a child under six years of age).

[502] Bible, Genesis 9:6.

[503] *Id*, Exodus 21:24.

the scope of the original crime. The same notion of proportionate punishment is found in Aristotle's Ethics.

3- Discretionary punishment (Taazir) is imposed for offenses not covered by fixed punishment or retaliation.

Death by capital punishment may be the sentence if convicted for any of the three types of offenses. The difficulties of proof mandated by strict evidentiary requirements and the Quranic restriction of the ultimate penalty to specified crimes form a strong legal reluctance to avoid imposing the death penalty in traditional Islam. As each category of crimes arises from its own authority and embodies its own set of values, the categories must be examined separately as we gauge Islamic support for capital punishment.

In the United States death penalty is not per se cruel and unusual punishment forbidden by the Eighth Amendment. The Eighth Amendment imposes restrictions on the types of offenses for which the death penalty may be imposed, and upon the manner in which it may be imposed in those cases in which it is permissible.[504]

We should consider that the non-homicide death penalty statutes, offenses for which the death penalty has been upheld other than murder in the U.S. include robbery, arson, kidnapping, espionage, assault, rape, and attempted rape. Non- homicide death penalty statutes make a reasonable contribution to the acceptable goals of punishment and are not solely concerned with the needless imposition of pain, we must still analyze

---

[504] Woodson v. North Carolina, 428 U.S. 280, 96 S. Ct. 2978, 49 L. Ed. 2d 944 (1976) (per Justice Stewart with two Justices concurring and two Justices concurring in the judgment); Jurek v. Texas, 428 U.S. 262, 96 S. Ct. 2950, 49 L. Ed. 2d 929 (1976) (per Justice Stevens with two Justices concurring and three Justices and the Chief Justice concurring in the judgment); U.S. v. Jones, 132 F.3d 232, 48 Fed. R. Evid. Serv. (LCP) 699 (5th Cir. 1998), 1998 WL 313347 (U.S. 1998); Ex parte Harrell, 470 So. 2d 1309 (Ala. 1985); People v. Fairbank, 16 Cal. 4th 1223, 69 Cal. Rptr. 2d 784, 947 P.2d 1321 (1997), as modified on denial of reh'g, (Feb. 18, 1998) (holding that the same is true under the California state constitution); Dillon v. State, 454 N.E.2d 845 (Ind. 1983); State v. Bass, 189 N.J. Super. 445, 460 A.2d 214 (Law Div. 1983); State v. Compton, 104 N.M. 683, 726 P.2d 837 (1986); Davis v. State, 665 P.2d 1186 (Okla. Crim. App. 1983); State v. Harbison, 704 S.W.2d 314 (Tenn. 1986); Woolls v. State, 665 S.W.2d 455 (Tex. Crim. App. 1983), 468 U.S. 1220, 104 S. Ct. 3592, 82 L. Ed. 2d 889 (1984); Stockton v. Com., 227 Va. 124, 314 S.E.2d 371 (1984).

whether a punishment is grossly out of proportion to the severity of the crime. It is important to note that the test is grossly disproportionate and not merely disproportionate. Thirteen states and the federal government have enacted laws which authorize the use of the death penalty for crimes in which no one was killed.

2   Proportionality Doctrine & 8th Amendment in the United States

Historical evidence from the Founding period indicates that the American Framers intended the Clause to forbid modes of punishment such as torture. Neither the English nor the Framers, however, intended to incorporate a guarantee of proportionality.[505]

The Supreme Court first recognized proportionality in ***Weems v. United States***.[506] In *Weems,* the defendant was convicted of falsifying documents and sentenced to fifteen years of hard labor in chains. He was also subjected to life-long civil disabilities, including the loss of the right to vote, to hold public office, and to receive retirement benefits. Additionally, the defendant was sentenced to a lifetime of government surveillance, including continuous reporting and inspections. The court reviewed a lot of evidence against the use of corporal punishment, but none, it would seem, in favor of it. It refers to two expert penologists whose testimony clearly demonstrated that the use of the strap in this day is unusual and we encounter no difficulty in finding that its use is cruel.

The Supreme Court, in this landmark decision, found proportionality to be part of the Eighth Amendment and held that the punishment imposed on Weems was improper in both method and quantity. After *Weems,* the Supreme Court vacillated between holding that proportionality was a legislative matter not fit for judicial review, except in extreme cases, and the "principle that a criminal sentence must be proportionate to the crime for which the defendant has been convicted," as determined by the judiciary.

---

[505] Stephen Parr, *supra* note 500.

[506] 217 U.S. 349 (1910).

In ***Solem v. Helm***[507], the Court announced three factors to be considered when examining a sentence for proportionality. The first factor is the "gravity of the offense and the harshness of the penalty." The second factor involves "the sentences imposed on other criminals in the same jurisdiction." The third factor involves examining "the sentences imposed for commission of the same crime in other jurisdictions."

Although the first factor relies on the subjective determinations of judges, the other two factors are objective. In creating these three factors, the Court's rationale was consistent with its prior holding in ***Coker v. Georgia***.[508] It was in *Coker* that the Court observed the following: "Eighth Amendment judgments should not be, or appear to be, merely the subjective views of individual Justices; judgment should be informed by objective factors to the maximum possible extent." The Court has also observed that deference to legislative determinations is mandated by both the Eighth Amendment and federalism concerns. In fact, the Court stated that "the clearest and most reliable objective evidence of contemporary values is the legislation enacted by the country's legislatures."

In ***Stanford v. Kentucky***[509], a post-Solem decision, the Court said that "in determining what standards have 'evolved,' however, we have looked not to our own conceptions of decency, but to those of modern American society as a whole." Because *Solem* involved a sentence of life imprisonment without parole, it appeared that proportionality analysis might play a significant role in no capital cases.

The role of proportionality in punishment for crime changed in 1991 with the ***Harmelin v. Michigan***[510] decision. *Harmelin* involved an offender convicted of possession of 672 grams of cocaine. The offender was sentenced to life imprisonment with no possibility of parole. On appeal, the offender challenged the sentence as disproportionate to the crime. The Supreme Court determined that individualized sentencing is required only in death penalty cases and affirmed the sentence. Justice Scalia rejected the contention that *Weems* stood for a general proportionality principle as

---

[507] Solem v. Helm, 463 U.S. 277, 290 (1983).

[508] 433 U.S. 584 (1977).

[509] Stanford v. Kentucky, 492 U.S. 361, 369 (1989).

[510] 501 U.S. 957 (1991).

part of the Eighth Amendment. Further, Justice Scalia, writing for himself and Chief Justice Rehnquist, examined the history of the Eighth Amendment and concluded that the *Solem* Court was simply wrong in its conclusion that the Eighth Amendment contains a proportionality guarantee in no capital punishment cases.

An analysis of the text and history of the Eighth Amendment and the English Bill reveals that the Framers did not intend to include a proportionality requirement in the Eighth Amendment. Before *Weems*, the Court agreed on this point. After *Weems*, the Court gradually developed an asymmetric proportionality principle. Although *Rummel* and *Hutto* significantly curtailed this principle, *Harmelin* revealed that the Eighth Amendment still contains a narrow, albeit asymmetric, proportionality requirement. The Court's vision of proportionality has no theoretical foundation. Utilitarian theories of punishment, by their very nature, cannot yield or justify a proportionality requirement. Retribution theory, on the other hand, provides a sound theoretical footing for symmetric proportionality. Symmetric proportionality is also more faithful to a Reconstruction reading of the Cruel and Unusual Punishment Clause. There are few, if any, obstacles to implementing a symmetric proportionality regime. Current or future Supreme Court doctrine could simply be extended to cover both severity and leniency analysis. In short, symmetric proportionality is a valid and superior incarnation of the proportionality principle.[511]

Therefore there is a trend In the United States where states have increasingly begun to favor using the death penalty for no homicide crimes. Despite the increase in the number of non-homicide death penalty laws, no one is currently on death row for a crime which did not involve the death of another person.[512]

In *Coker v. Georgia*,[513] the Court again confronted the use of the death penalty for a non-homicide crime and ruled that sentencing a defendant to death for the rape of an adult woman was unconstitutional. This decision set a precedent suggesting that the Court would closely examine, and possibly invalidate, any sentence of death for a crime not involving a homicide.

---

[511] Stephen. Parr, *supra* note 500.

[512] Jeffrey C. Matura, ***Campaign Finance Reform Symposium: Note: When Will It Stop? The Use of the** Death Penalty for **Non-Homicide Crimes***, 24 J. Legis. 249 (1998).

[513] Coker v. Georgia, 433 U.S. 584 (1977).

In Coker, the Court set forth a definition for proportionality and decided that proportionality is guided by the excessive nature of the punishment for the crime committed.[514] Also, the Coker Court viewed the proportionality test as merely one prong in the test for excessiveness.[515] Under Coker, if a punishment is disproportionate to the crime committed, then that punishment is excessive and unconstitutional. The real question, then, seems to be the test for excessiveness.

Even though the Supreme Court struck down the use of the death penalty for the rape of an adult woman only twenty years ago, Louisiana currently has legislation which provides for the death penalty for the rape of a child under the twelve years of age.[516] Georgia is also very close to enacting similar legislation.[517] The legislatures in these states have apparently decided to draw a distinction between the rape of an adult woman and the rape of a minor. However, the Coker Court did not make such a distinction, so whether the Court would uphold these statutes cannot be predicted. For example, Florida and Mississippi passed laws making the rape of a child a capital offense, but the Florida Supreme Court struck down their law under Coker and the Mississippi law was invalidated for other reasons. These invalidated laws were significant because they represent the state legislatures' general movement.

In addition to the use of capital punishment for the rape of a minor, strong support also exists across the country for the use of capital punishment for other crimes where the victim is not killed. In fact, thirteen states currently have laws that permit the death penalty for a non-homicide crime.[518] Most of these laws center around crimes of treason, aggravated kidnapping, and aircraft hijacking.[519] Several other states also

---

[514] *Id.*

[515] *Id.*

[516] La. Rev. Stat. Ann. § 14:42 (West 1996).

[517] House Bill 801, offered by Representative Warren Massey, was recently defeated in the Senate; however, it was sent back to the committee and will be reconsidered in January, 1998.

[518] Michael Higgins, *Is Capital Punishment for Killers Only*?, 83 A.B.A. J. (Aug. 1997).

[519] See Ark. Code Ann. § 5-51-201 (Michie 1995); Cal. Penal Code § 37 (West 1988); Colo. Rev. Stat. Ann. § 18-3-301 (West 1990); Ga. Code Ann. § 17-10-30 (1997); 720 Ill. Comp. Stat. Ann.

provide the death penalty for such crimes as espionage,[520] drug trafficking,[521] placing bombs near bus terminals,[522] and aggravated assault or kidnapping while incarcerated in state prison for murder or persistent felonies.[523] Further, in 1994, Congress passed a law authorizing the death penalty for drug kingpins who generate more than $ 20 million a year.[524] Also, the reason even more state legislatures have not enacted similar statutes is because many of them are waiting to see how the Supreme Court rules on the issue. Although no defendant has been sentenced under the one of these non-homicide death penalty statutes, each year more state legislatures are taking a serious look at enacting such laws.

3   Proportionality Doctrine v. Islamic Laws in Iran

As I mentioned in chapter two, capital punishment is applied to three different specify in Iran. Although it seems there is no way to limit the death penalty when it is not proportionate to the crime, there are solutions that can limit the imposition of the death penalty under Islamic law.

A   Hodoud Offenses

Had means restricted or restriction, prevention, hindrance or prohibition, and hence a restrictive ordinance or statute of God. Enforcement of these punishments in considered 'the right of Allah'. Indicating that such punishments are invariably clarify and imperative. Had warrants no [human] interference. High standards of proof required

---

5/30-1 (West 1993); La. Rev. Stat. Ann. § 113 (West 1986); Miss. Code Ann. § 97-767 (1972); Wash. Rev. Code Ann. § 9.82.010 (West 1988).

[520] N.M. Stat. Ann. § 20-12-42 (Michie 1978).

[521] Fla. Stat. Ann. § 893.13 (West 1997).

[522] Mo. Ann. Stat. § 578.310 (West 1996).

[523] Mont. Code Ann. § 46-18-220 (1996).

[524] Violent Crime Control and Law Enforcement Act of 1994, Pub. L. No. 103-322, 108 Stat. 1796 (codified as amended in scattered sections of 18 U.S.C.).

for conviction indicate that the application of the Hodoud penalties can be curtailed in practice. Attention to the affirmative defenses discussed above as they apply to Hodoud offenses is necessary to limit the scope of liability when the punishment is fixed and severe.[525] In reference to the defense of mistake, Abu Yusuf in his Kitab al-Ikhtiyar specified that if a man, in the darkness of night, finds a woman not his wife in bed and sleeps with her thinking she is his lawful wife, he has not committed adultery and may not be punished. If a woman does not tell a blind man she is not his wife and he sleeps with her, he is not criminally responsible.[526] Jurists in Iran may restrict Hodoud penalties by narrow construction of the law and by presuming the lawfulness of a defendant's acts when they resemble another, lawful one.[527] Although confessions are generally binding proof of guilt, a confession involving a had offense may be withdrawn. It is incumbent on the judge to recommend this option to the confessor.

Increasing procedural safeguards is another way to limit the imposition of the death penalty when there is a fixed penalty for conviction. To be admitted in to evidence, witnesses must meet strict requirements. Witnesses must possess the characteristics required for full legal capacity: sanity, legal age, and full responsibility. It has not been indicated in the Penal Code of Iran, witnesses must also be of 'good character' (Adl), i.e., they must not have committed 'grave sins and must not persevere in small ones.'[528] Limitations on the admissibility of witnesses may serve to increase the difficulty of obtaining a conviction leading to capital punishment to Iran.

Similar restrictions apply to the admissibility of confessions. Moharebeh, punishment for armed robbery, finds authority in the Quran: punishment of those who wage war against God And His Messenger, and strive with might and main for mischief through the land is: execution, crucifixion, cutting off of the offender's hand and foot from opposite sides, or exile: These punishments represent disgrace in the world, and a

---

[525] Safia M. Safwat, *Offences and Penalties in Islamic Law*, 26 Islamic Q. 149, 154 (1982).

[526] Saqlain Masoodi, *Criminal Liability at Islamic and Western Laws--Parallels and Distinctive Features*, 9-10 Islamic & Comp. L. Q. 1, 3 (1990-1991).

[527] Based on the Principle of Doubt.

[528] Joseph Schacht, *An Introduction to Islamic Law*, pp 124-125, Greenwood Pub Group, (1964).

heavy punishment; except for offenders who repent disgrace is: in the cases where offenders repent Allah is Oft-Forgiving, Most Merciful.[529]

The crime of armed robbery is serious. An array of punishments is authorized by God sometimes in an indifferent manner. The values of Islamic law support the imposition of punishment proportionate to the harm caused. When the brigand is not a murderer, a strong Islamic legal tradition prohibits the execution. In contrast, in cases of Moharebeh where the victim's death results, with or without the successful dispossession of property, the penalty is generally death.

It is not exaggeration that punishments for offenses forth in the Quran and the Sunnah are primarily deterrents. They are a signal to the believer of the gravity of the crimes. Dire theoretical consequences in the application of their punishment remain within the procedural and substantive limits of the classical Islamic law.

Furthering the tradition of juristic reluctance to facilitate the imposition of Hodoud penalties, some contemporary Iranian jurists argue that Hodoud punishments may not be inflicted absent the establishment of a 'true' Islamic society. Basic human needs must first be met, including the provision of adequate food, shelter, medical care, and employment.[530]

Careful parsing of offenses is proof of the desire to make the punishment proportionate to crime and has the effect of limiting the use of capital punishment despite the apparent discretion given by the text.

B   Qisas (Retaliation)

Retaliation is prescribed for offenses proscribed by the Quran or Sunnah of the Prophet, but subject of a private claim. Retaliation applies to crimes against persons (murder) and crimes against the body (injury), and distinguishes between degrees of intent. In cases of intentional murder Iran permits the death penalty as a right of the individual (i.e., the victim's family), not the State. Concepts of forgiveness and brotherly

---

[529] Holy Quran, 5: 33-34.

[530] Safia M. Safwat, *supra* note 525, p 155.

love' in reaction to the harm caused are preferable recourse. Judges in these cases are reminded to fulfill the letter, spirit, and values of the law God has revealed.

The Quranic verses do not seem to require a nuanced inquiry into the circumstances of the murder before permitting the imposition of Qisas. Classical Islamic law has limited the death penalty. It required a specific intent of the murderer, and granted certain family the right to override Qisas by accepting Diyat (blood-money) or other compensation in lieu of the murderer's death, also classical Islamic law took into account the status of the victim and murderer.

Restraints on the imposition of Qisas are still relevant to contemporary society.[531] These restraints involve an examination of the status of the murderer and the victim regarding both gender and religion.[532] Twelve Shiism contends that since the diyat for a woman is only half that of a man's. For a female victim's family to pursue Qisas against her male assassin, the victim's family must make up the difference in the blood-price. [533]

C Taazir (Discretionary Punishments)

Capital punishment for Taazir (Discretionary punishments) offenses, when permitted, are discouraged by the availability of other punishments which reflect concerns of proportionality and leniency. To the extent the imposition of the death penalty is motivated by the sovereign's desire to exercise control over the community. Space is opened to question whether punishment God's wishes or is merely a political choice of Muslim rulers sanctioned by the values or substance of Islamic religious law.

---

[531] J.N.D. Anderson, *Homicide in Islamic Law*, 13 Bull. of The School of Oriental & African Stud. 811, 815 (1951).

[532] Ahmed I. Ali, *Compensation in Intentional Homicide in Islamic Law*, 9 J. Islamic & Comp. L. 39, 45. (1980).

[533] J.N.D. Anderson, *supra* note 531.

Jurists disagree whether death may be imposed as a Taazir penalty. Ibn Farhun characterized Taazir as a 'disciplinary, reformative, and deterrent punishment.'[534] Emphasis on reformation and deterrence would seem to imply that the extinction of human life would not serve the purposes of Taazir. Indeed several jurists have conferred that capital punishment is not suited as Taazir penalty.[535] Abd al-Qadir Awdah, in his work, al-Tashri al-Jina'i al-Islami, argued that a Taazir punishment must be less severe than Hodoud punishments in proportion to the crime. While insisted the only justification for the establishment of Taazir offense is the protection of society.[536]

Codification of capital punishment for this offense, even when it espouse beliefs of some Muslim clerics, radically transforms the history and nature of the law.

II *Juvenile[537] Death Penalty*

Maturity is an important factor in evaluating whether a sentence of death is an appropriate response to juvenile crime. The juvenile justice system itself was formed on the principle that the relative immaturity of children warrants separate from adults. Whether juvenile offender sentences are appropriate depends in part on whether the juvenile is sufficiently responsible to deserve it. In the case of the death penalty, maturity is central to whether a punishment is consistent with societal norms, and whether it is proportionate to the harm caused.

However a juvenile offender may have known right from wrong enough to be considered guilty of the crime, such a determination does not mean that the juvenile offender is sufficiently culpable and incorrigible to warrant the death penalty. Unfortunately, most juvenile offenders do not receive an individualized consideration of their maturity, only their guilt. The transfer to adult court that makes the death penalty available is often based on the severity of the crime, not the mental state of the offender. Treating a juvenile like an adult simply based on the type of offense is illogical, because

---

[534] Mohamed S. El-Awa, **Punishment in Islamic Law**, p 96, American Trust Publications (1982).

[535] Safia M. Safwat, *supra* note 525, p 181.

[536] *Id*, p 176.

[537] As used in this section, "juveniles" refers to individuals who were under the age of eighteen when the crime at issue was committed.

juvenile offenders have troubled childhoods, and capital punishment for juvenile offender are only solution that falls to adhere to International law.

If civilized nations are serious about protecting children against hunger, homelessness, and hopelessness, how can they impose the death penalty on juvenile offenders who are mentally retarded, sexually and physically abused, those with chronic and congenital physical defects, represented by incompetent counsel and those refused treatment for their maladies by the state which will ultimately murder them. We engage in state murder of children who are our social trash. That's why there's a Geneva Convention on war crimes, and that's why judges who sentence children to death are guilty of war crimes.

Although the number of juvenile offenders affected by the death penalty is small, it is a direct conflict with international law, violates the right to life and is the ultimate cruel, inhuman and degrading punishment.

Over the last decade, the issue of the juvenile (definition of juveniles under national laws are different. There should be no juvenile execution in the world, because of that juvenile in this section is based on international law definition) death penalty has received significant public attention. Almost all nations, even those with a death penalty believe it is inherently cruel and they have agreed to put aside the death penalty for juvenile offenders. In the United States although American public opinion favors retaining the death penalty in general, it opposes executing offenders under the age of eighteen. In addition a long list of international agreements and protocols has prohibited the juvenile death penalty.

Eighteen years is the internationally accepted minimum age for the imposition of capital punishment. According to Amnesty International, since 1990, only five countries in the world are known to have executed juvenile offenders: China[538], Congo[539], Pakistan,[540] Iran,[541] and the United States.

---

[538] In China, although by law no one should be executed for a crime committed when they were under 18, children have continued to be executed because the courts apparently do not take sufficient care to determine their age.

[539] A 14-year-old child soldier was executed in January 2000 within half an hour of his trial by a special military court. The special military courts were abolished in April 2003.

Between 1990 and 2007, at least fifty four executions against juvenile offenders have been carried out around the world. China (2 children), Democratic Republic of Congo (1 child), Iran (24 children), Nigeria (1 child), Pakistan (3 children), Saudi Arabia (1 child) Yemen (1 child), Sudan (2 children) and the USA (19 children) (Figure 4-1).

Pakistan, China and Congo abolished the juvenile death penalty. The United States recently has abolished the juvenile death penalty and in Iran the bill to raise the minimum age to 18 is under consideration. Ayatollah Mahmoud Hashemi-Shahrudi, Head of Iran's Judiciary sent a directive to judges instructing them to stop issuing death verdicts for juveniles (Figure 4-2).

---

[540] The juvenile justice system Ordinance 2000 has abolished the death penalty for people under 18 at the time of the offense in most of the country. However, the Ordinance was not extended to the provincially and federally administered tribal areas in the north and west.

[541] On 17 October 2008 a high-ranking Iranian Judiciary official announced the issuance of a directive to judges that execution sentences for juvenile offenders must be replaced by life imprisonment sentences with the possibility of parole also a bill to raise the minimum age to 18 is under consideration in Iran.

Figure 4-1 Juvenile executions in the world (since 1990)

Source: Amnesty International Report, available at:

http://web.amnesty.org/library/Index/ENGACT500152004

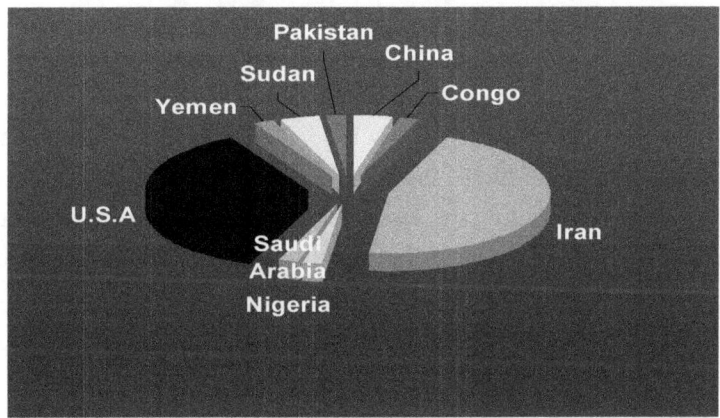

Figure 4-2 Executions of Child Offenders Since 1990 in the World

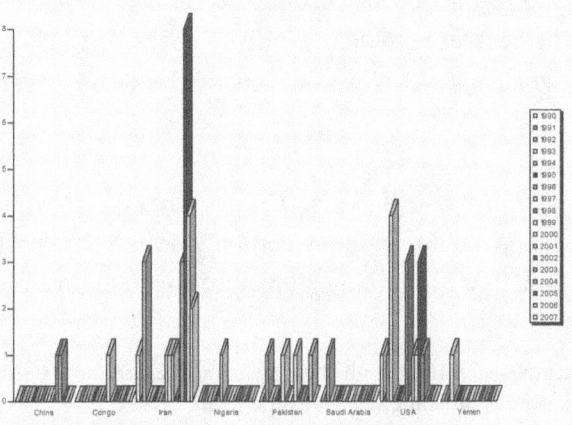

» Source: Amnesty International Report, available at:
http://web.amnesty.org/library/Index/ENGACT500152004

1   The Efficacy of Death Penalty for Juvenile Crimes & Violation of International Law

A   Penology View

The rules that people create as they form societies are enforced by the society itself, not individual members of the society. The collective entity determines whether the person charge of crime broke the rules, and society may impose punishment when appropriate. Society is willing to lend its muscle to regulate individual activity to maintain stability, provide for the common protection, and advancing society in accordance with the majority's wishes. Punishment serves these ends by modifying the behavior of potential lawbreakers by retribution, deterring people from engaging in crime, and by rehabilitating lawbreakers.

Retribution [542] is based upon the idea that punishment is justified when it is deserved. Punishment is deserved when the wrongdoer freely chooses to violate society's rules. In the context of the juvenile death penalty, the problem lies in applying these notions to a person that is not fully developed.

While juveniles convicted of homicide may know the difference between right and wrong, scientific findings about the incomplete formation of the adolescent brain raise questions about whether these children are freely choosing to violate society's rules. Such research directly challenges the justification of the death penalty on retributive grounds. [543]

The kids do not contemplate and plan before they kill. They do not think ahead before they do anything, apparently, and they certainly do not do a cost-benefit analysis of crime and punishment before committing homicide. Imagine, if you will, the kid in the

---

[542] Retributivism is sometimes identified with the particular measures of punishment such as an eye for an eye, or with a kind of punishment such as the death penalty.

[543] Phyllis Bookspan, *Too young to Die: Evolving Standard of Decency and the Juvenile Death Penalty in America*, 21 Delaware Lawyer 19 (Winter 2003-2004).

neighborhood thinking about robbing a store: "Well, the sentence has just been increased from ten to twenty years, so maybe I will not commit the robbery. Maybe I will go across the Michigan line and do it there, because I know they do not have the death penalty -- but I am not sure about the prison sentence. I will have to stop by the law library and check it out." Reflect for a moment on how kids plan so little of their behavior and you will understand that they do not go through that sort of cost-benefit research and analysis.[544]

By contrast, **deterrence** is not based upon the wrongdoer, but rather uses the wrongdoer as a means to an end, by punishing the wrongdoer; society sends a message to others to avoid similar bad acts.

The death penalty for juveniles is not a greater deterrent than is long-term imprisonment. In fact, the research indicates that the homicide rate goes up following an execution or even the announcement of a death sentence. Intuitively, it would seem that the homicide rate would decrease in the face of the death penalty, but in fact it goes up. I know you have heard political leaders tell you that they believe in the deterrent impact of the death penalty. In contrast, where we rely on research findings and the research findings are perfectly clear on this issue[545]. Despite significant increases and declines in juvenile homicide rates in the 1980s and 1990s (Homicide offending rates for teenagers and young adults increased dramatically in the late 1980's while rates for older age groups declined.), the rate of juvenile death sentences has remained constant at about 2% of all executions, raising the question of whether its use is even related to incidence of homicide[546]. (Figure 4-3)

---

[544] Victor Streib, *Sentencing Juvenile Murderers: Punish the last Offender or Save the next Victim*, 26 U. Tol. L. Rev. 765 (summer 1995).

[545] *Id.*

[546].U.S Department of Justice, Bureau of Justice Statistics, at: www.ojp.usdoj.gov/bjs.

Figure 4-3 Juvenile executions in U.S.A since 1990

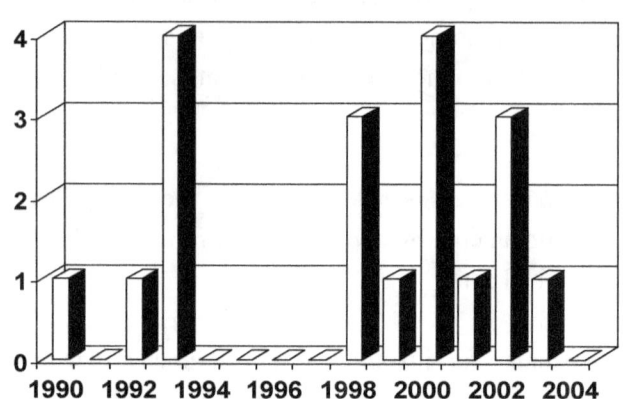

Source: Amnesty International, www.amnesty.org.

With respect to deterrence, scientific studies consistently fail to find convincing evidence that the death penalty deters crimes more effectively than other punishments. Recognizing this fact, U.S. Attorney General Janet Reno recently noted: "I have inquired for most of my adult life about studies that might show that the death penalty is a deterrent. And I have not seen any research that would substantiate that point." Deterrence is arguably even less persuasive when considering a juvenile offender, given evidence of the inability of children to comprehend long-term consequences. Psychological and sociological reports show juveniles live in an "intense present" whereby the "past and future seem pallid by comparison."[547]

---

[547] *Killing Kids: The Impact of Domingues v. Nevada on Juvenile Death Penalty as a Violation of International Law*, at:
http://www.bc.edu/bc_org/avp/law/wsch/journals/bclawr/41_5/04_TXT.htm.T24.

Based on ***child- centered interpretation*** [548] if juveniles do get any message from the death penalty, it is probably the wrong message. The children analysis is generally far more perceptive In fact, the message they have received is that killing is justified, even commendable if you have got the power. If you are "the man," killing is okay. If you are not, then killing is not okay.

Finally, the findings of impairment of rational decision making, the impulsive nature of adolescent actions, , plus the physiological and emotional impact of the traumas that most juvenile offenders have endured, all suggest no rational basis for deterrence as a sentencing theory for capital punishment for juvenile offenders.

Although, the goals of retribution and deterrence could not be met by imposing the death penalty on minors this dose not suggest that teenagers should not face punishment for violating society laws, but children should not be punished the same degree as adults. Also we should consider the goals of reform and ***rehabilitation*** for young people, because we know that people, particularly very young people, do change over a period of time.

Some people suggest that: Long-term imprisonment is only a stop-gap measure for juveniles who are killing. I do not see it as the long-term solution to the problem. I think the best long-term approach to the problem of juvenile homicide is to deal directly with the American cycle of violence, and the cycle of death. The question that I always hear is: "How do these kids do such violent things?" My response is that they are our children, they are American children. They are just a reflection of the nightmare side of the American dream. If you want to prevent homicide, you sentence the offenders to twenty or thirty years in a secure environment, give them strong training and rehabilitation programs, and get rid of almost everybody else in those prisons. When most of these present teenage offenders reach the age of thirty-five or forty, they will be releasable into society. Not all of them, as the focus are whether they are likely to kill again. What we know from almost everybody released at that level is that they are no more likely to kill than another forty-five year old who has never been to prison. Given that premise, there is no reason to keep these people locked up beyond that point.[549]

---

[548] Based on child –centered interpretation rule in interpretation of criminal laws consideration of children perspectives and benefits is necessary.

[549] Victor Streib, *supra* note 544.

Although, sever punishment is a solution for crimes but concentrating efforts on improving the odds of saving the next victim, rather than intensifying the punishment for the last offender is more important, and it is prevention, not revenge, that is the proper goal. Therefore instead of death penalty and other arbitrary and capricious penalties we must increase our Secure Correctional programs for youths with special rehabilitate and reformatory facilities for them, because killing (especially minors) would appear an accepted behavior and cause more violence.

B   International View

By execution of juveniles, states violate International law. International law has expressly determined that the death penalty, for crimes committed by juveniles is a human right issue. The International community has adopted human rights treaties that explicitly exclude child offender from the death penalty. Nearly all states in the world are now parties to these treaties and are therefore legally obliged to respect the prohibition. In addition, juvenile death penalty is violating customary international law and peremptory norm of international law.

Treaties are an important tool for comparing the policy of the United States with the world-view because they are sources that help to determine whether domestic laws comport with international treaties and policies. In deciding a juvenile death penalty case, domestic constitutional law may provide a basis for appeal, particularly the Eight Amendment dealing with cruel and unusual punishment, but international law may also be introduced.

International Covenant on Civil and Political Rights, Dec/16/1966, art. 6 (5) U.N.T.S. No 14668, Vol 999, p 171:

ICCPR, one of the primary human rights treaties, states in Article 6: "sentence of death shall not be imposed for crimes committed by persons below 18 years of age…" The ICCPR had been ratified by 152 states at mid-August 2004.Iran, China, Congo and Yemen have ratified the ICCPR.

When United States ratified the ICCPR in 1992, it made a reservation stating that it reserved the right to impose capital punishment for juveniles. This stipulation that is contrary to the terms of the ICCPR because Article 4 prohibits derogations from Article 6. The United States also included an affirmation of its right to try juveniles as adults in certain circumstances. Of the 144 signatories to the treaty, the United States was the only nation that entered a reservation to Article 6. This resulted in eleven foreign nations filing complaints against the United States with the Human Rights Commission.[550] However, if evidence exists that the United States intended to accept the treaty as a whole, it could be bound by all of the provisions regardless of the reservation

Convention on the Right of the Child, Dec/12/1989, art 37(a) U.N.G.A, Doc A/RES/44/25:

CRC indicates in Article 37 "Neither capital punishment nor life imprisonment without the possibility of release shall be imposed for offences committed by persons below 18 year of age".

CRC has been ratified by 192 states, except Somalia and the U.S.A. In 1993 Iran joined the CRC with a precondition that wherever the provisions of the convention conflicted with Iranian Civil Code and Islamic laws the Iranian government would not be bound to comply with them. To presume that Iran can disregard the provisions of the Convention under the pretext that they conflict with the Iranian Law is wrong and a willful breach of the Convention, because in that case there was no need for the country to join the Child Rights Convention. Meanwhile we must not forget that international law (including the Child Rights Convention) must be considered as compulsory in the same way that domestic law is also compulsory in Iran, otherwise it is senseless for a government to join an international convention or treaty and declare that it would comply with or will not comply with it whenever it deems prudent.[551]

African Charter on the Rights and Welfare of the Child, states in Article 5(3): ""The death sentence shall not be pronounced for crimes committed by children"". Article 2 of this treaty specifies that the term ""child"" refers to anyone under the age of 18. The African Charter on the Rights and Welfare of the Child has been ratified by 33 African countries.

---

[550] *Killing Kids: The Impact of Domingues v. Nevada on Juvenile Death Penalty as a Violation of International Law, supra note* 547.

[551] Shirin Ebadi, ***Children Rights***, *supra* note 23.

American Convention on Human Rights, Nov/22/1969, art 4(5) KAV 2307 (1965-1994):

"Capital punishment shall not be imposed upon persons who, at the time the crime was committed, were under 18 years of age…".

24 states in the U.S. have ratified the American convention on human rights.

International humanitarian law treaties also known as the laws of war exclude child offenders from the death penalty:

The **Geneva Convention Relative to the Protection of Civilian Persons in Time of War of 12 August 1949** (the Fourth Geneva Convention) states in Article 68: ""In any case, the death penalty may not be pronounced against a protected person who was under eighteen years of age at the time of the offence"".

The **Protocol Additional to the Geneva Conventions of 12 August 1949, and relating to the Protection of Victims of International Armed Conflicts** (Additional Protocol I of 1977) states in Article 77(5): "The death penalty for an offence related to the armed conflict shall not be executed on persons who had not attained the age of eighteen years at the time the offence was committed."

The **Protocol Additional to the Geneva Conventions of 12 August 1949, and relating to the Protection of Victims of Non-International Armed Conflicts** (Additional Protocol II of 1977) states in Article 6(4): "The death penalty shall not be pronounced on persons who were under the age of eighteen years at the time of the offence. . ." (Article 6(4)).

While the United States was the motivating force behind the first Geneva Convention in 1864 and a signatory to its multiple successive treaties, the United States has not ratified the two protocols from 1977. [552]

---

[552] Amy Eckhert, *"Unlawful Combatants" or "Prisoner of War": The Law and Politics of Labels*, 36 Cornell Int'l L.J. 59, 66 (2003). The United States did ratify the treaties that arose in 1883, 1907, 1929, and 1949. Id. Protocols I and II contain numerous clauses beyond the ones cited and it would be unfair to assume that the only reason that the United States has not ratified the treaty is because of these statements.

Safeguard Guaranteeing Protection of the Rights of those Facing the Death Penalty, ECOSOC resolution 1984/50, adopted 25/May/1984, endorsed UN General Assembly in resolution 39/118, 14/Dec/1984, art 3:

Safeguard 3 of this instrument states: "Persons below 18 years of age at the time of the commission of the crime shall not be sentenced to death…".

In 1984, the United Nations endorsed the Safeguards Guaranteeing Protection of the Rights of Those Facing the Death Penalty, which signified the strong agreement that existed among nations regarding the minimization, if not the abolition, of the death penalty. However, since the document was not voted upon, it is not legally binding. The document states that no person under the age of eighteen at the time of the crime will be sentenced to death nor will such a penalty be used on pregnant women, new mothers, or those who have become insane.

The exclusion of child offenders from the death penalty is now so widely accepted in law and practice that it has become a rule of **customary international law** – international rules derived from state practice and regarded as law *(opinio juris)* - and therefore binding on every state, except on those that have ""persistently objected"" to the rule in question.[553]

The Supreme Court has employed customary international law as a basis for deciding cases, and, as a result, the issue of whether or not the abolition of the juvenile death penalty has become customary and a jus cogens norm is raised. After evaluating Protocol I and Protocol II to the Geneva Convention, the American Convention on Human Rights, the Safeguards Guaranteeing the Protection of the Rights of those Facing the Death Penalty, the Covenant on the Rights of the Child, and the International

---

[553] In 2000 the UN Sub-Commission on the Promotion and Protection of Human Rights adopted a resolution affirming that "the imposition of the death penalty on those aged under 18 at the time of the commission of the offence is contrary to customary international law" and inviting the UN Commission on Human Rights to confirm the affirmation (resolution 2000/17 of 17 August 2000). In 2004 the Commission on Human Rights "reaffirmed" the Sub-Commission's resolution 2000/17 "on [in the Commission's words] international law and the imposition of the death penalty on those aged under 18 at the time of the commission of the offence" (resolution 2004/67 of 21 April 2004, Para. 2).

Covenant on Civil and Political Rights, a strong argument exists that the international norm is no longer one that supports the execution of juvenile offenders.[554]

There are two elements that must be satisfied, in order for customary international law to exist: 1- Are state practice and the belief that the practice is actually required by international law? The first element is clearly fulfilled, since only a few countries impose the death penalty on juveniles and all other countries have either abolished it or enacted legislation to prohibit it. In order to meet the second element, the nations that prohibit the juvenile death penalty must do so because they believe that they must in order to comply with international law.[555] Based on the four international agreements that prohibit the juvenile death penalty, it is arguable that the conforming nations believe that they are required to prohibit the juvenile death penalty by customary international law, but when most nations have signed at least one of the above-mentioned treaties, the prohibition of the juvenile death penalty in these nations may be based, at least in part, on their belief that it is a violation of customary international law.[556] These facts reveal that the juvenile death penalty may be in violation of customary international law.

Certain rules of international law are of such importance that they are considered to be ""*peremptory norms*"", otherwise known as *jus cogens*, which all states must abide by under any circumstance. The Vienna Convention on the Law of Treaties defines a norm of *jus cogens* as ""a norm accepted and recognized by the international community of States as a whole as a norm from which no derogation is permitted and which can be modified only by a subsequent norm of international law having the same character"". Amnesty International believes that the prohibition of use of the death penalty against child offenders should be recognized as such a norm.

Jus Cogens are "those from which no derogation can be justified and which can only be changed by a subsequent norm of the same character." The United States Supreme Court, as early as 1804, stated, "An act of Congress ought never to be construed

---

[554] Lori Edwards; *Critique of the Juvenile Death Penalty in the United States: A Global Perspective*, 42 Duq. L. Rev. 317, winter, 2004.

[555] Jessica Mishali, *Roper v. Simmons--Supreme Courts Rellance on International Law in Constitutional Decision-Making*, Touro Law Review (2006).

[556] *Id.*

to violate the law of nations if any other possible construction remains." It is clear that this ideology has filtered down to the lower courts as exemplified by a 1980 opinion that stated, "Upon ratification of the Constitution, the thirteen former colonies were fused into a single nation, one which, in its relations with foreign states, is bound both to observe and construe the accepted norms of international law."[557]

States parties to these treaties are required to submit periodic reports on the measures they have taken to give effect to the treaties' provisions. The reports are examined by the expert bodies set up to monitor implementation of the treaties – the UN Human Rights Committee and the UN Committee on the Rights of the Child respectively.

When representatives of governments that have executed child offenders have appeared before these committees during the examination of their countries' reports, they have generally avoided mentioning the matter or have given confusing replies. Iranian representatives told the UN Committee on the Rights of the Child in May 2000 that death sentences imposed on child offenders had not been carried out and that the death penalty was not "imposed on children under 18". The Committee strongly recommended that Iran "take immediate steps to halt and abolish by law the imposition of the death penalty for crimes committed by persons under 18".

Regarding this matter the UN Human Rights Committee stated in 1995 that it believed the reservation of U.S. to be "incompatible with the object and purpose" of the ICCPR and recommended that the reservation be withdrawn. The Committee also deplored provisions in a number of US state laws allowing for child offenders to be sentenced to death as well as "the actual instances where such sentences have been pronounced and executed" and exhorted the authorities "to take appropriate steps to ensure that persons are not sentenced to death for crimes committed before they were 18".[558]

---

[557] Lori Edwards, *supra* note 554.

[558] *Reports of UN Human Rights Committee on Protection of Human Rights*: http://www.ohchr.org/english/.

2 The Story of Juvenile Death Penalty Abolition in the United States

The application of death penalty to juvenile offenders is a concept that was older than the constitution of the United States. Thirty eight states and the Federal government had statutes authorizing the death penalty for certain forms of murder. In total, 31 states (along with the Federal government and District of Colombia) prohibited juvenile executions. Of the 19 states permitted juvenile executions, 14 states set the minimum age (at the time of offense) for execution at 16, and 5 states set the minimum age at 17 years.

While the juvenile death penalty was rare in the United States, it did exist. The American people had been executing their children in the pursuit of justice for more than three and one half centuries. The United States was one of very few countries that execute people for crimes committed when they were under the eighteen years old. The first documented juvenile execution was that of Thomas Graunger in 1642 in Plymouth Colony, Massachusetts. Since then, 366 persons for offenses they committed as juveniles (below the age of 18) had been executed in the United States and of those, 22 were executed between 1973-2003[559]. Finally on March 1, 2005 the juvenile death penalty in the United States was effectively abolished. The Supreme Court ruled 5-4 that the execution of offenders who committed crimes before the age of 18 was a violation of the cruel and unusual punishment clause of the eight Amendment. The court decision relied on national and International consensus, the current trend of legislation and court decisions, as well as medical documentation describing the "diminished capacities" of juveniles.

The rate of juvenile death sentencing fluctuated considerably in the early years of this current era but then settled in to consistent annual rate of about 2% of total death sentences in the mid-1980s. A change occurred from 1987 to 1989 when the juvenile death sentencing rate dropped considerably, presumably by the cases then pending before the United States Supreme Court. In 1990s, the rate appears to have returned to the previous pattern of about 6 to 12 juvenile death sentences each year for an annual rate of about 2% to 3% of all death sentences. Since 1977, the U.S. has executed 22 children

---

[559] *Id.*

who were under the age of 18 at the time of the offence. (For information about juvenile executions since 1977 please refer to figure 4-4).

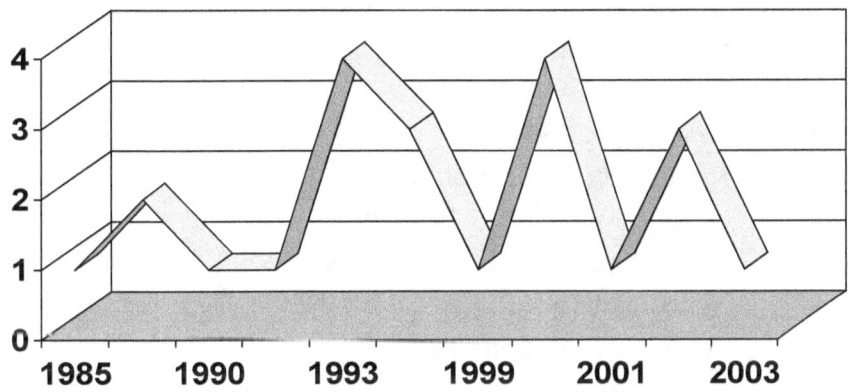

Figure 4-4 Juvenile executions in the United States since 1977.
Source: Streib, Victor, Juvenile death penalty today, available at
http://www.law.onu.edu/faculty/streib/juvdeath.htm.
And U.S. Department of Justice, Bureau of Justice Statistics: www.ojp.usdoj/bjs

A Legal Background

Eight Amendment indicates: "Excessive bail shall not be required, nor excessive fines imposed, nor cruel and unusual punishments inflicted."[560] To decide death penalty for juveniles violates 8th amendment of the U.S. constitution, the Supreme Court uses an analytical framework that includes 3 criteria. A punishment is cruel and unusual if: 1-It is a punishment originally understood by the frames of the Constitution to be cruel and unusual. 2-There is a societal consensus that the punishment offends civilized standards of human decency. 3-It is grossly disproportionate to the severity of the crime or makes no measurable contribution to acceptable goals of punishment.[561] Because many consider

---

[560] U.S. Const. amend. VIII.

[561] Cothern Lynn; *Juvenile and the Death Penalty*:
http://www.ncjrs.org/pdffiles1/ojjdp/184248.pdf

the death penalty a violation of the Eighth Amendment even when applied to adults, the issue of executing juveniles is extremely controversial.[562]

United States. Federal law set a minimum age of 18 at the time of the offence for application of death penalty.[563] And also Model Penal Code indicates:" Under this section minimum age for death penalty is 18".[564]

In State Statutes before Roper v. Simmons case, nineteen U.S. states allowed for the execution of people who were 16 or 17 at the time of the crime. In following states minimum age was expressed in statute:

- Alabama: ALA. Code § 12-15-34(a).
- Georgia: Ga. Code Ann. § 16-3-1.
- Kentucky: KY. Rev. Stat. Ann. § 635.020.
- Nevada: NV. Code § 5-194-010.
- New Hampshire: NH. Criminal Code § 628.1.
- North Carolina: N.C. Gen. State § 7A.608.
- Texas: TX Penal Code § 2-8-07.

In following states minimum age 16, required by the constitution, per the Supreme Court in ***Thompson v. Oklahoma***, 487 U.S. 815 (1988)[565]: Arizona, Arkansas, Delaware, Idaho, Louisiana, Mississippi, Oklahoma, Pennsylvania, South Carolina, Utah and Virginia.

In Florida minimum age 17, required by Florida constitution per Florida Supreme Court in ***Brennan v. State***, 754 So.2d 1(Fla.1999).[566]

---

[562] Robert F. Glass, ***Roper v. Simmons: A Dead-End for the Juvenile Death Penalty***, Mercer Law Review Summer (2006).

[563] 18 U.S.C. § 3591.

[564] MPC § 210.6(d).

[565] The outcome of decision was that: A state's execution of juvenile who had committed a capital offence prior to age 16 violated Thompson case, unless the state had a minimum age limit in its death penalty statute.

[566] 754 So.2d 1(Fla.1999).

Texas and Florida were leaders in this practice, each impose many more juvenile death penalties than any other jurisdiction. Only 5 of the states had imposed 10 or more such sentences. Before Roper v. Simmons 12 states had 73 inmates under sentence of death who were juveniles at the time of the crime, one-third in Texas. Since 1977, 7 states known to have executed people under 18, these states are: Texas, South Carolina, Oklahoma, Louisiana, Virginia, Georgia and Montana. (Figure 4-5) Only three states – Oklahoma (in Oklahoma in spite of other states that executed people at age 16 and 17 the jurisdictional age under juvenile court is 18.), Texas and Virginia- had executed child offenders from 2000-2005.

Figure 4-5 Juvenile executions in U.S.A since 1977 (by states)
Source: Streib, Victor, Juvenile death penalty today, available at
http://www.law.onu.edu/faculty/streib/juvdeath.htm

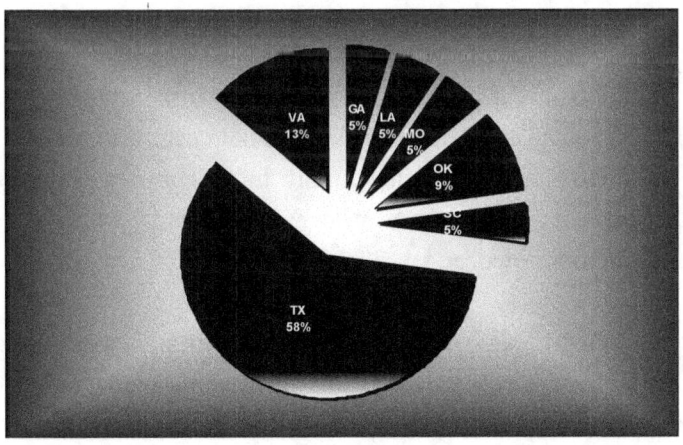

Although the United States Supreme Court has devoted considerable attention to constitutional issue in death penalty cases generally, the court did not consider the constitutionality of imposing the death penalty on juvenile until recently. In various cases throughout the 1980s, the Supreme Court consider the minimum age for imposing capital punishment. The issue in these cases was whether applying the death penalty to children constituted cruel and unusual punishment in violation of the 8th amendment.

- **Edding v. Oklahoma, 455 U.S. 104, 102 S.Ct. 869 (1982):**

It was the first case the Supreme Court agreed to hear based on the defendant's age. Without ruling on the constitutionality of the juvenile death penalty, the court vacated the juvenile's death sentence on the grounds that the trial court had failed to consider additional mitigating circumstances.

- **Burger v. Kemp, 483 U.S. 776, 107 S.Ct. 3114 (1987):**

The government prosecuted petitioner, and he was convicted of murder and sentenced to death. Petitioner seeking habeas relief contended that his counsel was ineffective. Because of his alleged conflict of interest and his failure to offer mitigating evidence. The court agreed with the lower court that the overlap of counsel, if any, did not so infect counsel's representation as to constitute an active representation of competing interests. The court also agreed that petitioner had made no showing that the justice of his sentence was rendered unreliable by a breakdown in the adversary process caused by deficiencies in counsel's assistance.

- **Thompson v. Oklahoma, 487 U.S. 815, 108 S.Ct. 2687 (1988):**

Thompson (15-year-old defendant) had participated in the murder of his former brother in law. United States Supreme Court held that death penalty can not be constitutionality imposed on a person who was under 16 years of age when the underlying crime was committed.

- **Stanford v. Kentucky, 492 U.S. 361, 109 S.Ct.2969 (1989):**

The Supreme Court expressly held that the eight Amendment does not prohibit the death penalty for crimes committed at age 16 or 17. In this case Supreme Court upheld the death penalty sentence.

- **Roper v. Simmons:**

The Missouri Supreme Court (112 S.W.3d 397, 2003) held the juvenile death penalty to be unconstitutional under Federal law and voted 4-3 to overturn the death sentence of Christopher Simmons, who was 17 at the time of the crime.

The Supreme Court granted certiorari, and in affirming the decision, held that the Eighth Amendment prohibits the imposition of capital punishment on offenders under the age of eighteen at the time of offense.[567] The Eighth Amendment explicitly prohibits the imposition of cruel and unusual punishment on criminal offenders.[568] In addition to those acts considered cruel and unusual at the time of adoption of the Bill of Rights, the Supreme Court measures the challenged punishment against "the evolving standards of decency that marks the progress of a maturing society." The Court relies foremost on well-established, objective indicia of consensus. While the Court has ruled that the death penalty itself is not unconstitutional on a number of occasions, the Court has found the death penalty to be cruel and unusual punishment for certain crimes or as imposed on particular offenders.[569]

B Diminished Responsibility

Diminished capacity or *diminished responsibility* is an impaired mental condition that is caused by intoxication, immaturity, trauma, or disease and that prevents a person from having the mental state necessary to be held responsible for a crime. In some jurisdictions, a defendant's *Diminished capacity* can be used to determine the degree of the offense or the severity of the punishment. The doctrine of "*diminished responsibility*" is likewise limited to reducing murder to manslaughter that means punishment exist but the immaturity of offender suggests that less punishment is justified by reason of the offender immaturity.

The criminal law should include a generic, doctrinal mitigating excuse of partial responsibility that would apply to all crimes, and that would be determined by the trier of fact. This partial excuse would apply in cases in which a defendant's behavior satisfied the elements of the crime charged, but the defendant's rationality was non-culpably compromised and thus the defendant was not fully responsible for the crime charged. Current Anglo-American criminal law contains no such generic partial excuse. Some doctrines, such as provocation/passion and extreme mental or emotional disturbance for

---

[567] Roper v. Simmons, 540 U.S. 1160, 1160 (2004).

[568] U.S. Const. amend. VIII.

[569] Steven J. Wernick, *Constitutional Law: Elimination of the Juvenile Death Penalty Substituting Moral Judgment for a True National Consensus,* Florida Law Review April (2006).

which there is reasonable explanation or excuse, appear to operate in effect as partial excuses. They typically apply only in limited contexts, however, such as to reduce a homicide that would otherwise be murder to manslaughter. Criminal law already recognizes the moral importance of "partial responsibility" for determining just punishment. Despite the lack of a generic mitigating excuse and strict limitations on the few doctrines that serve this purpose, the relevance of diminished rationality and diminished responsibility to sentencing is widely and generally accepted. For example, *Atkins v. Virginia*, which categorically prohibited capital punishment of people with retardation on Eighth Amendment grounds, was based precisely on this recognition.[570]

Recent medical studies on adolescent brain development contradict with previously-held notions that a person's brain is fully developed by age 14. According to research conducted by Harvard Medical School, the frontal and prefrontal lobes, which regulate impulse control and judgment, are the last to develop. Thus, "the very brain system necessary for inhibition and goal-directed behavior comes 'on board' last and is not fully operational until early adulthood (about 18-22 years)."[571]

Anyone who lives with adolescents might readily agree that they suffer from an inability to regulate emotions, and often act with little regard for consequences. Yet, does this adequately explain why some juveniles become homicidal? The problem is further complicated by the trauma and shocking life experiences commonly found in the backgrounds of juvenile offenders. For example, in a 1987 study of 14 juvenile males awaiting execution for offenses committed between the ages of 15 years, 10 months and 17 years, 10 months, researchers found that 12 of the 14 had been brutally physically abused, five had been sodomized by relatives, and only two had IQ scores above 90. Alcoholism, drug abuse, and psychiatric hospitalization were prevalent in their parents' histories. Such traumas most often occurred for these offenders during pre-puberty -- in the pre-sculpting, brain-building period. The psychological consequences arising from exposure to violence, abuse, neglect, and childhood trauma have generally been acknowledged, but "now it has been found that these experiences may cause physical changes in the brain and fundamentally alter brain development." While researchers previously believed that the effects of trauma were most pronounced during the

---

[570] Stephen Morse; ***Diminished Responsibility***, 1 OHSTJCL 289 (Fall 2003).

[571] Phyllis Bookspan, *supra* note 543.

developing years, more current understanding of the adolescent brain's "pruning process" suggests that such early-occurring events cause a state of fear-related activation in the brain, resulting in hypervigilance, anxiety, and impulsivity. The abuse essentially becomes an ingrained part of the teen's physical and biological makeup, and therefore determines behavior and responses. [572]

Despite the universal acceptance of immaturity in doctrines of infancy and the widespread acceptance of reduced levels of responsibility in early teen years, there has been little analysis of the aspect of immaturity that are relevant to mitigation of punishment. The lesser maximum punishment of serious crimes in juvenile court can be seen as testimony to the belief in youthful diminished culpability, but when this concept of proportionality is expressed only in the institutional output of one court system, the transfer of offenders from the juvenile to criminal court would risk changing the applicable penal principles without justification. [573]

Concerns about diminished capacity may be the reason for minimum age standards in states and nations that observe all limits for the death penalty, but it is the age limits rather than the rationale for them that have center stage in the constitutional debate. [574]

The only legal issue concerning the diminished capacity of adolescent killers that has received sustained attention in the United States is the constitutional question of whether the Eighth Amendment's prohibition of cruel and unusual punishment implies that very young killers cannot be executed. The reasoning of the justices in *Eddings v. Oklahoma* and *Thompson v. Oklahoma* does not provide clear exposition on questions of diminished responsibility for adolescent killers for three reasons. First, the issue comes up in a death penalty context, and strong categorical sentiments about capital punishment dominate the responses of many observers to detailed questions about death penalty policy. In order to put great weight on the importance of a defendant's youth as a

---

[572] *Id.*

[573] Franklin Zimring, *Youth on Trial: A Development perspective on juvenile justice*, p 278, edited by Thomas Grisso & Robert G. Schwartz, University of Chicago Press (2000).

[574] Franklin Zimring, *The Hardest of the Hard Cases: Adolescent Homicide in Juvenile and Criminal Courts*, 6 Va. J. Soc. Pol'y & L. 437(Spring 1999).

diminishment of responsibility after Thompson, it is first necessary to remove the principles to be found in the cases from a solely death penalty context. A second major restriction in the Eighth Amendment cases is the limited basis for constitutional review. It is not the self-appointed duty of the federal Supreme Court to draw a minimum age for execution eligibility that would be appropriate on policy grounds. Instead, the Court will only limit state power when clear violations of contemporary standards of decency would otherwise occur. The third reason is the method of analysis in the Supreme Court put its emphasis on the practices in various punishment systems rather than the reasons behind those practices. [575]

In *Roper v. Simmons* case the instant Court identified three major differences between juveniles and adults that demonstrate diminished culpability in juvenile offenders. The first major difference noted was a lack of maturity and sense of responsibility in juveniles. The second major difference discussed was a vulnerability to negative influences predicated on a lack of financial and legal freedom to escape from negative environments. Third, the instant Court noted that juveniles still have a transitory personality and undefined character. Thus, the Court reasoned that the social purposes of the death penalty-retribution and deterrence-are without merit when applied to juveniles.[576]

Based on these differences, the instant Court dismissed the idea that juveniles could be among the worst offenders in society. While youth is considered a mitigating factor in sentencing guidelines, the instant Court stated that juries are too likely swayed by evidence of the brutal nature of murder to adequately consider mitigating arguments. Thus, the instant Court's own judgment confirmed its findings of a national consensus against the execution of juvenile offenders.[577]

Finally it is important to mention that the diminished responsibility is not merely a doctrine of juvenile justice system but a principle of penal proportionality, therefore, immaturity raise the same issue we know confront in juvenile justice even if all young offenders were tried in criminal court that means changes in the jurisdictional boundaries

---

[575] *Id.*

[576] Roper, 125 S. Ct. at 1195.

[577] Steven J. Wernick, *supra* note 569.

of juvenile and criminal courts do not remove the necessity of determining variations in moral desert.[578]

C Facts behind the Juvenile Death Penalty in the United States

Although, American public opinion favors retaining the death penalty in general, it opposes executing those under eighteen. In 2002, a Gallup survey found that 69% of Americans oppose capital punishment for juvenile offenders.[579]

But most importantly the horror of executing children cannot be fully understood until we look at the children who have been murdered by the state in America. Consistently, pervasively, and invariably the children have been executed have four common characteristics: (1) they were mentally ill or mentally retarded at the time they committed they crime; (2) they were victims of horrifying sexual and physical abuse; (3) they were victimized by a society which has one of the highest child poverty and infant mortality rates in the world and which consigns many children to lives of hopelessness and grinding poverty; and, (4) they were represented by inexperienced, unskilled, and incompetent counsel. So the truth of juvenile executions in the United States is that the state executed the ill and infirm without providing them with any advocacy. To say that such a policy reeks of eugenics and "ethnic cleansing" is almost an understatement.[580]

Furthermore, the juvenile death penalty was racist. Over the half of the children executed in the United States since 1977 have been African-Americans. In addition, all of the children executed in the United States for the crimes of rape or attempted rape (40 children in all) have been black. Almost two- thirds of the current population of juvenile offenders on death row was persons of color. In addition, the issue of bias by victim race was also present in juvenile death penalty cases. Since 1977-2003 seventy-seven percent of the juvenile executions in the United States in the post-*Furman* era involved a white victim. (For Information regarding race bias in juvenile executions please refer to following figure 4-6).

---

[578] Franklin Zimring, ***Youth on Trial***, *supra* note 573, p 282-283.

[579] http://www.galluppoll.com.

[580] *Fact Sheet: The Juvenile Death Penalty*, at:http://www.mokids.org.

Figure 4-6 Juvenile executions in U.S.A by race of defendants / victims (since 1977)

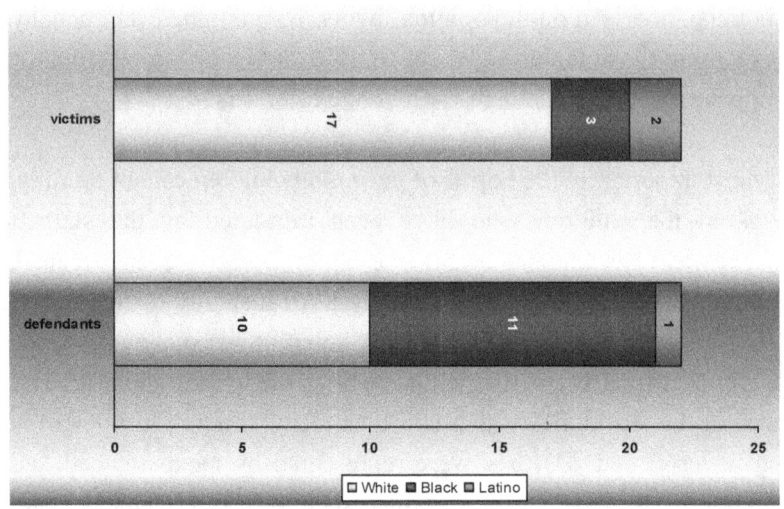

- Source: Amnesty International Report, available at: http://web.amnesty.org/library/Index/ENGACT500152004

As of October 1, 1998 sixty-five percent (33 blacks and 15 Latinos compared to 26 whites) of the children on death row in the United States were minority offenders (Strieb, 1998). Additionally, questions of age and gender bias also arise in view of the fact that 83% of the victims in these cases were adults and half were women. Ninety-eight percent of the juveniles sentenced to death were male (Strieb, 1998: 12). Only four cases involved females.[581]

Because the American juvenile death penalty was authorized in 19 separate state jurisdictions, each essentially authorized to go its own way; the justifications for this

---

[581] Victor Streib, *The Juvenile Death Penalty Today*, OH: Ohio Northern University (1998).

practice among these 19 states could be expected to differ. However, common themes can be detected:

- Violent juvenile crime, particularly homicide, is apparently worse in America than in any other country;
- Juvenile homicide is increasing substantially, even as adult homicide is decreasing;
- Juvenile murderers seem to be particularly brutal and unresponsive to civilized pleas to stop the killing;
- Almost every political leader is pushing strongly for harsher punishments for violent juvenile crime; and
- Correcting the societal conditions which breed violent juvenile crime seems to be a huge task which is probably impossible to achieve.[582]

Arguments against the juvenile death penalty typically focus on a similarly wide spectrum of concerns:

The juvenile death penalty contradicted with every other law concerning children in the United States. The law in most states assumes that juveniles are not of sufficient maturity and judgment to exercise a wide range of rights. In most states the age of majority is 18; 21 is earliest age at which alcohol may be bought, possessed and consumed; children may not enter into contracts until the age of 18; children may not buy cigarettes until the age of 18; children must be 18 before agreeing to donate their organs; children must be 18 before they may execute a will; children must be 18 before entering into a marriage; and, of course, the 26th Amendment to the Constitution sets the voting age in the United States at 18.

The contradictions inherent in the laws which assume that juveniles do not have sufficient responsibility, maturity or judgment to make these many decisions, while at the same time assuming that they are fully in control of their judgments when they engage in criminal behavior is a horrific and illogical contradiction in the law. This is particularly the case in homicides where much evidence indicates that (1) children have an

---

[582] Gary Potter, *The Juvenile Death Penalty*:
http://dpa.state.ky.us/library/advocate/nov99/juvdp/html.

undeveloped and unsophisticated concept of death; and (2) the children are often impulsive and reckless in their actions.[583]

In addition, in many states persons under the age of 18 are deemed not mature enough to obtain abortions but sufficiently mature to be sentenced to death. The decisions to apply the death penalty and to deny abortions seem to depend primarily on maturity.[584]

Finally considering, juvenile death penalty, abortions, voting, drinking alcoholic beverages and marriage provides a consistent framework for evaluating the maturity of minors facing serious deprivations of their rights. If these are dangerous, emotional, and irresponsible people, it seems that we can not have it both ways. We cannot deny those adult rights and privileges but nonetheless impose upon them adult punishments.

3 Juvenile Death Penalty in Iran

The criminal responsibility age was eighteen under former Penal Code of Iran. Juvenile execution is a product of the Islamic Revolution of 1979. The establishment of the Iranian juvenile court goes back to year 1959. In 1982, following the ratification of Islamic Penal Code, the modern Penal Code of Iran was regulated in accordance with novel concepts of crime and punishment was abolished. The present criminal justice system in Iran is based on the Twelve Imami Shii version of Sharia law (Islamic law). This system of law formed in the early 1980s during the tenure of the Ayatollah Ruhullah Musavi Khomeini. Islamic law replaced the secular system that two Pahlavi monarchs established in Iran during their consecutive reigns.

---

[583] Victor Streib, *The juvenile Death Penalty in the United States and Worldwide*, 4 Loy. Poverty L.J. 173 (Spring 1998).

[584] Nicole, Saharsky, *Consistency as a Constitutional Value:*
A Comparative Look at Age in Abortion and Death Penalty Jurisprudence, 85 Minn. L. Rev. 1119 (April 2001).

A Legal Background

The Iranian Civil Code states: "In Iranian law childhood is attributed to a person who has not reached puberty age". Under Article 1210-1: "A girl achieves puberty after nine lunar ages and a boy after completing fifteen lunar years".[585]

Iranian Penal law applies to those who have reached puberty. [age nine years for girls and fifteen years for boys].[586] For example under Iranian law if a ten years old girl murders, she will be tried and punished in the same way a forty years old woman is tried and penalized. Thus under the Islamic Penal Code of Iran it is permissible to issue a death sentence for a female juvenile who has reached nine years age.

Despite this statute by Ayatollah Mahmoud Hashemi-Shahrudi, head of Iran's Judiciary directive, judges cannot issue death sentences for juveniles. Although the bill to raise the minimum age to 18 is now under consideration in Iran. If trial courts judges consider the current statute, it will be reversed in the Supreme Court. Because all death sentences must be upheld by the Iranian Supreme Court before they can be implemented.

Amnesty International has recorded at least 10 incidents of juvenile death penalty in Iran since 1990: (Figure 4-7).

---

[585] Iran Civil Code [C.CIV] Art. 1210-1 (1991).

[586] Iran Penal Code [C. PEN] Art. 49-2 (1997).

Figure 4-7 Juvenile Executions in Iran & U.S.A
(since 1990)
Source: Amnesty International Report, Recorded executions of child offenders,1990-2004, available at: http://web.amnesty.org/library/Index/ENGACT500152004.

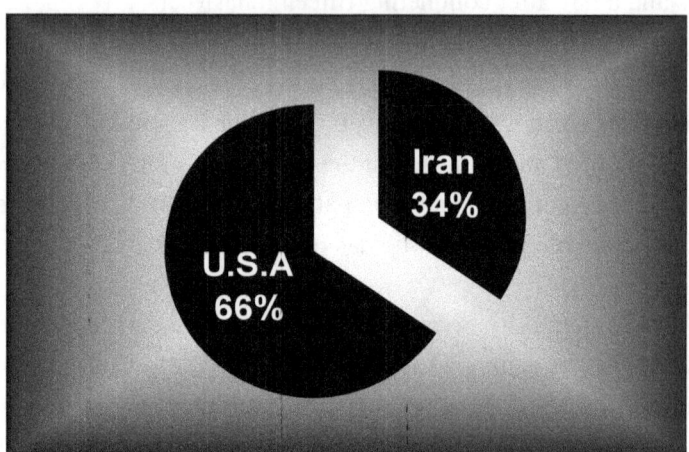

Mehrdad Yousefi (May/29/2001):
The Iranian official news agency reported that Mehrdad Yousefi, aged eighteen, had been hanged for a crime committed two years earlier.
Mohammad Zadeh (Jan/25/2004)
Salman (May/12/2004):
Mohammad Zadeh and Salman were executed, while were seventeen at the time of the crimes.
Atepheh Rajabi (Aug/15/2004):
Sixteen years old female, Atepheh Rajabi was executed for "acts incompatible with chastity." She was publicly hanged in the city center of Neka (Northern Iranian province of Mazandaran).[587]

---

[587]*Which Countries still Use the Death Penalty against Child Offenders*, at http://web.amnesty.org.library.

B Rational behind the Juvenile Death Penalty in Iran

As previously mentioned after Islamic revolution in 1979, a modern legal system was replaced by Islamic legal system based on Shiite version of Sharia law. Shiism has been particularly influenced by the opinions of the sixth Imam, Abu Abdullah Jafar bin Mohammad Sadegh, and hence its legal school is known as the Jafari School of Jurisprudence. According to the Jafari School, the only sources of Islamic law are the Holy book, tradition (Hadith), the consensus of the jurist (Ijma), and reason (Aql).[588]

Under Iranian law there are three stages for childhood in Iran:
1. Stage one: Birth to sixth year. Child should not be punished on criminal grounds disciplinary or reformatory measures.
2. Stage two: Six years to puberty age. Some disciplinary actions applied.
3. Stage three: Begins at puberty. Child is criminally accountable for offence.[589]

Based on the Shiite school, the criminal responsibility age starts at puberty. As the sign of puberty is nocturnal pollution, an adolescent boy's coming of age is signified by potency to impregnate. Similarly a girl's puberty is signified by menstruation, nocturnal pollution and pregnancy. Since signs of puberty vary and may appear in advance or by delayed, it has been deemed necessary to fix the age limits. There is no special age for puberty based on Holy book and there are different views about puberty age in tradition. Islamic jurists are not united in their opinion. The majority of jurists in Shiite believe that the age of puberty is nine years old for girls and fifteen years old for boys. Some jurists argue that puberty age is for praying obligations not for penal obligations. Therefore Iran needs puberty age plus maturity age for purposes criminal responsibility. Maturity can be set at different ages according to conditions of the time. It is based on criminal perception.[590] Even some jurists build on Imam Jafar saying that

---

[588] Nader Entessar, *Criminal Law and the Legal System in Revolutionary Iran*, p 91-102, 8 Boston College third World law Journal (Winter 1988).

[589] Iraj Goldouzian, *General Criminal Law*, pp 273-274, Tehran, Iran: Mizan Publication (1999) [In Farsi].

[590] Abdoreza Asghari, *Age of Criminal Responsibility in Islam*, p 80, Razavi University law review (2000) [In Farsi].

childhood can be divided in to three seven year periods, and conclude that childhood ends at the age of twenty one.[591]

In Iran marriage age is equivalent to puberty. There are several instances where end of the childhood is not puberty in the Iranian law. For example jurisdictional age under juvenile court is eighteen, but the problem is establishing juvenile court is not mandatory in each jurisdiction and that judges just can apply mitigation factors for Taazir punishments. The Islamic Penal Code has divided crimes in to the four categories of Hodoud,[592] Qisas,[593] Diyat,[594] and Taazir,[595] based on the type of punishment for each category of offense. In most circumstances capital crimes are under Hodoud and Qisas punishments. In Election law sixteen is the age of responsibility, Labor law fifteen, eighteen years old for financial transaction if a person has not reached the age of eighteen can perform financial transaction after receiving a verdict from the court. The court must determine whether a girl over nine or a boy over fifteen achieved the age of maturity.[596] Islamic law does not prohibit the increasing of lawful maturity age. Considering the social conditions in Iran and the need to address the failure of the juvenile death penalty to adhere to International law, hope the bill to raise criminal responsibility to age eighteen will be passed in the near future.

In December 2004 the Iranian Parliament approved a bill raising the minimum age to eighteen for imposition of the death penalty. The bill is awaiting approval by the Guardian Council, Iran's highest legislative body. If this bill is approved by the Guardian

---

[591] *Children Rights Convention and Child's Rights in Iran*:http://www.netiran.com.

[592] Hodoud crimes are acts prohibited by God and punishable by mandatory penalties, such as adultery, sodomy, rape....

[593] Qisas crimes included murder, and manslaughter. These offenses are acts against the victim and family. They allow for inflicting an injury exactly equal to the injury inflicted.

[594] Diyat is blood money which is to be paid to the victim or his family as reparation for an injury or murder.

[595] Taazir offenses are those for which no specific penalties are mentioned in the Holy book or tradition.

[596] According to unique verdict issued by the general council of the Iranian Supreme Court on December 24, 1995.

Council, offenders under age of eighteen would no longer be executed except for Qisas and Hodoud crimes. There is a distinction between "Qisas" (retribution – the sentence issued in cases where defendants are found guilty of murder), Hodoud (such as adultery, sodomy, rape), and other crimes carrying the death penalty. Because "Qisas" was a private-not a state matter-and Hodoud crimes are prohibited by God and punishable by mandatory penalties. Attempts are being made to address the failure of "Qisas and Hodoud" to adhere to International law in Iran.

The bill currently under consideration falls of the reform measures needed in Iran if Iran is to meet international obligations under the ICCPR and the CRC. The majority of executions of juvenile offenders in Iran are cases of "Qisas" where the individual has been found guilty of murder. It is unacceptable for the Iranian authorities to separate cases of murder from other crimes carrying the death penalty. Legislation is urgently required to ensure that no person in Iran is sentenced to death for any crime, including murder, when the crimes were committed when the offender was under the age of eighteen.

Finally on 17 October 2008 a high-ranking Iranian Judiciary official announced the issuance of a new directive to judges that execution sentences for juvenile offenders must be replaced by life imprisonment sentences with the possibility of parole.

This decision is a significant step towards honoring international law. This directive will put an immediate end to any more executions of juvenile offenders for nearly 130 juveniles on death row.

According to this directive, punishments for offenders under the age of 18 in capital crimes, will be reduced to life in prison in the first stage and in the second stage of parole will be reduced to 15 years in prison. In addition, in cases of good behavior and signs of rehabilitation, juvenile offenders may qualify for conditional release.

Iranian officials have previously made a distinction between execution for capital offenses and executions for Qisas & Hodoud (retaliation-Prescribed punishment), claiming Qisas & Hodoud sentences cannot be reduced by judges. While this directive did not explicitly address this issue, Iranian Judiciary officials announced that "offenders under the age of 18, no matter what their offence is, will not be subject to executions but will receive other punishments according to the law."

The next and urgently needed step is for the parliament to act on this issue and abolish the death penalty for children through legislation.

III   *Miscellaneous Conditions & Proportionality*

1   Mandatory Death Sentences

Mandatory penalty denies the judiciary the necessary discretion to sentence fairly and appropriately. The mandatory death penalty is in violation of the international prohibition on cruel, inhuman or degrading treatment or punishment. The provision of mandatory death sentences deprives the courts of the discretion to weigh the evidence in capital cases in order to consider mitigating circumstances. This can result in decisions which are arbitrary and disproportionate to the circumstances of the case.

According to the UN Special Rapporteur on extrajudicial, summary or arbitrary executions the death penalty *"should under no circumstances be mandatory."*[597] The mandatory death penalty makes it difficult, if not impossible, for the court to take into account mitigating or extenuating circumstances that may remove a particular offense from the category of most serious crimes.[598] The Special UN Rapporteur has expressed concern at the imposition of a mandatory death penalty for crimes which do not constitute "most serious crimes" or where fair trial standards were not respected.[599]

Many countries have ended the use of mandatory death sentences. In a landmark judgment on April 2001, the East Caribbean Court of Appeal ruled that the mandatory death penalty is unconstitutional in all seven countries under its jurisdiction. The Court ruled that, "dignity of human life is reduced by a law that compels the court to impose death by hanging upon all convicted of murder, granting none an opportunity to have the

---

[597] A/55/288, para.34.

[598] UN document: E/CN.15/2001/10, para. 96.

[599] UN document: E/CN.4/2002/74, para. 114.

individual circumstances of his case considered by the court that is to pronounce sentence."[600]

To prevent the imposition of mandatory death sentences individualized sentencing is required. Individualized sentencing allows the sentencing authority to consider mitigating, and aggravating circumstances. The Court by considering maintaining aggravating circumstances can adequately limit and reduce the risk of the arbitrary and capricious imposition of the death penalty.

In Iran based on Islamic definition of punishments the mandatory death sentence is applicable for some capital crimes. These capital crimes include murder, adultery sodomy, rape, armed robbery, incest, and other capital crimes under prescribed punishments.[601] There is a distinction between "Qisas" (retaliation – the sentence issued in cases where defendants are found guilty of murder), Hodoud (such as adultery, sodomy, rape), and other crimes carrying the death penalty. The distinct exists in part because "Qisas" is a private, not state matter and Hudoud crimes are acts prohibited by God and considered 'the right of God indicating that such punishments are invariably fixed, imperative and punishable by mandatory penalties.[602] As mentioned before the crimes for which Islamic law mandates the death penalty—adultery, murder…—cannot by legal or religious interpretation be deemed to be the "most serious crimes." The death penalty may only be legally imposed in accordance with International conventions.

For non retaliatory and prescribed capital crimes[603] (Hodoud and Qisas) the sentencing authority in Iran is allowed to consider mitigating, as well as aggravating

---

[600] Spence and Hughes v. The Queen, Criminal Appeal No. 20 of 1998, East Caribbean Court of Appeal, Judgment, 2 April 2001. See also Roger Hood, The Death Penalty, A Worldwide Perspective", Third Edition.

[601] The death penalty in Iran is now applicable to an extremely broad range of crimes in addition to murder: incest, rape, sex between a non-Muslim and a Muslim female; adultery, sodomy; homosexual acts after a fourth conviction, drinking liquor after three convictions, drawing arms to create fear, defamation to sanctities, drug trafficking in special amount, corruption on earth, fornication (fourth time), false accusation of unlawful intercourse (4th time), and had theft.

[602] Safia M. Safwat, *supra* note 525.

[603] Taazir (discretionary punishment) by which public authorities set their own punishment and in which the judge has wide discretion. Under Taazir, public authorities may provide for capital punishment, but no religious text requires them to do so.

circumstances. The Court by considering aggravating circumstances can more adequately limit and reduce the risk of the cruel and unusual capital sentencing.

In the United States mandatory death penalties statute eliminated all sentencing discretion of the jury in capital cases, it had complied with Furman's mandate. [604] The reason that the plurality provided for overturning the mandatory death sentences statute was "its failure to provide a constitutionally tolerable response to Furman's rejection of unbridled jury discretion in the imposition of capital sentencing."[605] The plurality of the court observed that no standards had been provided by the state's mandatory death penalty statute "to guide the jury to its inevitable exercise of the power to determine which first-degree murderers shall live and which shall die." [606]

In 1976, the United States Supreme Court, in *Woodson v. North Carolina* ,[607] held mandatory death penalty statutes for first degree murder to be unconstitutional. State legislatures that had interpreted *Furman v. Georgia* to require a mandatory death penalty were compelled to return to the drawing board. Prior to *Furman*, the North Carolina death penalty statute provided for unbridled jury discretion in the determination of whether to impose the death penalty.[608] In *Woodson*, the Court considered for the first time the constitutionality of a mandatory death penalty statute.[609] After presenting a detailed history of the mandatory death penalty, the Court concluded that jurors, and society as a whole, have an aversion to automatic death sentences.[610] The Court maintained that the mandatory death penalty statutes enacted did not reflect a renewed societal acceptance of mandatory death sentencing. The Court invalidated mandatory

---

[604] Woodson v. North Carolina, 428 U.S. 280 (1976).

[605] *Id.*

[606] *Id.*

[607] 428 U.S. 280 (1976).

[608] *Id.*

[609] *Id.*

[610] *Id.*

death sentences they conflicted with contemporary standards of decency and thus violated the eighth amendment's prohibition against cruel and unusual punishment.[611]

2   Mentally Retarded Offenders

Mental retardation is a lifelong condition of impaired or incomplete mental development. According to the most widely used definition of mental retardation, it is characterized by three criteria: significantly subaverage intellectual functioning; concurrent and related limitations in two or more adaptive skill areas; and manifestation before age eighteen.[612]

The practice of executing people of diminished culpability - including people with mental retardation - is particularly abhorrent. The United Nations Economic and Social Council (ECOSOC) resolution recommended "eliminating the death penalty for persons suffering from mental retardation or extremely limited mental competence."[613] The U.N. Commission on Human Rights adopted resolutions in 1999 and 2000 urging states that retain the death penalty not to impose it "on a person suffering from any form

---

[611] *Id.*

[612] American Association on Mental Retardation (AAMR), "Definition of Mental Retardation," available at *www.aamr.org/policies/faqmentalretardation.html*, visited September 15, 2000. For the most part, statutes prohibiting the execution of persons with mental retardation adopt a version of this AAMR definition. Seven states and the federal government do not specify an I.Q. level in their definition, making this an issue for the court to determine based on expert testimony. Two state statutes say that an I.Q. of 70 or below "shall be presumptive evidence of mental retardation," thus leaving open the possibility that a person whose I.Q. is above 70 may also, through expert testimony, establish his or her mental retardation.

[613] U.N. Economic and Social Council resolution 1989/64, "Implementation of the safeguards guaranteeing protection of the rights of those facing the death penalty," ESC/RES/1989/64, adopted May 1989.

of mental disorder," a term that includes both the mentally ill and the mentally retarded.[614]

Prohibition on "cruel and unusual punishment" and application of the proportionality principle-the can be extended to strike down death penalty for mentally retardation offenders on proportionality grounds. A punishment can be excessive not because the penalty in and of itself is unacceptably cruel, but primarily because the penalty is harsh in relation to the conduct at issue. Moreover, even if a serious offense were at issue, a diminished mental culpability can cause an otherwise permissible penalty to become disproportionate.[615]

By focusing on whether the two "penological purposes" of capital punishment, retribution and deterrence, are advanced by the execution of the mentally retarded we can conclude the immediate prohibition of that is necessary. Retribution[616] and deterrence[617] are the two principal justifications for punishment, especially when that punishment is the death penalty.

For retribution purposes, "the severity of the appropriate punishment necessarily depends on the culpability of the offender."[618] Since capital punishment is reserved for the most deserving of execution it is "excessive" to execute mentally retarded persons.

As for deterrence, "the increased severity of the punishment inhibits criminal actors from carrying out their murderous conduct."[619] But, mentally retarded persons are "less likely" than average offenders to "control their conduct," even when the severity of

---

[614] U.N. Commission on Human Rights Resolution, "Question of the Death Penalty," E/CN.4/RES/1999/61, adopted April 28, 1999; U.N. Commission on Human Rights Resolution, "The Question of the death penalty", E/CN.4/RES/2000/65, adopted April 27, 2000.

[615] Boyde v. California, 494 U.S. 370, 400 (1990).

[616] "Retribution" refers to society's "need to offset a criminal act by a punishment of equivalent 'moral quality."

[617] "Deterrence refers to the use of punishment to discourage future criminal conduct."

[618] Mary Sigler, *Contradiction, Coherence, and Guided Discretion in the Supreme Court's Capital Sentencing Jurisprudence,* 40 Am. Crim. L. Rev. 1151, 1155 (2003).

[619] *Id.*

punishment is increased.[620] Hence, executing the mentally retarded does not measurably further the goal of deterrence.

In recent years, the U.N. special rapporteur on extrajudicial, summary or arbitrary executions has received reports of the execution of people with mental retardation in only three countries - Japan, Kyrgyztan, and the United States.[621]

The common law prohibition against punishing 'idiots' for their crimes suggests that it may indeed be 'cruel and unusual' punishment to execute persons who are profoundly or severely retarded and wholly lacking the capacity to appreciate the wrongfulness of their actions.[622] Although the common law prohibition against punishing idiots and lunatics for their criminal acts was the precursor of today's insanity defense[623]. An idiot was generally considered to be a person with a total lack of reason or understanding, corresponding to a person with "profound" or "serious" retardation today.[624]

In *Penry v. Lynaugh* (1989)[625], defendant's IQ was between 50 and 63, indicating mild to moderate mental retardation, and he had a mental age of 6 1/2 years. He claimed that to execute a mentally retarded person with his reasoning capacity would constitute cruel and unusual punishment. The Supreme Court rejected the argument. In this case the Supreme Court of the United States recognized that mental retardation was a mitigating

---

[620] *Id.*

[621] U.N. Commission on Human Rights, "Extrajudicial, summary or arbitrary executions: Report by the Special Rapporteur," E/CN.4/1997/60, para. 89 (1996); U.N. Commission on Human Rights, "Extrajudicial, summary or arbitrary executions: Report by the Special Rapporteur," E/CN.4/1995/61, para. 380 (1994); U.N. Commission on Crime Prevention and Criminal Justice, "Capital punishment and implementation of the safeguards guaranteeing the protection of the rights of those facing the death penalty: Report of the Secretary-General," E/CN.15/1996/19, para. 74, (1996).

[622] 109 S.Ct. 2954, 106 L.Ed.2d 287.

[623] *Id.*

[624] *Id.*

[625] 492 U.S. 302, 109 S.Ct. 2934, 106 L.Ed.2d 256.

factor of constitutional significance,[626] which had to be considered by the sentencer in capital cases;[627] but the Court held that the execution of mentally retarded offenders does not violate the Eighth Amendment's prohibition on "cruel and unusual punishment." [628]

Finally in *Atkins v. Virginia*[629] court held that the Eighth Amendment bars the execution of mentally retarded persons, thereby overruling the 1989 case of *Penry v. Lynaugh*.[630] In overruling Penry, Atkins effectively held that the mental retardation mitigator was so significant that it made the mentally retarded categorically ineligible for the death penalty.[631] In addition the recent trend in many states' legislation to eliminate capital punishment for the mentally retarded, as well as other indicators of public opinion, showed that society now viewed mentally retarded offenders "as categorically less culpable than the average criminal."[632]

3   Challenging the Imprisonment as Excessive

Punishment by imprisonment is not per se cruel and unusual; it may be offensive when the duration of a sentence is so excessive or disproportionate to the crime committed as to shock the conscience and reason of people generally.

In determining what punishments should be regarded as incompatible with human rights standards, the result has been that in many societies long periods of

---

[626] *Id.*

[627] *Id.*

[628] *Id.*

[629] 536 U.S. 304 (2002).

[630] Penry v. Lynaugh, 492 U.S. 302 (1989).

[631] Mark Alan Ozimek, Note, *The Case for a More Workable Standard in Death Penalty Jurisprudence: Atkins v. Virginia and Categorical Exemptions under the Imprudent "Evolving Standards of Decency" Doctrine,* 34 U. Tol. L. Rev. 651, 684 (2003).

[632] See www.deathpenaltyinfo.org.

imprisonment, sometimes but not always or necessarily for life, has emerged as the ultimate penalty for the most serious offences.

Anti cruel and unusual principles have also played a part in deciding how imprisonment must be implemented to meet the requirements of international human rights law. One insight is that it requires the imposition and implementation of punishment, including imprisonment, to be viewed holistically.[633] Thus, for example, the International Covenant on Civil and Political Rights (ICCPR) contains mutually reinforcing provisions. The prohibition on cruel, inhuman or degrading punishment in Article 7 and on servitude and forced or compulsory labor in Article 8, combine with a further prohibition on loss of liberty without due legal process in Article 9.[634]

Further development of international human rights standards relating to prisons may eventually be achieved through the implementation of an optional protocol to the International Convention against Torture and Other Cruel, Inhuman and Degrading Treatment or Punishment.[635] The Optional Protocol provides for the establishment of a regular system of visits by independent international bodies to all places where persons who are deprived of their liberty are detained.[636] Inevitably the proposed Subcommittee on Prevention, which will be responsible for such inspections, will have to develop guidelines for what is to be regarded as torture and as cruel, inhuman or degrading punishment or treatment. In doing so it is bound to draw on existing international standards.

These issues emerging international standards become even greater when one considers that a similar process of standard setting is underway at the regional level. In Europe this is most prominent. The European Court of Human Rights, by interpreting the prohibition on inhuman or degrading treatment or punishment in Article 3 of the European Convention on Human Rights, has somewhat haltingly developed its own

---

[633] *Mbenge v Zaire*, Communication No. 16/1977 (25 Mar 1983), UN Doc CCPR/C/OP/2 at 76 (1990).

[634] Also see Rule 71(1) of the United Nations Standard Minimum Rules for the Treatment of Prisoners.

[635] GA Res 39/46, 10 Dec 1984, 39 UN GAOR Supp (No 51) 197, UN Doc E/CN 4/1984/72.

[636] GA Res A/Res/57/199, 18 Dec 2002.

standards for the imposition[637] and implementation of punishment, as well as for imprisonment generally.[638] The 1987 European Prison Rules and other recommendations of the Council of Europe on punishment and prisons have bolstered this process.[639]

Cruel and unusual punishment is aimed primarily at the kind of punishment imposed, not its duration. Nevertheless, where the duration of a sentence imposed on one convicted of crime is so disproportionate to the offense committed as to shock the moral sense of the community, the punishment is prohibited.[640] In determining whether the length of a sentence offends a prohibition against cruel and unusual punishment, the courts will look to such matters as the nature of the offense, the character of the offender, the penalties imposed in the jurisdiction for other offenses, and the penalties imposed in other jurisdictions for the same offense.[641] Therefore increased sentence statutes, multiple sentence in single prosecution, indeterminate sentences and unequal sentences for codefendants are successful challenges to imprisonment that to some may appear disproportionately harsh.

Statutes imposing life imprisonment upon *habitual criminals*[642] have been challenged as cruel and unusual punishment on several grounds. They should not inflict double jeopardy, violate ex post facto clauses or deny equal protection of law[643], except where such punishment is disproportionate to the gravity of the prior crimes alleged and proved.[644]

---

[637] B Emmerson, A Ashworth, ***Human Rights and Criminal Justice***, pp 479-514, Sweet & Maxwell London (2001).

[638] *Peers v Greece* (2001) 33 EHRR 1192.

[639] Recommendation R (87)3 of the Committee of Ministers of the Council of Europe and Recommendation R (82) 16 of the Committee of Ministers of the Council of Europe on Prison Leave.

[640] 21A Am Jur 2d Criminal Law § 973.

[641] *Id.*

[642] Habitual offender statutes, variously known as increased sentence statutes, enhanced punishment statutes, recidivist statute, and multiple offender statutes.

[643] See Graham v. West Virginia, 224 U.S. 616 (1912), McDonald v. Massachusetts, 180 U.S. 311 (1901), and Moore v. Missouri, 159 U.S. 673 (1895).

Life sentence without possibility of parole does not per se constitute a cruel and unusual punishment. In United States Statutes prescribing life sentences without possibility of parole have been upheld in cases involving murder,[645] kidnapping,[646] bank robbery,[647] drug or narcotic offenses,[648] and aggravated rape.[649] Although, regarding juveniles[650] a statute providing a penalty of life imprisonment without benefit of parole for the offense of rape has been held to constitute cruel and unusual punishment.

The idea of ***indeterminate sentences*** was to individualize punishment to better fit the needs of prisoner and society. Indeterminate sentences are four types: 1. Most provide for minimum and maximum limits. 2. Set the minimum but allow the judge or jury to establish the maximum. 3. Set the maximum but allow the judge or jury to set the minimum. 4. Authorize the judge or jury to fix the either minimum or maximum.[651] There are several objections to these sentences because they permit an unlawful delegation of judicial power to an administrative body, that they interfere with the pardoning power of the executive, also they violate the separation of powers doctrine, and they are void for uncertainty[652], therefore they inflict cruel and unusual punishment.

There are three possibilities when the defendant participating in a single activity may be sentenced to ***multiple terms of imprisonment***: 1. When the stature separates each step in a given process.[653] 2. Unrelated statutes may overlap and allow multiple sentences

---

[644] 21A Am Jur 2d Criminal Law § 974.

[645] State v. Farrow, 118 N.H. 296, 386 A.2d 808 (1978).

[646] Beard v. State, 262 Ind. 643, 323 N.E.2d 216 (1975).

[647] People v. Ferguson, 60 Mich. App. 302, 230 N.W.2d 406 (1975).

[648] State v. Stetson, 317 So. 2d 172 (La. 1975).

[649] State v. Iaukea, 56 Haw. 343, 537 P.2d 724 (1975).

[650] Workman v. Com., 429 S.W.2d 374, 33 A.L.R.3d 326 (Ky. 1968).

[651] *"Indeterminate Sentence Law"* Harvard Law Review 50 (winter 1937).

[652] *Id.*

that single act may result in conviction on several counts.[654] 3. A defendant may be sentenced to multiple terms of imprisonment as a result of a single act, when more than one victim is involved.[655]

The last challenge to imprisonment as an excessive punishment is ***unequal sentences for codefendants.*** Disparate sentences are often imposed on codefendants charged with the same offense. In some cases the most obvious disparities result when the trials are separated. Although sometimes we can not consider unequal sentence for codefendants as violation of cruel and unusual, generally because the facts of the case justify the disparity or that the sentence was well within statutory limits.[656]

By considering the nature of the offense, the character of the offender, the penalties imposed in the jurisdiction for other offenses, and the penalties imposed in other jurisdictions for the same offense the difficulty is asserting the gravity of offense comparing similarly grave offence and comparing the offence in different jurisdictions.

Of course some offences involving violent harm to human beings will always and anywhere be regarded as serious but the problem is what else should be regarded to be as serious as these offences or to be more serious than some of them.[657] It is easy to prove a mandatory sentence of life imprisonment for a minimum of thirty years as applied to a 15-year old child convicted of murder after standing trial as an adult is neither cruel nor unusual punishment within the meaning of the this prohibition but 3

---

[653] For instance when prosecution of counterfeiting allows for prosecution for possessing plates, concealing, manufacturing and possessing counterfeit money as well as buying, selling, exchanging, transferring, receiving, delivering or passing counterfeit money.

[654] For instance when an Act allows prosecution for the purchase, sale, distribution, exchange, or gift of narcotics, also prohibits the purchase, sale or concealment of illegally imported drugs as well as the importation itself.

[655] See 18 U.S.C. secs. 471-74, 21 U.S.C. sec, 173 (1952), also Islamic Penal Code of Iran, Art 46-7 (1997).

[656] Howard Alperin, ***Length of Sentence as Violation of Constitutional Provisions Prohibiting Cruel and Unusual Punishment,*** 33 ALR3d.

[657] Kristin O'Donnell Tubb, ***Freedom from Cruel and Unusual Punishment,*** pp 106-8, Greenhaven press (2005).

years for conviction of adultery under Idaho Code[658] constitutes cruel and unusual punishment. But would it be grossly excessive to provide life imprisonment for mere possession of a certain amount of drugs. Moreover, what is the possible dissemination of drugs can be as grave as to impose life imprisonment.

The second difficulty is there is no subjective standard of gravity for judges to compare. Sometimes two offences that are judicially determined to be similarly grave receive dis similar penalties. We can not say harsher penalty is cruel and unusual because similarly the grave crimes would not necessarily be comparable since there are other justifications such as deterrent or rehabilitation effects to consider. Deterrent is not only depends on the amount of penalty but upon its certainty, crimes that are less grave but more difficult to detect may warrant higher punishment or grave crimes of that sort that are committed once in lifetime by law abiding citizens will profit from rehabilitation.[659]

The final difficulty is comparing the offense from jurisdiction to jurisdiction. In federal system some states will always bear the distinction of treating particular offenders more severely than other state or a state may criminalize an act that other states do not criminalize at all. Though the difference needs and concerns of other states may induce them to treat possession of 672 grams of cocaine as relatively minor offence.[660]

The legislature, and likewise a city council under a delegated authority, may prescribe definite terms of imprisonment for crimes or violations of statutes or city ordinances without depriving the judiciary of discretionary power to fix reasonable limits, so long as the rights of citizens have not been violated or invaded a sentence within the limits of a statute cannot be said to be cruel and inhuman.

---

[658] Idaho code, secs 18-6601.

[659] Kristin O'Donnell Tubb, *supra note 657,* pp 108-9.

[660] *Id.*

4   Cruel and Unusual due to the Status of Offender

Offenses have traditionally defined in terms of acts or failures to act.[661] Despite the general rule that a crime requires a prohibited act or omission, certain atypical offenses, have at times been defined in terms of a person's status or condition of being, rather than in terms of acts committed by him or her.[662] For example being a vagrant, prostitute, drunkard, gambler, beggar, narcotic addict and homosexual. The more recent tendency in the law seems to disfavor such statutes in favor of the notion that a person should be held criminally culpable only for specific acts.[663] Thus, it has been violated prohibition against cruel and unusual punishment to punish a person for his physical condition, as distinguished from an act.

Since the late 1960 Europe has engaged in decriminalization of moral offences. Various kinds of sex and intoxication offences that would once have carried a prison term have been stricken entirely from the books.[664] The criminal offense generally known as "*prostitution*" has persisted since biblical times, and has acquired the traditional meaning of indiscriminate illicit intercourse for hire.[665]

An early attempt in United States was made to control prostitution by limiting the moves of known prostitutes or otherwise penalizing them for their status as prostitutes. While there was some early authority that an ordinance could prohibit prostitutes from walking the streets at night, except in case of reasonable necessity,[666] more recently it has been recognized that what the law brands as criminal is not the status

---

[661] Forrest Lacey, *Vagrancy and Other Crimes of Personal Condition,* Harvard Law Review 66 (May 1953).

[662] 21 Am. Jur. 2d Criminal Law § 31.

[663] *Id.*

[664] James Whitman, *supra* note 145, p 80.

[665] 63C Am. Jur. 2d Prostitution § 1.

[666] Coker v Ft. Smith, 162 Ark 567, 258 SW 388; Braddy v Milledgeville, 74 Ga 516.

of being a prostitute, but the act of offering to engage in some sort of sexual conduct with another in exchange for a fee.[667] Thus, a statute prohibiting "common nightwalkers, both male and female," has been held to apply only to a person abroad at night attempting to solicit someone to have illicit sexual intercourse.[668] Thus, making the status of prostitution as an offense knowingly to associate with persons having the reputation of being prostitutes is cruel and unusual.

Another challenge as status statutes is being *homosexual*.[669] The question is homosexuality properly equal with an individual's sexual conduct or, homosexuality is a status that is independent of that person's sexual behavior and to be equated with an individual's orientation? If homosexuality is a status and sodomy is an act and it is different from homosexuality we can not use the explanation of status and cruel punishment for sodomy statutes.

There are many homosexuals, who choose not to engage in sodomy. Some individuals who self-identify as homosexual may lead lives of celibacy. Other self-identified homosexuals may engage in kissing, hugging, erotic massage, and/or mutual masturbation with same-sex partners-some of which may be prohibited by the sodomy statutes. In spate of that, based on their own observed affectional attraction to persons of the same sex, all of these individuals consider themselves to be homosexual.[670]

---

[667] Similarly, a more recent ordinance making it unlawful to "knowingly congregate" in or about a place where prostitution is permitted or carried on has been held unconstitutional for violation of the right of free and peaceful assembly. Also, an ordinance prohibiting any prostitute from wandering about the streets or frequenting places of public resort is too indefinite, restrictive and liberty-depriving to constitute a valid use of the police power. Ordinances that forbid any prostitute to reside in or stay in any house or room within the city, and forbid the renting of any such premises to a prostitute without regard to its use, or that provide that prostitutes shall not live outside houses of prostitution in such places as they select as dwelling houses, are invalid.

[668] Thomes v. Commonwealth, 355 Mass 203, 243 NE2d 821.

[669] For more information see: Sanaz Alasti, *Comparative study of Cruel & Unusual Punishment for Engaging in Consensual Homosexual Acts*, 7 Annual Survey of International & Comparative Law (2006).

[670] Terry Kogan, *Legislative Violence Against Lesbian and Gay Men*, 1994 Utah L. Rev. 209 (1994).

In addition, the complicated results of equality between homosexuality and sodomy is because the fact that the definitions sodomy varies in criminal sodomy statutes. If we can say that homosexuality cannot be equated to sodomy, instead is homosexuality properly considered a status? Some homosexuals may consider their own sexual identity with particular behavior, and perceive themselves to be homosexual do not.[671] Studies indicate that a significant majority of lesbians and gay men sensed same-sex affectional attraction long before they reached an age at which sexual conduct was even contemplated. For many of these individuals, homosexuality is perceived as an orientation. Still others who engage in sexual relations with same-sex partners may view themselves as heterosexual.[672] Thus, there is no simple way, to resolve whether homosexuality is equal to conduct or status, or whether any individual is precisely portrayed as homosexual.

Second question: Is homosexuality involuntary or not? If we say it is voluntary, the explanation of depenalizing status crimes will not apply to homosexual acts. If a legislator is asserting that when an individual engages in same-sex sexual conduct he or she "chooses" to engage in that conduct, that legislator is surely correct. Absent rape or similar duress, human sexual conduct is chosen action, as opposed to involuntary actions like breathing or choking. Sexual conduct entails intentional action, not action resulting from the autonomic nervous system. In this sense, heterosexual conduct is also chosen action, no different from homosexual conduct.[673]

Although, the claim that homosexuality is chosen behavior indicates that homosexuality is equal with homosexual behavior. If, it is a distortion of homosexual identity to equate it in every case with homosexual behavior, then the question of choice becomes far more complex.[674] Moreover, studies indicate a significant majority of homosexuals describe same-sex attraction as having existed from youth, long before engaging in sexual

---

[671] *Id.*

[672] *Id,* see also Richard Isay, ***Being Homosexual: Gay Men and their Development***, p 82, Harpercollins Publisher (1989).

[673] Terry Kogan, *supra* note 570.

[674] *Id.*

behavior with other persons. This attraction often manifests itself in dreams and fantasies during early stages of sexual identity.[675]

The third question is whether homosexuality should be regarded as a sickness like addiction and whether, it is cruel to punish persons convicted solely of being with another consent adult? Research shows that efforts to change an individual's sexual orientation are often "psychologically wrenching and sometimes physically painful." By focusing on homosexuality: with a view toward the origins of sexual orientation and the possibility of reorientation we can conclude the individual homosexual orientation is innate. Homosexual identity is no more chosen than a heterosexual's sexuality identity. There are hidden rhetorical advantages in distorting the nature of human sexuality to describe homosexuality as a matter of choice.[676]

In Iran drug *addiction* as a status has been considered as a crime. In Iran drug addicts are sentenced to the following punishments: 1- The first time, fine of five hundred thousand up to one million rials and four to twelve months of imprisonment. 2- The second time, cash fine of one million to four million rials and one to three years of imprisonment. If the offender is a Government employee, in addition to the cash fine and the imprisonment, he shall be permanently dismissed from Government offices. 3- The third time onwards, the punishment prescribed in paragraph two shall be two to four-fold, plus fifty lashes.[677]

The punishment of the drug addicts who are offered after treatment in rehabilitation centers: 1- The first time, cash fine of five hundred thousand to one million rials, and four to twelve months of imprisonment. 2- The second time, a cash fine in the amount of one million to four million rials with one to three years of imprisonment plus permanent dismissal from Government service. 3- The third time, the punishment stipulated in paragraph two shall be two to four-fold, plus fifty lashes.[678]

---

[675] *Id.*

[676] Richard Isay, *supra* note 572.

[677] The Anti Narcotic Drugs Statute, Art 16 (1989).

[678] *Id,* Art 17.

While In the United States it is state law which may be used imprisons a narcotics addict, regardless of whether the addict has ever touched any narcotic drug within the state or been guilty of any irregular behavior there. Such situations inflict cruel and unusual punishment in violation of the Federal Constitution's Fourteenth Amendment. States generally have the power, in the interests of discouraging the violation of laws against drug traffic or of protecting the general health or welfare of their inhabitants,[679] to establish a program of compulsory treatment for those addicted to narcotics, including involuntary confinement, with penal sanctions for failure to comply with the compulsory treatment.[680] Accordingly, statutes providing for the civil commitment of narcotic addicts who have been arrested have been held constitutional.[681]

A statute criminalizing the mere status of being an *alcoholic* would probably be struck down because it is criminalized the mere status of being alcoholic like addiction to narcotics. However, statutes criminalizing public intoxication have been upheld as against the contention that they improperly punish the status or disease of chronic alcoholism, at least where the accused has failed to show that it was impossible for him both to refrain from becoming intoxicated and to avoid public places when intoxicated.[682]

Vagrancy statutes are void for vagueness where its language fails to give a person of ordinary intelligence notice that contemplated conduct is forbidden, or, encourages arbitrary and erratic arrests.[683] Vagrancy statutes which permit convictions on the basis of conduct is also overbroad.

---

[679] In the United States Federal courts, have the power to suspend the imposition or execution of sentence and to place a defendant on probation, may impose as one of the conditions of probation that the defendant, if an addict or other person with a drug abuse or other drug dependence problem, must submit him- or herself for drug treatment.

[680] Robinson v. Caalifornia, 370 U.S. 660, 82 S. Ct. 1417, 8 L. Ed. 2d 758 (1962).

[681] People v. Gilmore, 37 A.D.2d 912, 325 N.Y.S.2d 455 (4th Dep't 1971).

[682] Powell v. State of Tex., 392 U.S. 514, 88 S. Ct. 2145, 20 L. Ed. 2d 1254 (1968).

[683] Papachristou v. City of Jacksonville, 405 U.S. 156, 92 S. Ct. 839, 31 L. Ed. 2d 110 (1972); State v. Pugh, 369 So. 2d 1308 (La. 1979).

It has been observed that in contrast to most crimes, vagrancy traditionally has been defined not in terms of an act or acts, but in terms of a status or condition of being—the vagrant having a certain personal condition or being a person of a specified character. Although authority exists for the punishment of vagrancy or related crimes as status offenses, it has also been held that the state may not punish vagrants simply for being vagrants, absent the commission of culpable acts independently punishable as criminal.[684]

In Iran, unlike the United States vagrancy is punishable by one to three months imprisonment under existing statutes.[685] There is no implicit definition for what constitutes vagrancy in Iran. In the United States some jurisdictions have repealed such traditional statutes in favor of laws prohibiting specific conduct and making no use of the term "vagrancy" or "vagrant".[686] However, the mere fact that a statute prohibits specific conduct and eschews the terms "vagrancy" and vagrant does not make it proof against a challenge on vagueness grounds.[687]

As a result of cruel and unusual prohibition, individuals may not be punished for being an addict, alcoholic, prostitute, homosexual, or vagrant, but may be prosecuted for the acts of or acts accompanying, addiction, alcoholism, prostitution, homosexuality and vagrancy.

---

[684] Am. Jur. 2d, Criminal Law § 31.

[685] Islamic Penal Code of Iran, Art 712 (1997).

[686] People v. Weger, 251 Cal. App. 2d 584, 59 Cal. Rptr. 661 (2d Dist. 1967) (explaining that California enacted disorderly conduct laws specifically to replace its vagrancy laws).

[687] Akron v. Rowland, 67 Ohio St. 3d 374, 1993-Ohio-222, 618 N.E.2d 138 (1993).

Chapter 5

Corporal Punishment

Corporal punishment is "A practice than which nothing tends more to harden and degrade"[688] *v. Corporal punishment may be reactionary, but it is better than nothing.*[689]

Corporal punishment is almost nonexistent today in industrialized democratic countries, except for disciplining children in families and schools. Corporal punishment is the punishment of body. It is defined as "physical punishment as distinguished from pecuniary punishment or a fine; any kind of punishment of or inflicted on the body." [690]

Corporal punishments are the most obvious acute punishments, but there are many different kinds of corporal punishment, and not all have the same physical and mental effects. Most corporal punishments are discrete acts that visibly harm the offender's body. Their consequences are ordinarily foreseeable and clearly intended. Hence, the state's culpability is not in question.

Corporal punishments typically inflict readily apparent physical injuries, such as the lacerations caused by whippings. There are five degrees of corporal punishment: whipping - first degree; burning skin - second degree; mutilation - third degree; merciful death - fourth degree; and prolonged death - fifth degree.[691] The drafters of the Eighth Amendment intended to prohibit all but the first and fourth degrees.

---

[688] Report of the Committee on Juvenile Delinquents (1817).

[689] Dostoyevsky, Notes from Underground.

[690] Steven Hatfield, *supra* note 181.

[691] Pieter Spierenburg, **The Body and the State, in The Oxford History of the Prison,** pp 49-53, Norval Morris & David J. Rothman eds.(1995).

I *History*

Corporal punishment was mild in comparison to other punishments of the era. The use of physical punishments has a history in nearly all cultures. Europeans used several forms of punishment intended either to inflict pain, to publicly humiliate offenders, or both. Branding, mutilation, the stock and pillory, the Bilbo, the ducking stool, hard labor, and flogging were all used by the British government to punish criminals.

1 History of Corporal Punishment in the United States from Colonial Times to Twentieth Century

In the colonial America another category of punishments were the "bodily punishments." These punishments, which would later become known as corporal punishments, were directed at the body of the offender and intended to cause pain. Aware of the "shocking apparatus of death and torment" employed throughout the world at the time, colonial legislatures were concerned with establishing limits on the severity of these types of punishments. The Massachusetts Body of Liberties, which established the original capital laws of the colony, placed a restriction on bodily punishments stating, "We allow amongst us none that are inhumane, barbarous, or cruel." A review of the bodily punishments commonly used in seventeenth century America reflects the ideas of the day as to what was or was not barbarous, inhumane, and cruel.[692]

Corporal punishment was the most common form of punishment for no capital offenses in colonial America. Devices used for corporal punishment included the pillory, the whipping post, and the ducking stool. The corporal punishments inflicted upon offenders were public and highly ceremonial. Colonists used public beatings to prevent recurrences of illegal or sinful conduct and to deter potential offenders from committing such crimes themselves. While the physical abuse was severe, the accompanying shame was often the most painful ingredient of the punishment. "The sting of the lash and the contortions of the stocks were surely no balm, but even worse for community members

---

[692] Steven Hatfield, *supra* note, 181.

were the piercing stares of neighbors who witnessed their disgrace and with whom they would continue to live and work."[693]

When corporal punishments dominated penal policy in the American colonies, sanctioning authorities often administered them for public viewing. Onlookers saw the body visibly marked and displayed. Punishment had become theater and education: The large whipping-post painted red stood conspicuously and prominently in the most public street in Boston. It was placed in State Street directly under the windows of a great writing school which I frequented, and from there the scholars were indulged in the spectacle of all kinds of punishment suited to harden their hearts and brutalize their feelings. Here women were tied to the post with bare backs on which thirty or forty lashes were bestowed among the screams of the culprit and the uproar of the mob.

A Corporal Punishment in Early America (1597-1740)

In *Virginia and Southern Colonies* from its earliest days colonial authorities relies on brutal corporal punishments. For instance a Virginian colonist was severely punished for making false charges against another colonist. As punishment, the offender was sentenced to be disarmed and have his arm broken and his tongue bored through with an awl and was then forced to walk through a gauntlet of forty men and battered by each one. In 1618, a more moderate law code was introduced, but there were few alternative to the tradition of harsh corporal punishment. Public shaming or exhibitory punishments were often effective in curbing petty crime. Malefactors were forced to sit in the stocks or stand in the pillories or offer public penance in church for violating conventional moral standards. The ducking stool astride a prominent riverbank saw frequent use when women acted outside their traditional gender rules. Women who committed bastardy, or childbirth outside marriage and could not afford to pay a fine, they were liable to be publicly whipped while naked to the waist. Since slaves were always a valuable commodity, mutilation, whipping and other corporal punishment were administered quickly and visibly to set an example and not interfere with agricultural work.[694]

---

[693] Scott Sanders, *Scarlet Letters, Bilbo's and Cable TV: Are Shame Punishments Cruel and Unusual or are they Viable Option for American Jurisprudence?*, 37 Washburn L.J. 359 (1998).

[694] Mitchell. Roth, *supra* note 163, pp 54-55.

In ***Massachusetts and the New England Colonies*** in lieu of the death penalty, several examples suggest that fines and whipping were the normal modes of punishment. Other public sanctions exposed offenders to an array of corporal punishments, including whipping, the stocks, and pillories. (Whipping was administered for fornication.) These punishments were administrated publicly before the assembled community, usually on the market, lecture or military training day. Habitual drunker wore the shame letter D, for drunken, for an entire year. An unscrupulous baker sometimes stood in the stocks supporting a lump of dough on his head. Chronic property offenders were branded on the cheek or forehead or mutilated, living the mark of infamy to warn the community of their criminal disposition. Like the wearing of shame letters, which sent a message to the community, specific form of maiming also sent a warning to potential miscreants. Among the more grotesque punishment administrated but Puritans were the amputation of ears, slitting of nostrils, and branding of faces and hands.[695]

In ***Pennsylvania and the Mid-Atlantic colonies*** individuals arrested for civic disorder or physical violence was punished severely, particularly in rape cases. One individual facing the shame and the pain of a public whipping for rape slit his own throat before the sentence could be carried out. Whipping remained in fashion in Pennsylvania throughout the eighteenth century. Neighboring Delaware, heavily influenced by early Quaker Code, even had a name for its permutation of this device known as "Red Hannah". Anachronism Delaware authorities continued to whip prisoners in to 1940s.[696]

B   Corporal Punishment in Revolutionary Times (1718-1797)

The eighteenth century is often referred to as the age of reason, or the enlightenment. During this ear great thinkers such as Becaria, Bentham, Howard, and Penn had a great impact on the treatment of criminals. Their efforts resulted in transition from corporal punishment to correction and laid the groundwork for the modern

---

[695] *Id*, PP 55-56.

[696] Robert Graham Caldwell, ***Red Hannah, Delaware Whipping Post***, pp 69-82, University of Philadelphia Press (1947).

penitentiary. Becaria harshly condemned the use of torture in punishment, the corruption of state official, and disproportionalty sever penalties for minor offences.[697]

C Corporal Punishment in the New Nation (1777-1857)

With population growth, increasing mobility and migration the emergence of a distinct poor population made sanctions such as fines, whipping, and the pillory less effective than in the past. While the use of capital punishment had diminished, corporal punishment was another matter, with many criminal offences still being punished with the public infliction of pain and suffering. Most towns in New England boasted whipping posts and stocks near the commons or meetinghouse. As late as 1805, the penalty in Massachusetts for counterfeiting was the amputation of an ear after sitting in a pillory for an hour. The penalty for manslaughter consisted of having one's forehead branded in public, and many communities flogged perpetrators of petty theft. But by the 1830s, public corporal punishment began to disappear from statutes books as prison became a more accepted sanction for most crimes. In 1790, Pennsylvania began the movement to prohibit flogging, and in 1805, Massachusetts followed suit. The movement to abolish corporal punishment was haphazard at best, with Connecticut constables continuing to whip petty criminals until 1828 and Delaware officials flogging black and white prisoners well to twentieth century.[698]

D Corporal Punishment in the Civil War Era (1856-1876)

Corporal punishment, with few exceptions, had all but disappeared by the Civil War.[699] Penal historians have attributed the near extinction of corporal punishment to

---

[697] Mitchell Roth, *supra* note 163, pp 89-90.

[698] *Id*, p 110.

[699] State and federal authorities, however, continued to inflict capital punishment. States conducted fifty seven reported executions from 1864 to 1890. See Margaret Werner Cahalan, U.S. Dep't of Justice, Historical Corrections Statistics in the United States, 1850-1984, at 10 tbl.2-1 note a (1986). They carried out one hundred fifty five reported executions in the 1890s. Whippings continued well into the twentieth century. See generally Robert Caldwell, Red Hannah: Delaware's Whipping Post (1947) (documented nearly three hundred years of whippings in Delaware). In some state prisons, whipping as a disciplinary sanction was practiced as late as the 1960s. Discussing changing judicial attitudes toward the whipping of inmates). See generally

three factors: 1) the new republic's eagerness to abandon Old World criminal sanctions, one being corporal punishment; 2) "riotous disorder" in the nation's rapidly growing cities, resulting in a loss of confidence in the traditional mechanisms of social control; and 3) a new perspective on deviance that attributed criminality to a familial defect, "a failure of upbringing." [700]

E Corporal Punishment in the Young Nation

Gradually, criminal punishment in America evolved away from its emphasis on corporal and humiliating punishments until by the end of the first half of the nineteenth century, imprisonment was virtually the only method of criminal punishment used by most states besides capital punishment and monetary fine. This evolution can be attributed in large part to the birth of the modern science of penology.[701]

In the young America, attempts to reform the severe penal code of England took place, calls for further reform met eager ears. In 1793, in a pamphlet entitled "An Enquiry How Far the Punishment of Death is Necessary in Pennsylvania," William Bradford advanced the ideas of Beccaria and Montesquieu. In his introduction, Bradford cites these philosophers as the basis for three important propositions: the prevention of crimes is the sole end of punishment, that every punishment which is not absolutely necessary for that purpose is a cruel and tyrannical act, and that every penalty should be proportioned to the offense.[702]

Bradford argued that milder forms of punishment were as effective at curbing offenses as the most severe. He pointed to the lenient departure from the English penal

---

Graeme Newman, Just and Painful 7-8 (2d ed. 1995) (calling for a return to human corporal punishments for the majority of offenders who do not need to be locked away).

[700] James Robertson, *Houses of the Dead: Warehouse Prisons, Paradigm Change, and the Supreme Court*, 34Hous. L. Rev. 1003 (1997).

[701] *Id.*

[702] William Bradford, "*An Enquiry How Far the Punishment of Death is Necessary in Pennsylvania*", American Journal of Legal History 12 158. *18 U.S.C. 3567* (1968).

system that William Penn orchestrated in the colony of Pennsylvania between the years 1683-1718, when corporal punishment was replaced with prison, and argued, "During this long space of thirty-five years, it does not appear that the mildness of the laws invited offences, or that Pennsylvania was the theatre of more atrocious crimes than the other Colonies."[703]

Bradford also pointed to one of the major problems with a severe penal code, jury nullification, and related it to the writings of Montesquieu. Faced with the awesome responsibility of sending an individual to the gallows or some other heinous punishment, juries would often acquit if they felt sympathy for the prisoner. According to Bradford, "the unwillingness of witnesses to prosecute, the facility with which juries acquitted, and the prospects of pardon, created hopes of impunity which invited and multiplied the offense."[704]

2   History of Corporal Punishment in Iran from the Ancient Times to the Revolutionary Restatement of Corporal Punishment

A   Corporal Punishment in the Ancient Era

In ancient Persia punishments were harsh and in the majority of cases the death penalty was applied. Whipping under Achaemenian and Sassanian dynasty was widely practiced. Punishment for poisoning of shepherd dogs was two hundred lashes. In this era whipping was a religious concept because based on Zoroastrian[705] religion, when humans commit a crime the devil exerts influence. Because the death penalty and imprisonment do not any effect the devil the punishment is whipping. For this reason whipping was an important punishment in Zoroastrian laws.[706]

---

[703] *Id.*

[704] *Id.*

[705] The ancient Persian religion founded by the prophet Zoroaster, espoused the worship of the daily Ormazd in the context of a universal struggle between the forces of light and of darkness.

[706] Mosa Javan, ***Zoroaster Laws or Vandidad of Zoroaster's Holy Book***, p525, Iran, Tehran (1953) [In Farsi].

In addition to whipping, mutilation, taking off the skin, scalding, branding and shame punishments such as shaving head, beard and wearing wooden signs in public for months for petty crimes were practiced.[707]

B Corporal punishment in the Islamic Era

After the Islamic era, the criminal justice system of ancient Iran was replaced by Islamic laws. Muslims enforced Islamic criminal rules to establish order, security and the promotion of Islam. After the invasion by the Arabs corporal punishment was based on Islamic rules.[708] Islamic punishments were administrated up to ratification of Penal Code in Iran, when the Pahlavi Dynasty replaced the Qajar Dynasty (1779-1925).

C Corporal Punishment under the Pahlavi Monarchy (1925-1979)

Iran's secular criminal justice system was formed under the Pahlavi Dynasty and its two monarchs, Reza Shah (1925-1941) and Mohammad Reza Shah (1941-1979). Modern criminal law in Iran was based on modern capitalist notions of crime and punishment. The first penal Code of Iran was ratified in 1926. Based on Iran's Penal Code the only applicable corporal punishment was flogging for knife-stabbing,[709] vagrancy[710] and gaining ownership of another person property.[711] In 1966 Iran's parliament ratified "Abolition of Flogging Statute" and after that time we have not observed any kind of corporal punishment in Iran.[712]

---

[707] See Mohammad bagher Karami, *supra* note 190; Ava Vahedi, *supra* note 94.

[708] Morteza Ravandi, *supra* note 33.

[709] General Penal Code of Iran, Art 173 (1923) [In Farsi].

[710] *Id,* Art 273.

[711] Statute Regarding the Transferring of Property, Art 3 (1923) [In Farsi].

[712] Abolition of flogging Statute, Single Clause (1966) [In Farsi].

D Corporal Punishment after Islamic Revolution (1979)

The present criminal justice system in Iran regarding some punishments is based on the Twelve Imami Shii version of the Sharia law. This system formed in the early 1980s during the tenure of the Ayatollah Ruhullah Mosavi Khomeini. In 1983 the first specific Islamic penal Statute was ratified. The Statute of Retaliation prescribed punishments such as flogging, mutilation and shame punishments for those crimes with fixed punishment in the Holy Quran and tradition. Therefore for other crimes jurists refer to the modern penal Code of Iran. In 1984 discretionary punishment statute was ratified in Iran. Under this statute flogging was considered as a punishment for sixty four different crimes. Chapter two and three of the Islamic Penal Code outline retaliation and prescribed punishments (ratified in 1992). Immediately after, chapter five of Islamic Penal Code was ratified in 1997 (discretionary and preventive punishments). This statute also includes flogging for different crimes but, the incidence of flogging decreased when compared to 1984 statute.[713] (For more information please refer to chart 5-1 & Figure 5-1). Furthermore, Article 729 of this statute abolished all contrary statutes including modern penal Code of Iran.[714]

---

[713] Iraj Goldouzian, *Special Criminal Law*, Iran, Tehran: Mizan Publication (2001) [In Farsi].

[714] Islamic Penal Code of Iran, Art 729 (1991) [In Farsi].

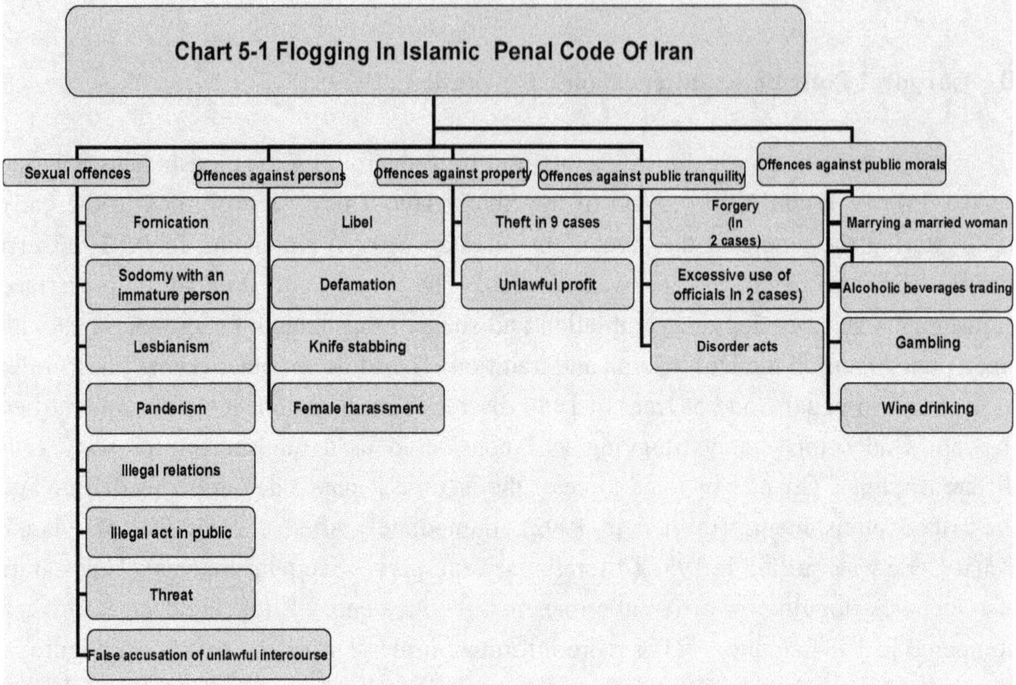

218   Cruel and Unusual Punishment

Chart 5-1 Flogging In Islamic Penal Code Of Iran

- **Sexual offences**
  - Fornication
  - Sodomy with an immature person
  - Lesbianism
  - Panderism
  - Illegal relations
  - Illegal act in public
  - Threat
  - False accusation of unlawful intercourse
- **Offences against persons**
  - Libel
  - Defamation
  - Knife stabbing
  - Female harassment
- **Offences against property**
  - Theft in 9 cases
  - Unlawful profit
- **Offences against public tranquility**
  - Forgery (In 2 cases)
  - Excessive use of officials In 2 cases
  - Disorder acts
- **Offences against public morals**
  - Marrying a married woman
  - Alcoholic beverages trading
  - Gambling
  - Wine drinking

* In Forgery, gambling, defamation and alcoholic beverages trading flogging is voluntary principle punishment.

Figure 5-1 Incidences of Flogging as a Discretionary Punishment in Islamic Penal Code (1997) in Compare to Discretionary Statute (1984)

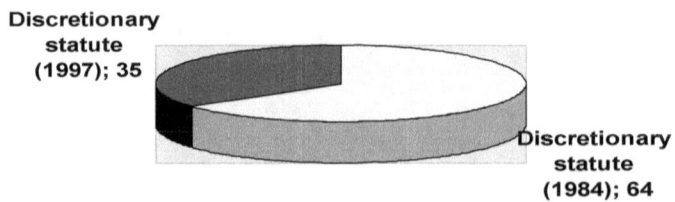

Discretionary statute (1997); 35

Discretionary statute (1984); 64

3 Contemporary Corporal Punishment

At the beginning of 21st century, corporal punishment is no longer a legal sanction in most countries around the world. At the same time, in some countries corporal punishment has been retained and even extended.

At least 16 nations punish offenders with corporal punishment. Newsweek reported that the laws of the following nations provide for corporal punishment: Afghanistan, Bahamas, Brunei, Iran, Isle of Man, Malaysia, Pakistan, Saudi Arabia, Singapore, South Africa, Sudan, Swaziland, Trinidad and Tobago, United Arab Emirates, Yemen, and Zimbabwe. And the recent trend in the United States reflects a desire to impose stricter punishments like those of Iran.[715]

It has already been shown that early American courts approved of whipping. The same is true of the contemporary courts that have considered the issue, with one major exception. Courts have reviewed the use of corporal punishment by prison authorities to discipline inmates by whipping them and have concluded that corporal punishment is not unconstitutional per se.

In the wake of rising crime rates, an increase in the number of youthful offenders, a growing public dissatisfaction with the prison system and the rehabilitative corrections model, and media accounts of the success of foreign systems using a retributive approach in deterring crime, the possible use of corporal punishment in the United States has evoked the public's interest. In addition to the popular interest, several public officials have considered the use of corporal punishment, especially for youthful offenders.[716]

---

[715] In United States we still have shame punishments and bills that have proposed whipping as a punishment.

[716] Daniel Hall, *When Canning Meets the Eighth Amendment: Whipping Offenders in the United States*, 4 Widenr J. Pub. L. 403, 1995.

Two states may have provided the avenue toward reinstituting whipping as a viable form of punishment. There are currently bills pending in Maryland and Mississippi that would provide for whipping if enacted into law,[717] and several other states have considered it in the past. In Maryland, juveniles aged fourteen and older could be caned up to ten times with a rattan cane for "stealing or destroying property worth more than $ 300" and for other serious crimes. The legislation proposed in Mississippi would amend the state constitution and grant the legislature the authority to use caning to punish the defendant for appropriate criminal convictions.[718] In addition, whipping has been considered in at least four other jurisdictions.

Since California first proposed its paddling bill, at least eight other states have attempted to pass similar legislation. Various versions of paddling laws were introduced in Missouri, New Mexico, and New York. Some states, including Louisiana, Mississippi, and Tennessee, have even considered public canings for a series of property crimes including vandalism. The most radical proposal, however, was the Arkansas bill that would allow jury-sanctioned public hangings.[719] This recent renewed interest can be at least partially credited to the 1994 caning of Michael Fay in Singapore for vandalism.[720] His case has made people willing to reexamine why corporal punishment fell into such disfavor.

Some scholars suggest that we can adopt Halachic corporal punishment. Halachic corporal punishment, or flogging, was the standard form of punishment for crimes that did not have biblically prescribed penalties. There were two forms of flogging, biblical and rabbinic. Biblical flogging was limited to thirty-nine lashes, and served as a metaphoric substitute for the death penalty. Rabbinic whipping served to

---

[717] H.R. 1077, Legis. Sess., 1995 Md. Laws; H.R. 106, Reg. Sess., 1995 Miss. Laws.

[718] H.R. 106, Reg. Sess., 1995 Miss. Laws.

[719] Ann O'Hanlon, *New Interest in Corporal Punishment*, Wash. Post, Mar. 5, 1995, at A21 (explaining that although California's paddling bill did not pass, it was reintroduced by Assemblyman Mickey Conroy in February, 1995).

[720] See ***Singapore to Cane Second Foreigner for Vandalism***, Reuters Info. Services, Apr. 22, 1994, available in LEXIS, World Library, Allwld File (acknowledging worldwide controversy over the justifications for caning).

discipline an offender who had flouted a rabbinic precept, and was not limited to a specific number of lashes. Theoretically, a candidate for rabbinic whipping could be flogged to death.[721]

The Talmudic scholars applied three unique procedures to corporal punishment. First, all whipping candidates received a physical examination immediately before being flogged. Only those deemed physically able to withstand the beating were lashed. Second, Halachic corporal punishment was imposed publicly to promote deterrence. Third, the sentencing judges had to attend and monitor the imposition of corporal punishment. Their presence ensured that the whipper did not whip excessively and if criminals became ill during punishment, whipping would cease. These requirements established that Halachic corporal punishment was not a form of torture or cruel and unusual punishment, but served as both general and specific deterrent. It may be because Halachic corporal punishment was considered to be both a humane act and an effective deterrent. However, exactly copying of Halachic punishment methods by the American legislature and judiciary would be inappropriate. American legal society can benefit from Talmudic penology by adapting sanctions modeled after the principles of Halachic punishment.[722]

In *Iran* based on Article 12 of Islamic Penal Code there are five different punishments:
1. Hodoud[723]: crimes with fixed punishment in the Holy Quran and Sunnah. The punishment in Hodoud is not subject to any amendment, alteration or commutation, substation, change or waiver by the judge, ruler or any person in authority. Hodoud punishments are to be prevented in case of doubt. This based on the prophetic tradition says: "Prevent the application of Had punishment as much as you can whenever any doubt exists."[724] The standard of proof in Hodoud punishment is very high and difficult. It is recommended by Sharia law that judges should suggest withdrawal of confession to

---

[721] Kenneth Shuster, **Halacha as a Model for American Penal Practice: A Comparison of Halachic and American Punishment Methods,** 19 Nova L. Rev. 965(1995).

[722] *Id.*

[723] The word Hudoud is the plural form of Had (prescribed punishment) meaning restraint, obstruction, hindrance or prohibition.

[724] Mohammad Bahrami, *supra* note 463.

an accused who has confessed to the commission of crime.⁷²⁵ The infliction of the Had punishment is restricted by repentance of the accused. For instance, if a thief repented and returned the stolen property before the application for prosecution is made the Had lapse.⁷²⁶

In Iran the sanction for prescribed punishment in many cases is corporal punishment. Had punishment includes flogging and mutilation. Because Had is the principle punishment in Iran there is no alternative sanction.⁷²⁷

2- Organ Retaliation (Qisas) for injuries is prescribed in the Holy Quran:" We ordained therein for them, life for life, eye for eye, nose for nose, ear for ear, tooth for tooth and wounds equal to equal.⁷²⁸ Conditions before Qisas injuries are applicable:
   a) The injury must be deliberate and not accidental.
   b) The part of the body on which Qisas may be inflicted must be the same, and in the same condition as the part of the victim's body which was injured by the culprit.
   c) Qisas must be practicable to inflict.⁷²⁹

3 - The word Taazir (discretionary punishment) means to prevent, to respect, and to reform. In the Islamic legal context, Taazir is defined as follows: discretionary punishment to be delivered for transgressions against God, or against individuals for which there is neither fixed punishment nor penance. Taazir denotes a punishment aimed at the prevention of crime and reformation of the criminal. It is stated by Islamic scholars that the aim of Taazir punishment is: disciplinary, reformative and deterrence.⁷³⁰ Taazir punishment is not specified in either the Holy Quran or Sunnah of the Holy Prophet. Crimes for which there is no fixed punishment and concerning are left for the judge or

---

⁷²⁵ *Id.*

⁷²⁶ Islamic Penal Code of Iran, Art 198/4 (1991) [In Farsi].

⁷²⁷ See Islamic Penal Code of Iran.

⁷²⁸ Holy Quran, Maedeh Surah, 45 Verse.

⁷²⁹ See Islamic Penal Code of Iran, Art 271-272.

⁷³⁰ Matthew Lippman, Sean McConville, and Mordechai Yerushalmi, **Islamic Criminal Law and Procedure: An Introduction,** New York: Praeger publication (1988).

the ruler to decide punishment and the manner of infliction (such as imprisonment, fine and flogging less than prescribed punishments).[731]

4- Preventive punishment is prescribed by Iranian government in order to protect order and compliance with governmental regulations.[732] Examples include imprisonment, fine.

5- Blood money (Diyat) as compensation for victims of crimes prescribed by holy Quran and tradition.[733] There is no corporal punishment under preventive and blood money punishments.

II *From Different Methods to International Restrictions*

1 Corporal Punishment Methods in the United States & Iran

A Whipping

Foremost among the bodily punishments was *whipping*. Whipping is also known as flogging, lashing, strapping, beating, or caning. All of these methods involve striking the accused with an object to produce immediate, and acute pain. Various tools have been used to flog people including metal rods, straps, branches, logs, whips, rubber hoses, cat-o-nine tails, and rattan canes.[734]

Whipping was a widely accepted form of punishment throughout the world at the time. In colonial America it was meted out by the stripe. In other words, accused were sentenced to twenty stripes, a stripe being the mark made by the whip on the accused. A limit of forty stripes at one time was recognized throughout the colonies. This limitation, like many other laws of the time, was biblical in origin and based on the Book of Deuteronomy: "Forty stripes he may give him, and not to exceed: lest, if he should exceed, and beat him above these many stripes, then thy brother should seem vile unto thee."

---

[731] See Islamic Penal Code of Iran, Art 498-729.

[732] *Id*, Art 17.

[733] *Id*, Art 15.

[734] Robert G. Caldwell, Criminology, 451-52 (2d ed. 1965).

With regard to whipping, as well as the other bodily punishments, the higher the offender's socio-economic status, the less likely the offender is to receive whipping punishment. In addition to the forty stripe limit the Massachusetts Body of Liberties stated, ". . . nor shall neither any true gentleman, nor any man equal to a gentleman be punished with whipping, unless his crime be very shameful, and his course of life vicious and profligate."[735] Men of standing in the community would receive a fine and even this would be remitted after a period of good behavior. Thus, whipping appears to have been reserved for those who could not afford to pay fines.

Whippings were administered in public as were all other forms of corporal punishment. The great majority of whippings took place at a centrally located whipping post where the offender was bound and the whip applied to his bare back.[736] If the crime was particularly offensive, the culprit was bound to the back of a cart and forced to walk behind it. The stripes were applied as the cart was pulled through the town.[737]

In colonial America, judges commonly sentenced criminals to the whipping post. Nearly every crime, no matter how petty, was punished by whipping. Whipping was abolished crime by crime, finally disappearing as late as 1986.[738]

In ancient Iran, whipping was administered in amount of five lashes to two hundred and fifty lashes (two hundred lashes for poisoning shepherd dog and ninety lashes for manslaughter). Judges could convert whipping punishment to a fine.[739] Following crimes had whipping as punishment: theft, violation of covenant, sodomy, unsuitable dog feeding, dog killing, heating the dog, carrying arms, causing wounds and

---

[735] Edwin Powers, *Crime and Punishment in Early Massachusetts: 1620-1692, p 254*, Boston: Beacon Press, (1966).

[736] Alice Earle Morse, *Curious Punishments of Bygone Days*, pp 70-85, Chicago: Herbert S. Stone and Company (1896).

[737] Edwin Powers, *supra* note 735, p 174.

[738] *Id.*

[739] Mohammad bagher Karami, *supra* note 190, p 57.

injuries.[740] Whipping was practiced before Pahlavi Dynasty. Following the reign of the Pahlavi monarchs it was imposed for three crimes. Whipping finally abolished in Iran in 1966. However with Islamic government approval whipping is permitted in Iran. (Flogging is a common punishment in Had and Taazir offenses).

B Branding

Serious offenses warranted branding. ***Branding*** was an alternative when it was necessary to mark the criminal so that those who might have later dealings with him would be put on notice. The practice of branding survived in England until at least 1699. The practice of branding was also adopted by the American colonies. In some colonies, branding was replaced with requiring offenders to conspicuously wear a badge or a sewn letter indicating the committed crime. Under the East Jersey Codes of 1668 and 1675, first convictions for burglary were punishable by the branding of a "T" on the hand, and second convictions for the same offense were punishable by the branding of an "R" on the forehead of the offender. The Maryland colony branded the letter "B" on the forehead of convicted blasphemers, and adulteresses were required to wear the "scarlet letter" in many New England colonies. The letter "A" sewn to the adulterer's clothing was common, but some victims were branded with the letter.[741] Branding, ear cropping, piercing and burning of tongues, and similar forms of punishment continued until at least the time of the American Revolution.[742]

C Mutilation

Mutilation was another example of early punishment used in England and later administered in the American colonies. There were three classes of punitive mutilation. First, where punishment mirrored the crime committed, the *lex talionis* method of punishment was administered. Mayhem was met with mayhem--an eye for an eye. The

---

[740] Parviz Saneiee, ***General Criminal Law,*** p 287, Iran, Tehran: Ganje Danesh Publication (Fall 1992).

[741] Daniel Hall, *supra note* 716.

[742] See Mitchell Roth, *supra note* 163.

second class included cases where the government removed the offending appendage. For example, thieves had their hands severed, and perjurers had their tongues removed. This type of punishment dates back to at least 1700 B.C.[743] Finally, in early European history, severe and brutal mutilations were used solely for retribution and deterrence purposes. In such cases, there was no nexus between crime and mutilation. Noses, ears, and lips were slit; eyes were plucked out; and scalps were torn from the heads of offenders. Mutilating punishment reserved for serious offenses was the cutting off of one or both ears. The cropping of ears was not always neatly accomplished. Sometimes the ears were nailed to the pillory (a description of this device to follow) during the prisoners stay there. When the prisoner's time was up he was permitted to leave; his ears, however, were expected to stay.[744]

Other mutilating punishments, popular in England and on the European continent at the time, such as slitting nostrils, removing noses and scalps, and cutting out or piercing tongues with hot irons, never received widespread acceptance in the colonies.[745] This is not to say that tongues were totally safe. Lying, mild blasphemy, and gossip were punishable by fastening a cleft stick to the tongue to prevent talking. The offender was then made to stand in some public place in that condition so that all could see his predicament. An alternative to the cleft stick was gagging. Again the gagged individual was made to stand in public in that condition.[746]

Mutilation was not a common punishment in ancient Persia. It practiced for crimes involving usurper theft, abortion and adultery. Blinding was a punishment for rebellious princes achieved by dipping hot needles in the eyes of criminals. These punishments were imposed only by the king's sentence.[747] Under Islamic laws, mutilation was only a punishment for special kind of theft,[748] resorting to arms to

---

[743] Drapkin Israel, *Crime and Punishment in the Ancient World*, p 26 Lexington Bks (1989).

744 *Id.*

[745] Steven Hatfield, *supra* note, p 181.

[746] Edwin Powers, *supra* note 735, p 185.

[747] Ava Vahedi, *supra* note 94, pp 86-87.

[748] Islamic Penal Code of Iran, Art 201 (1991) [In Farsi].

frighten people[749] and organ retaliation (Qisas) for injuries.[750] Mutilation punishments are rare in practice. (Please see chart 5-2).

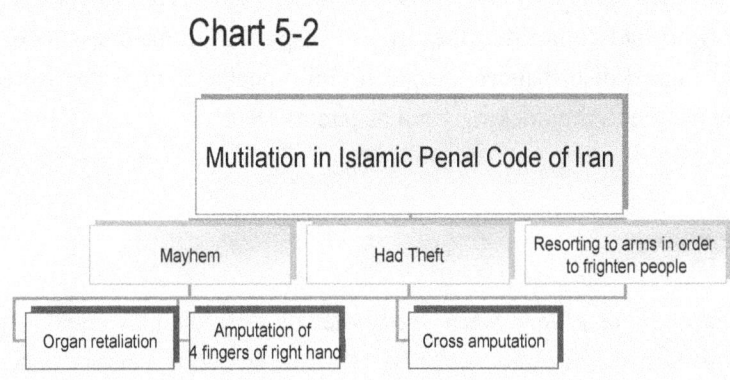

For this **Theft** 16 special conditions must be proven: puberty and sanity for thief, without threat and coercion on thief, intention for theft, knowledge that property belongs to somebody else, knowledge that this act is unlawful, property should be located in the safe custody, breaking to the safe custody, the minimum value of property, lack of necessity for the theft, thief is not the father of the owner, safe custody had not belonged to thief previously, the act is for stealing, lack of famine, proportionate of safe custody, and stolen goods are not government property unknown ownership.

D Ducking Stool

The *ducking stool* was not at all a popular means of punishment. The ducking stool was a device in which the prisoner was restrained and repeatedly dunked in water. The device itself was complicated to build and had to be built near a body of water sufficiently deep enough to submerge the victim. The necessity for a deep body of water conflicted with the desire that the punishment be in a central public place so that the greatest percentage of the community could view the spectacle. Thus, while there is

---

[749] *Id,* Art 183.

[750] *Id,* Art 269.

evidence of the existence of the ducking stool in colonial America, there is little evidence of its actual use.[751] Most often women received the ducking stool as a punishment. Gossips, slanderers, public scolds, and unruly women were ducked. Although the ducking stool was used primarily to punish women, men were also subject to the punishment. Men who had committed the offense of public drunkenness, had sold bad bread or beer, had caused disturbances, or had brutally beaten their wives were dunked. Georgia sentenced people to the ducking stool as late as 1811.[752]

E   Stocks & the Pillory

The *stocks and the pillory* were used when it was felt that public shame and humiliation would best serve justice.[753] By the seventeenth century, though, the humiliating effect of sitting in the stocks was being utilized as a punishment. The stock held prisoners in a seated position with their legs and hands secured. The pillory held the prisoner in a standing position with head and hands secured in a locked frame. Offenders were subject to public ridicule, pelting, and stoning while held in either the stock or the pillory. In some cases, the prisoner received an additional form of punishment, such as flogging or branding, while he was confined to the stock or the pillory. For example, in the case of the pillory, as described above, the ears of the offender were nailed to the pillory, and, when the time for release came, the offender would either have to tear his ears loose or the ears would be severed by the official in charge. Both the stock and pillory were commonly used during colonial times and the times following the ratification of the Constitution. The use of the pillory survived until as late as 1905.[754]

---

[751] Edwin Powers, *supra* note 735.

[752] Daniel Hall, *supra note* 716.

[753] Graeme Newman, *supra* note 195, p 114.

[754] Daniel Hall, *supra* note 716.

2 International Aspect

A Treaties & International cases

Numerous existing international human rights *documents* prohibit torture and cruel, inhuman, or degrading punishment:

The oldest of the existing conventions is the *Universal Declaration of Human Rights*, adopted in 1948, which protects individuals from torture and cruel, inhuman, or degrading punishment. Since the Universal Declaration, the United Nations ratified the Convention for the Protection of Human Rights and Fundamental Freedoms in 1950, followed by the International Convention on Civil and Political Rights in 1966. Both of these conventions also contain provisions prohibiting cruel or torturous punishment. Whereas the three aforementioned documents are general conventions which target a variety of human rights concerns, a more recent agreement focuses specifically on problems regarding punishment.[755] Article 5 of the Universal Declaration of human rights provides that "no one shall be subjected to torture or to cruel, inhuman or degrading treatment or punishment".

Article 7 of the *International covenant on civil and political rights* (ICCPR) provides that "no one shall be subjected to torture or to cruel, inhuman or degrading treatment or punishment. In particular, no one shall be subjected without his free consent to medical or scientific experimentation." Article 10, paragraph 1 of the ICCPR states that "all persons deprived of their liberty shall be treated with humanity and with respect for the inherent dignity of the human person." The *United Nations Human Rights Committee*, in its authoritative general comment on Article 7 of the ICCPR, emphasized that the absolute prohibition of cruel, inhuman or degrading punishment must extend to corporal punishment.

---

[755] See Convention Against Torture and Other Cruel, Inhuman or Degrading Treatment or Punishment, 39 U.N. GAOR, 39th Sess., Supp. No. 51, at 197, U.N. Doc. A/RES/39/46 (1984); Universal Declaration of Human Rights, G.A. Res. 217 (III), U.N. GAOR, 3d Sess., at 71, U.N. Doc. A/810 (1948) Freedoms, Nov. 4, 1950, 213 U.N.T.S. 221]; International Covenant on Civil and Political Rights, G.A. Res. 2200 (XXI), U.N. GAOR, 21st Sess., Supp. No. 16, at 52, U.N. Doc. A/6316 (1966).

Article 5 of the ***American Convention of human rights***[756] provides: 1. every person has the right to have his physical, mental, and moral integrity respected. 2. No one shall be subjected to torture or to cruel, inhuman, or degrading punishment or treatment. All persons deprived of their liberty shall be treated with respect for the inherent dignity of the human person.

Also Article 5 of the ***African Charter of human rights***[757] provides: Every individual shall have the right to the respect of the dignity inherent in a human being and to the recognition of his legal status. All forms of exploitation and degradation of man, particularly slavery, slave trade, torture, cruel, inhuman or degrading punishment and treatment shall be prohibited.

Various ***international cases*** have dealt with corporal punishment. Courts have, however, ruled that whipping and flogging violate international law, but only as punishments for property crimes. Although the ***European Court of Human Rights*** held that "birching" in the Isle of Man violated international human rights, the ***European Commission of Human Rights*** concluded that corporal punishment in Scottish schools did not.[758]

In ***Campbell & Cosans v. United Kingdom***,[759] two plaintiffs filed separate applications with the European Commission, each contending that the use of corporal punishment violated Article 3.[760] The court recognized that a mere threat of prohibited

---

[756] Nov. 22, 1969, O.A.S. Treaty Series No. 36, O.A.S. Official Records OEA/Ser. L/V/II, Doc. 21, rev. 6 (1970).

[757] African [Banjul] Charter on Human and Peoples' Rights, adopted June 27, 1981, OAU Doc. CAB/LEG/67/3 rev. 5, 21 I.L.M. 58 (1982), *entered into force* Oct. 21 (1986).

[758] Jordan J. Paust, ***Human Dignity as a Constitutional Right: A Jurisprudentially Based Inquiry into Criteria and Content***, *27 How. L.J. 145, 176 (1984).*

[759] Campbell & Cosans v. United Kingdom, 48 Eur. Ct. H.R. (ser. A) (1982).

[760] Campbell attended a school that disciplined students using corporal punishment. The Regional Education Council refused to guarantee that Campbell would not face such measures. Cosans also attended a school that used corporal punishment. He was to receive punishment for allegedly taking a prohibited shortcut through a cemetery on his way home from school.

conduct may violate Article 3. Nevertheless, the court found that the mere threat of corporal punishment did not meet the minimum level of severity as defined in *Ireland v. United Kingdom*: In the present case, no "punishment" has actually been inflicted... . "Treatment" itself will not be "degrading" unless the person concerned has undergone - either in the eyes of others or in his own eyes - humiliation or debasement attaining a minimum level of severity.[761]

To determine whether the boys suffered humiliation or debasement, the court observed that a threat directed to an exceptionally insensitive person may have no significant effect on him but nevertheless be incontrovertibly degrading; and conversely, an exceptionally sensitive person might be deeply affected by a threat that could be described as degrading only by a distortion of the ordinary and usual meaning of the word.[762]

The preceding cases illustrate that conduct must transcend a minimum level of severity to merit judicial review. To determine whether particular conduct meets that standard, the court examines the totality of circumstances. It considers the "nature and context of the punishment itself and the manner and method of its execution,"[763] as well as the prospective physical and psychological effects on the individual.[764]

B Amnesty International

Amnesty International repeating the proclamation that the caning is torture. Amnesty International opposes the use of corporal punishment as a violation of the right not to be subjected to torture or cruel, inhuman or degrading treatment or punishment guaranteed by Article 5 of the Universal Declaration of Human Rights.

---

[761] Ireland v. United Kingdom, 25 Eur. Ct. H.R. (ser. A) at 66 (1978) ("The [European] Convention, with its distinction between 'torture' and 'inhuman or degrading treatment', should by the first of these terms attach a special stigma to deliberate inhuman treatment causing very serious and cruel suffering.").

[762] *Id.*

[763] Campbell & Cosans, 48 Eur. Ct. H.R.

[764] Tyrer v. United Kingdom, 26 Eur. Ct. H.R. (ser. A) At 15, 17 (1978).

Amnesty International understands that there is a need for effective deterrents against rape and that rape is a truly repugnant crime, the perpetrators of which should be brought to justice. However, the organization believes that no crime, no matter how serious, justifies the use of punishments that constitute torture or cruel, degrading or inhuman treatment.[765]

Amnesty International considers that the imposition of corporal punishment is also contrary to Articles 7 and 10(1) of the International Covenant on Civil and Political Rights (ICCPR): Article 7: "No one shall be subjected to torture or to cruel, inhuman or degrading treatment or punishment. In particular, no one shall be subjected without his free consent to medical or scientific experimentation"; Article 10: "All persons deprived of their liberty shall be treated with humanity and with respect for the inherent dignity of the human person". In its General Comment 20 on Article 7, the Committee emphasized that the absolute prohibition of cruel, inhuman or degrading punishment in Article 7 of the ICCPR "must extend to corporal punishment." This contention is strongly supported by other expert bodies and international jurisprudence.[766]

C Applying International Norms in Domestic Courts

There are three principal means by which domestic courts have applied or incorporated international law as a part of their domestic legal system: (1) by directly applying the terms of international treaties entered into by their respective governments; (2) by using international law to guide the interpretation of the state's own domestic law; and (3) by applying customary international law.[767] In countries which have incorporated

---

[765] See www.amnesty.org.

[766] For example the UN Commission on Human Rights, resolution 1997/38 of April 1997; Nigel Rodley, Special Rapporteur on Torture, in his report to the Commission on Human Rights, 10 January 1997 E/CN.4/1997/7; the European Court of Human Rights in Tyrer v The United Kingdom, Application no. 2865/72, European Court of Human Rights, Series B, No. 24.

[767] Article 38(1) of the Statute of the International Court of Justice identifies the sources of international law: (a) treaties, (b) international custom, as evidence of a general practice accepted as law (customary international law), (c) general principles of law, and (d) judicial decisions and teachings of the most highly qualified publicists.1947 I.C.J. Acts & Docs. 77. See also Restatement (Third) of the Foreign Relations Law of the United States, s102 (1) (1987).

international human rights law into their own jurisprudence, an appeal can be made directly to international law in a domestic case. Countries differ substantially in the extent to which they incorporate international law directly into their national law. Some countries such as Austria, Belgium, the Netherlands, and Romania accept international law as equal to, or supreme over, their own domestic law. Other countries, such as the United Kingdom, do not consider international law to be judicially enforceable unless it is implemented by domestic legislation.

The *United States* combines these two approaches.[768] There is significant interplay among these different ways of applying international law domestically, and it is

---

[768] In the United States, a treaty ratified by the United States is part of the supreme law of the land, of equal dignity with federal statutes. Article VI, paragraph 2 of the U.S. Constitution states the following: This Constitution, and the Laws of the United States which shall be made in Pursuance thereof; and all Treaties made, or which shall be made under the Authority of the United States, shall be the supreme Law of the Land; and the Judges in every State shall be bound thereby, any Thing in the Constitution or Laws of any State to the Contrary notwithstanding. (Emphasis added). Conflicts between treaty clauses and existing U.S. law are resolved according to three rules, (1) a treaty may not infringe on certain provisions of the U.S. Constitution, Reid v. Covert, 354 U.S. 1 (1957); (2) if there is a conflict between a treaty and a federal statute, the more recent prevails, and (3) if there is a conflict between a treaty and state law, the treaty controls, Zschernig v. Miller, 389 U.S. 429, 440-41 (1968). Customary law enjoys, in theory, a status under United States law similar to the U.S. Constitution, although there is some controversy over whether it is in fact equal in status. U.S. courts have, nevertheless, recognized the domestic authority of international customary law in certain cases. See The Paquete Habana, 175 U.S. 677, 700 (1900)(customary law is "part of our law, and must be ascertained and administered by the courts of justice of appropriate jurisdiction as often as questions of right depending upon it are duly presented for their determination"). In one of the most important cases to address the issue of domestic application of customary international law, the court in Filartiga v. Pena-Irala, 630 F.2d 876 (2d Cir. 1980), stated that "where the nations of the world have adopted a norm in terms so formal and unambiguous as to make it international 'law,' the interests of the global community transcend those of any one state." The Circuit Court noted that "although there is no universal agreement as to the precise extent of the 'human rights and fundamental freedoms' guaranteed to all by the U.N. Charter, there is at present no dissent from the view that guaranties include, at a bare minimum, the right to be free from torture. This prohibition has become part of customary international law, as evidenced and defined by the Universal Declaration of Human Rights." (Emphasis added). In Committee of United States' Citizens Living in Nicaragua v. Reagan, 859 F.2d 929 (D.C. Cir. 1988), the Circuit Court noted the supremacy of peremptory norms of international law (jus cogens) over domestic and customary international law. The court stated in dicta that "[s]uch basic norms of international law as the proscription against murder and slavery may well ... restrain our government in the same way that the Constitution restrains it. If Congress adopted a foreign policy that resulted in the enslavement of our citizens or other individuals that policy might well be subject to challenge in domestic court under international law."

somewhat artificial to discuss these forms of incorporating international law under discrete rubrics. For example, the acceptance of a treaty by a wide number of nations may lead a court to accept a treaty provision as part of customary international law and apply such provisions domestically even if the nation has not signed the treaty.[769]

The recent caning of an American teenager (Michael Fay) in Singapore has prompted world-wide debate over the international laws governing criminal punishment. Although international law consistently prohibits torture and cruel, inhuman, or degrading punishment, the question remains whether caning fits in that category of punishment. Although American medical organizations, including the American Medical Association (AMA), condemn the presence of doctors at canings, their presence is one element of Singapore's caning laws which distinguishes caning from cruel and inhuman punishment. By restricting the class of people eligible for caning, requiring the presence of doctors at canings, and establishing the size and type of instrument that constitutes a cane, Singapore's laws safeguard citizens from cruel, inhuman, or degrading punishment. Although the West condemns Singapore's punishment of caning as cruel and inhuman, the West must remember that the Republic of Singapore is only thirty years old. Consequently, caning does not always violate international prohibitions against torture and cruel, inhuman, or degrading punishment. Although international law prohibits torture and cruel, inhuman, or degrading punishment, caning is no more cruel and inhuman than capital punishment which is regularly practiced by the United States.[770]

---

[769] For example, with respect to the Vienna Convention on the Law of Treaties, the Legal Advisor of the United States Department of State wrote a Letter of Submittal to the President in which he stated: While the United States has not yet ratified the Vienna Convention on the Law of Treaties, [the United States has] consistently appl[ied] those of its terms which constitute a codification of customary international law. Most provisions of the Vienna Convention, including Articles 31 and 32 on matters of treaty interpretation, are declaratory of customary international law. Marian L. Nash, *Contemporary Practice of the United States Relating to International Law*, 75 Am. J. Int'l L. 142, 147, reprinted in Newman & Weissbrodt (1981).

[770] Firouzeh Bahrampour, *Note and Comment: The Canning of Michael Fay: Can Singapore's Punishment withstand the Scrutiny of International Law*, 10 Am. U.J. Int'l L. & Pol'y 1057(1995).

Applying international standards to United States legal principles may be problematic. In *Stanford v. Kentucky*[771], Judge Rehnquist, writing his plurality opinion stated neither "norms' nor the legal standards of other countries should disposition the Eighth Amendment." The government believes domestic laws provide more protection than international treaties and customary laws. Furthermore, even if the United States were to adopt the international definition of torture, application of this norm to lawful sanctions may be inappropriate. The Convention on Torture, for example, states, "[torture] does not involve pain or suffering arising only from, inherent in or incidental to lawful sanctions." Since capital punishment is legal in the United States, this treaty would not forbid states from using methods of execution which involve torturous treatment. As a result, the treaty becomes a futile attempt to satisfy human rights activists.[772]

However, while it is reasonable for judges to grant national standards greater influence when assessing what is cruel and unusual, judges should allow international trends to shed light on the issue as well. Especially because the United States is a party to international agreements that bear on the issue, it seems legally necessary to consider international trends at least relevant to an inquiry into contemporary standards of decency.

The United States is, of course, a founding participant in and the permanent host of the United Nations, the preamble of whose charter lists among the purposes of the organization, "to reaffirm faith in fundamental human rights, [and] in the dignity and worth of the human person, and to promote social progress and better standards of life." Further, in 1994, the United States ratified the Convention against Torture and Other Cruel, Inhuman or Degrading Treatment or Punishment. However, in ratifying the latter Convention and other such international instruments calling for adherence to international human rights standards, the United States has attached reservations intended to keep these pacts from forcing any change in United States law or policy. However, "reservations designed to reject any obligation to rise above existing law and practice of

---

[771] Stanford v. Kentucky, 109 S. Ct. 2969, 2975 (1989).

[772] Garry Ledbetter, *The International Norms: An Interpretation of the "Evolving Standard of Decency"*, 2 San Diego Justice J. 263 (1994).

dubious propriety .... . Even friends of the United States have objected that its reservations are incompatible with that object and purpose and are therefore invalid."

Setting aside the valid question of whether American law is subject to international human rights standards by force of these instruments of international law, the assent of the United States generally to the United Nations Charter, and to various treaties and international agreements promoting the dignity and worth of the human person and social progress suggests strongly that the United States has opened the door to the influence of the international community in assessing contemporary standards of decency.[773]

In contrast to the international community, the United States adheres to a "cruel and unusual punishment" clause. The Supreme Court interprets this clause by determining the "evolving standards of decency." International norms are indicative of the view of the global community on specific issues. As already mentioned the international community has spoken on the issue of torture and called for a ban on such practices. Application of a world opinion gives a greater indication of the "evolving standards of decency" than does the regional bias of separate jury panels and state criminal codes. Therefore, using international norms will not invade our sovereignty but will provide a better guideline in deciding what "cruel and unusual" punishment is.[774]

In *Iran*, Islamic penal law sets forth a number of crimes and penalties that are the object criticism from the international human rights community. These penalties, although protecting Islamic religious principles mete out harsh penalties that violate the right to life and, in many cases, may reach the threshold of torture or cruel, inhuman or degrading punishment.

International human rights discourse texts do not discuss punishments for specific violations of criminal law. However, the prohibition against torture would apply to death by crucifixion and cross amputation. A death sentence might be acceptable if able to be carried out in a humane manner for particularly serious acts. Forcibly expelling

---

[773] Steven Manley, *The Constitution. The Punishment of death, and Misguided Originalism*, 1999 L. Rev. M.S.U. D.C.L. 913 (1999).

[774] *Id.*

a convicted brigand from his country with no right to ever return may violate international norms.

Judicial corporal punishment in the forms of flogging and amputation for the offenses of theft, alcohol consumption, robbery, adultery, and rape in the Sharia Penal Code constitute torture or cruel, inhuman or degrading punishment under Article 7 of the ICCPR (For more information please refer to chart 5 & 6).

Despite international human rights treaties to which Iran is a party, there are a number of cases documented by Amnesty International where courts have ordered amputations for theft and robbery. Iranian courts have ordered public floggings these severe penalties have forced dissenters subject to Sharia law to renounce Islam, reflecting the internal dissent among Muslims that has resulted from the adoption of Sharia penal law in Iran.

The crime of robbery is considered one of the most serious crimes under Sharia law. Robbery is punishable by amputation of the right hand for the first offense, amputation of the left foot for a second offense, life imprisonment for a third offense, and death penalty for a fourth offense.[775] These penalties are seriously contested by members of the international human rights community, such as Human Rights Watch, as violations of the right to life and the right to be free from torture or cruel, unusual, or degrading punishment. Furthermore, these crimes are not uniquely offensive to an Islamic value system, but constitute common crimes that require regulation by a standard system of law enforcement.

Flogging may cause "severe pain or suffering," it is a "lawful sanction" in Iran. Similarly, the death penalty causes severe pain and suffering, and is considered cruel and unusual by the European Court on Human Rights,[776] The death penalty remains in

---

[775] Islamic Penal Code of Iran, Art 201 (1991) [In Farsi].

[776] See M. Cherif Bassiouni, *Human Rights in the Context of Criminal Justice: Identifying International Procedural Protections and Equivalent Protections in National Constitutions*, *3 Duke J. Comp. & Int'l L. 235, 262-63, nn.118-28 (1993)* (observing that the right to freedom from torture and cruel, inhuman, or degrading punishment appears in numerous international agreements as well as 81 national constitutions), Also See Highet and Kahale, (citingTyrer v. United Kingdom, 26 Eur. Ct. H.R. (1978) (ruling that the punishment of birching is degrading and

practice as a legal sanction in the United States and Iran. Consequently, a comparison of flogging in Iran and the death penalty in the United States reveals that both countries are potentially guilty of violating international law.

The UN Special Reporter on Torture corporal punishment is inconsistent with the prohibition of torture and other cruel, inhuman or degrading treatment or punishment.[777] The UN Human Rights Committee found that corporal punishment is excessive under Article 7 of the ICCPR, which prohibits cruel, inhuman or degrading treatment.[778] According to the language in the international human rights treaties to which Iran is bound, corporal punishment provided for in the Islamic Penal Code does not adequately protect the rights of Iranian citizens to be free from cruel, inhuman or degrading treatment.

According to General Comment 22, freedom of religion[779] is wholly protected to the extent that it does not infringe on other fundamental rights protected by the ICCPR. In terms of consistency, Islamic criminal law conflicts with Iran's international human rights obligations. A state is not prohibited from adopting an official religion, but it must not infringe on the rights of others to practice their own religions or profess no faith at all. This provision in the ICCPR is particularly relevant because non-Muslims and some Muslims prefer to be judged under modern criminal court rather than an Islamic court.

Iran is party to a number of international human rights treaties, which bind Iran to respect and ensure the human rights of all individuals within its territory. Iran is a party to the International Covenant on Civil and Political Rights (ICCPR). In addition, a number of international instruments such as the Universal Declaration of Human Rights

---

therefore violates the European Convention on Human Rights); Warwick v. United Kingdom, Eur. Comm'n H.R., Report of July 18, 1986 (unreported) (holding that corporal punishment, even one cane stroke on the hand, is degrading and violates the European Convention on Human Rights).

[777] See http://www.universalhumanrightsindex.org/documents/843/802/document/fr/text.html.

[778] *Id.*

[779] General Comment No. 22: The right to freedom of thought, conscience and religion (Art. 18) 30/07/93.
CCPR/C/21/Rev.1/Add.4, General Comment No. 22.

and the Declaration on the Rights of Persons Belonging to National or Ethnic, Religious and Linguistic Minorities (Minorities Declaration) are binding as customary international law.

According to (Article 14) the *Vienna Convention on the Law of Treaties*[780], once international treaties have been ratified a state party is bound to carry out its international obligations and may not invoke its domestic law as justification for non-implementation. Thus, the government of Iran has the ultimate responsibility to ensure that human rights are respected in the territory of Iran. As a result, Islamic Penal Code is not a valid reason for non-implementation of Iran's international human rights obligations.

Indeed, the prohibition of torture is a peremptory norm of international law which means it applies to all countries, whether or not they have consented to be bound by it. As such, it can protect the citizens of a country that has not signed any of the international instruments prohibiting cruel punishment.

Thus the utilization of the definition of the international norm of torture is more indicative of the "evolving standards of decency" rather than the opinions of juries and legislatures. The international norm displays the opinion of the global community giving the national courts a better interpretation than the regional decision making of juries and state governments.[781]

III   *Cruel & Unusual Analysis*

1   Cruel & Unusual Per se

At first glance corporal punishment is barbaric, per se although some scholars believe that corporal punishment is not per se "cruel and unusual" under either original or

---

[780] Vienna Convention on the Law of Treaties, May 23, 1969, 1155 U.N.T.S. 331; 8 I.L.M. 679 (1969).

[781] Garry Ledbetter, *supra* note 772.

modern understandings, but legislative, judicial history and pain infliction of corporal punishment are important factors that are against this hypothesis.

For instance, mutilating punishments are barbaric because they violate the body's integrity which is a value we deeply respect in our civilization, and because they seem like a throwback to our cannibalistic past.

The main challenge to the proposed systems of corporal punishment constitutes cruel and unusual punishment. However, the predecessors clearly accepted corporal punishment as a viable alternative to other forms of criminal punishment. The prison system did not truly begin to develop in that era. Before that, towns had stocks, pillories, and whipping posts to deal with criminals.

A survey of mild punishment provides further enlightenment perspective on cruel and unusual punishment. *"Cruel"* is defined as brutal, savage, or barbarous. *"Unusual"* means scarce, peculiar, or abnormal. ***"Cruel and unusual punishment"*** means "unnecessary and wanton infliction of pain." *"Wanton"* means unconscionable, unbridled, or unrestrained. *"Unnecessary"* is defined as needless or gratuitous.[782]

We will now consider corporal punishment is a savage and barbarous practice. But it is still question whether whipping was intended by the predecessors to be excluded per se as a form of punishment. It appears, however, that the predecessors did not consider whipping to be cruel and unusual. This view is evidenced by several facts. First, the evidence from the history debates indicates acceptance of corporal punishment. Second, corporal punishment was not a severe form of punishment in ancient era. Third, the early laws of the nations provided for the corporal punishment of offenders.

As mentioned earlier flogging is punishment for certain types of consensual homosexual acts and other crimes after Islamic revolution in Iran.[783] Imposing corporal punishments, such as flogging based, on Islamic Penal Code of Iran is inherently cruel and unusual. Flogging is an inhumane and barbarous type of punishment.

---

[782] Oxford Unabridged Dictionary.

[783] Punishment for any homosexual activity without intercourse is one hundred lashes; punishment for lesbianism is one hundred lashes.

Wiedeman[784] believed, the cruel and unusual punishment standard to be flexible, and open to wider interpretation than other constitutional provisions. It is important to note that at no time has corporal punishment been ruled unconstitutional. Second, if the state can impose corporal punishment on children, through teachers, without a hearing, surely the state can impose a substantially similar penalty on criminals after they have been duly convicted in a court of law. Wiedeman preferred the method of administering the punishment would be by flogging for violent, non-capital crimes and also for the more serious property crimes. Less physically painful punishment such as the pillory could be used for less serious crimes and the majority of "victimless" crimes.[785]

2 Pain Infliction

Throughout history, pain has proven to be important to medicine, philosophy, and religion. Without pain, pleasure would be unknown. Without pain, some forms of punishment would be ineffective. The total elimination of pain from punishment is wrong, or at least, unwise. On the other hand, unnecessary pain is also wrong. Pain inflicted for sadistic purposes or to achieve an improper objective (for example, obtaining a confession) is wrong. The Framers had such matters in mind when they ratified the Fifth, Eighth, and Fourteenth Amendments. Of course, drawing the line between permissible and impermissible pain is the challenge. In the context of criminal justice, the infliction of pain is valid when used to achieve a legitimate purpose.

The recognition of mental and emotional pain is also important to this inquiry. It is generally accepted that the emotional and psychological needs of inmates are protected by the Eighth Amendment. Justice Brennan stated that pain is not the only reason primitive punishments, such as the rack, thumbscrew, and stretching of limbs, is violative of the Eighth Amendment. He asserted that "the true significance of these punishments is that they treat members of the human race as nonhumans." The decision in *Trop v. Dulles*

---

[784] Whitney Wiedeman, *Special Issue: Juvenile Justice and the Criminal Law: Comment: Don't Spare the Rod: A Proposed Return to Public, Corporal Punishment on Convicts*, 23 Am. J. Crim. L. 651(1996).

[785] *Id.*

stands for the proposition that cruelty can transcend corporeal interests. The Court held that denationalization for the crime of desertion amounts to the "total destruction of the individual's status in organized society. It is a form of punishment more primitive than torture, for it destroys for the individual the political existence that was centuries in the development." Whipping does not transgress these limits. Although it does rely on pain and, to some extent, humiliation to achieve its objectives, it does not destroy a person's status in society. Nor does it serve only to satisfy sadistic desires. Moreover, in some cases, it may be more humane and penologically sound than other generally accepted forms of punishment, such as imprisonment.[786]

Considering above hypothesis it appears that a number of punishments still utilized today are extremely suspect. Whipping and mutilation are obvious candidates for extinction. But will all scholars agree to rule out these penalties? Following legislative and judicial approval shows certainly not.

3   Legislative Story

In the United States the Northwest Territory adopted an act which provided that people convicted of arson, robbery, burglary, or obstructing authority could be publicly whipped in addition to other forms of punishment(1788).[787] An act in 1795 made larceny punishable by a lashing and an act in 1805 punished horse thieves with as many as two hundred stripes as well as other penalties.[788]

In contrast to these penalties, other crimes were punishable with fewer lashes. For example, a Boston court sentenced a burglar to be hanged, "five thieves to be whipped, two greater thieves to be set on the gallows, and one counterfeiter set on the pillory." Later, the same Boston court ordered eleven offenders to be whipped. Another offender, appointed to execute the whipping, "persisted in being 'tender of strokes,'" contrary to the orders of the official supervising the punishment. Eventually, the official

---

[786] Graeme Newman, *supra* note 195, p 141.

[787] See www.corpun.com.

[788] *Id.*

seized the whip, turned it on the whipper, and then completed the task personally. According to one account, "'the citizens who were assembled complimented the Sheriff with three cheers for the manly determined manner in which he executed his duty.'" [789]

In 1790 Congress enacted the Nation's first criminal law that provided for public whipping of thieves.[790] There were other federal statutes that provided for whipping as a form of punishment. For example, certain postal crimes were punished with up to forty lashes under a statute enacted in 1799,[791] and in 1801 a federal statute was enacted delegating to justices of the peace in Washington, D.C., the authority to punish offenders with whipping, imprisonment, and a fine of 500 pounds of tobacco.[792] Whipping and standing in the stock continued to be punishments under federal law until 1839.[793] In 1898 the Virginia Legislature provided for the whipping of male youths.[794]

Although whipping was abolished for federal offenders in 1839, whipping continued in several states well into the twentieth century. For example, the final whipping in Maryland took place in 1948. Whipping was not statutorily abolished in Maryland until 1953.[795] Similarly, the last statutorily authorized whipping as punishment for a crime in Delaware was on June 16, 1952.[796] The crime was breaking and entering,

---

[789] Kenneth Shuster, *supra* note 721.

[790] Act of Apr. 30, 1790, ch. 9, § § 15, 16, 1 Stat. 112, 115-16 (repealed 1839). Convicted persons could be punished with as many as 39 stripes under this statute.

[791] Act of Mar. 2, 1799, ch. 43, § 15, 1 Stat. 733, 736 (repealed 1810).

[792] United States v. More, *7 U.S. (3 Cranch) 159, 167 (1805)*.

[793] The Act of February 28, 1839, abolished whipping and standing in the stocks. Act of Feb. 28, 1839, ch. 36, § 5, 25 Stat. 321, 322 (1839).

[794] Simeon. Baldwin, *The Restoration of Whipping as a Punishment for Crime*, 13 GREEN BAG 65, 66 (1901).

[795] Daniel Hall, supra note 716.

[796] DEL. CODE ANN. tit. 29, § *901* (1983) was amended to abolish flogging as a punishment by 65 Del. Laws 425 (1986). The effective date of the amendment was July 3, 1986. The crime to which the whipping penalty attached was altering, defacing, or otherwise destroying a bill or act

for which the defendant received twenty lashes.[797] Although not administered after 1952, whipping was provided for by statute in Delaware until 1986. In fact, defendants in two separate cases during the 1960s were sentenced to be whipped. For reasons discussed below, however, neither sentence was executed. A total of 1607 individuals were subjected to whipping in Delaware between 1900 and 1942.[798] State legislatures, enacted chemical castration laws and recently by way of the caning of Michael Fay in Singapore, have expressed renewed interest in corporal punishment.

In *Iran,* the legislature has approved corporal punishment in three different categories:

    a   *Prescribed punishments* (Hodoud) such as:

-The punishment of *fornication* is 100 lashes as stated in the Holy Quran.[799]

-*Sodomy* entails execution if both the active and passive persons are mature, of sound mind and have free will. If a mature man of sound mind commits sexual intercourse with an immature person, the doer will be killed and the passive one will be subject to Taazir (Discretionary punishment awarded by the judge) of 74 lashes if not under duress. When the active person is non-Muslim and the passive person is Muslim punishment for the passive person is death penalty. If an immature person commits sexual intercourse with another minor, both will be subject to Taazir (74 lashes) unless one was under duress.[800]

---

of the General Assembly. Whipping was abolished for most other crimes in 1973. Act of Apr. 1, 1973, ch. 497, 58 Del. Laws 2.

[797] Although no whippings were executed after 1952, it appears that a few judges continued to view corporal punishment as part of the state's sentencing scheme. For example, in *Balser v. State,* the defendant was sentenced to 20 lashes for a robbery conviction, *Balser v. State, 195 A.2d 757 (Del. 1963);* In *Cannon v. State,* a defendant was sentenced to three years imprisonment and 20 lashes for the crime of larceny. *Cannon v. State, 196 A.2d 399 (Del. 1963);* For reasons discussed in this Article, neither offender was flogged. In *Osburn v. State,* the trial judge commented, during the sentencing of an armed robber, that he would not sentence the defendant to be whipped because of the defendant's youth, indicating that the trial judge believed lashing adult offenders convicted of armed robbery was acceptable. *Osburn v. State, 224 A.2d 52 (Del. 1966).*

[798] Daniel Hall, *supra* note 716.

[799] Holy Quran, Soreh Noor, 2 verse.

[800] Islamic Penal Code of Iran, Art. 110-113, 121.

-*Lesbianism* (Mosaheqeh) is homosexuality of women by genitals. Punishment for lesbianism is one hundred (100) lashes. Punishment for lesbianism will be established Vis-a-Vis someone who is mature, of sound mind, has free will and intention. Punishment for lesbianism makes no distinction between the doer and the subject as well as a Muslim or non-Muslim. If the act of lesbianism is repeated three times and punishment is enforced each time, the death sentence will be issued the fourth time.[801]

-*False accusation of unlawful intercourse*[802] is prohibited under Islamic Penal Code by 80 lashes.

-*Theft* is an act of taking other people's property without any lawful claim to it. The following punishment for theft is prescribed in the Holy Quran: "As to the thief, male or female, cut off his or her hands as punishment by way of example from Allah for their crime. And Allah is exalted in power."[803] According to a tradition of Prophet Mohammad, this harsh punishment does not apply to petty larceny. However, the classical jurists differ as to the definition of petty larceny in terms of value of the property stolen. For this reason under Islamic Penal Code sixteen different thefts are regulated. Just punishment for one type of theft -with specific restrictions- is amputation. Punishment for nine types of thefts is both imprisonment and flogging.[804]

-Punishment for *Wine drinking* during the time of Holy Prophet was public beating with shoes, sticks, and hands without specifying the number of lashes.[805] Under Islamic Penal Code the punishment of wine drinking is 80 lashes.[806]

-Moharebeh (*Resorting to arms in order to frighten people*) is defined as an act of robbery by a group of armed men within the territory of the Islamic state so as to create anarchy under which the property, privacy, safety, dignity, and religious values of

---

[801] *Id*, Art. 127, 129, 130, 131.

[802] *Id*, Art 139.

[803] Holy Quran, Soreh Maedeh, 38 verse.

[804] Islamic Penal Code of Iran, Art 651-667.

[805] Matthew Lippman, Sean McConville, and Mordechai Yerushalmi, *supra* note 730.

[806] Islamic Penal Code of Iran, Art 174.

the people would be violated. The crime is regarded as a war against God and his messenger. There are several alternative punishments, i.e. execution, crucifixion, amputation of hand and foot and exile. Therefore, it is open to judge to pass any one of these sentences which he thinks fit under the circumstances of each case.[807]

b *Organ Retaliation* (Qisas):

Qisas is explained as follows in Article 269 of the Islamic Penal Code: "cutting off bodily organ or its injury if it were to be intentional is subject to retaliation in kind and the wronged party is allowed for retaliation against the criminal based on the prescribed norms and religious judge's decree." Article 271 defines three types of intentional cutting or injury as follows: (a) when the criminal intends to inflict such a cut and/or injury by the commission of a certain act whether that the acts results to inflict such a cut and/or injury; (b) when the criminal intentionally commits an act that somewhat results in a cut and/or injury although this were not intended to cut and/or injure; and (c) when the criminal does not intend to cut or injure an organ, and his act does not effectuate that result, but, due to the advanced age and/or infancy, the act effectuates the severance or injury of organs and it is known to the criminal. But by providing equity conditions in the health of organs, in originality of organs, in the place of injury, the retaliation is not fatal and it is not more injurious than the crime,[808] legislature goal in Iran is to restrict the application of organ retaliation. Therefore judges in majority of cases convert Qisas sentences to that of imprisonment.

c **Discretionary Punishments** (Taazir):

Taazir punishments are the third category of punishments that involve corporal punishment. Islamic Penal Code considered flogging as a discretionary punishment for different crimes as a principle punishment, or as a voluntary principle punishment. In these cases judges can sentence flogging or fine / flogging or imprisonment. As to whether Taazir punishment may exceed the Had punishment, there is a Prophet tradition

---

[807] Abolghasem Gorji, ***Legal Injunctions of the Quran***, pp 186-8, Iran, Tehran: Mizan Publication (2004).

[808] Islamic Penal Code of Iran, Art 272.

which says: "The man who shall inflict scourging, to the amount of punishment in case where Had is not established shall be counted an aggravator."[809] (For more information regarding corporal punishment in Quran refer to chart 5-3).

Chart 5-3 Corporal punishment in the Quran and tradition

Crime category	Punishment in the Quran	Punishment in the tradition
Maiming	Retaliation in kind or monetary restitution	monetary restitution based on authentic tradition
False accusation of unlawful intercourse	Public flogging	Different tradition
Resorting to arms in order to frighten people	Crucifixion or Amputation of alternate hand and foot	Different tradition
Thievery	Amputation of four fingers	Amputation of four fingers based on tradition
Adultery	Public flogging of the two parties involved in adultery	Different tradition
Sodomy	Public flogging	Different tradition
Wine drinking	Public flogging	Different tradition
Lesbianism	Public flogging	Different tradition
False Witness	Public flogging	Different tradition

4   Judicial Story

Some early state courts specifically declared whipping constitutionality permissible. Despite the court decisions, whipping as a mode of punishment has historically been subject to constant attack. During the nineteenth century it fell in to general disuse. Many scholars and jurists apposed its utilization altogether. Others while not entirely opposing it, favored strict limitations on its use. In 1820, for example, Justice Taylor writing an opinion for the North Carolina Supreme court, asserted: "Public

---

[809] Matthew Lippman, Sean McConville, and Mordechai Yerushalmi, *supra* note 730.

corporal punishment for any offense impresses an indelible stigma on the character and ought to be inflicted on those offenses only which are infamous in their nature." In 1851, Justice Lipscomb of the Texas Supreme court went so far as to assert: "Among all nations of civilized man, from the earliest ages, the infliction of strips has been considered more degrading than death itself."

The fact is courts routinely sentenced offenders to be lashed is another reason for believing that the framers of the United States Constitution did not consider corporal punishment to be cruel and unusual punishment. One can surmise that the judges must have believed that whipping punishment was consistent with their new Constitution. In addition to the other evidence of judicially imposed whippings discussed above, there are several reported decisions from which the constitutionality of whipping can be inferred. For example, the Illinois Supreme Court stated in 1930 that "the law is well settled that the record shall affirmatively show the defendant was present in court when sentence was imposed, if there is any corporal punishment administered."[810] Courts often assumed that corporal punishment was constitutional if the defendant's other rights were not violated. Where the issue was not addressed by the courts, the reason for the assumption was presumably because the parties did not raise the issue or that whipping was so commonly accepted that a defendant would not have raised the cruel and unusual defense.[811]

In support of the assertion that corporal punishment was not considered cruel and unusual punishment is that several courts directly addressed the issue and concluded that whippings were not repugnant to the Constitution. In *Foote v. State*[812], a defendant, sentenced to sixty days in jail and seven stripes for beating his wife, challenged the

---

[810] People v. Moran, 174 N.E. 532, 533 (Ill. 1930); see also Ritchey v. People, 43 P. 1026, 1027 (Colo. 1896) (asserting the rule that there will be no bail in cases of corporal punishment); People v. Russell, 91 N.E. 1075 (Ill. 1910) (recognizing that the whipping of thieves is provided for by statute).

[811] Kie v. United States, 27 F. 351, 358 (C.C.D. Or. 1886) (observing that the imposition of corporal punishment was constitutional if the defendant was present during the trial and sentencing proceedings); Ely v. Thompson, 10 Ky. (3 A.K. Marsh) 70, 74 (1820) (holding the imposition of corporal punishment unconstitutional where a statute deprived a defendant of due process of law); Ex parte Deane, 7 F. Cas. 306, 307 (No. 3712 C.C.D.C. 1816) (assuming the constitutionality of a Virginia law that imposed corporal punishment by allowing a town to provide a choice between corporal punishment and the imposition of a fine).

[812] 59 Md. 264, 1883 WL 4110, Md., January 26, 1883.

imposition of whipping as violative of the Eighth Amendment and its counterpart provision in the Maryland Constitution. Although the Maryland court concluded that the Eighth Amendment was not applicable against the state, it analyzed the case under the cruel and unusual punishment clause of the Maryland Constitution. The court held:

> The terms "cruel and unusual pains and penalties," and "cruel or unusual punishment," have been incorporated in each successive Constitution in this State from 1776 to the present time. That the punishment of whipping was not considered a "cruel or unusual punishment," and, therefore, coming within the prohibition of the Constitution, is most conclusively shown by the fact that the punishment by whipping was recognized by the statute law of the State under all these Constitutions, certainly down to the Constitution of 1864.[813]

When, therefore, we find that the people who made this Constitution, and who must be presumed to understand the meaning of the terms they use, have, from the time these words were first incorporated, in 1776 down to 1882, a period of more than a hundred years, through the several successive Legislatures, uniformly held that the punishment of whipping was not included in that class which the Constitution forbids, we should violate the plainest principles of the construction of statutes now to decide otherwise. We have not only the contemporaneous, but the continued, exposition of the meaning of the words in this long course of legislative construction, upheld and continually enforced by the Courts, in the imposition of the punishment.

If authority be wanted for the position we have taken, that whipping is not the cruel or unusual punishment forbidden by the Bill of Rights, it may be found in the decisions of some of the States as well as of the Federal Courts. Thus the Maryland Court of Appeals held that whipping did not violate the cruel and unusual punishment clause of the Maryland Constitution.

In 1824 the Virginia Supreme Court, in ***Aldridge v. Commonwealth***[814], relied on the principle of separation of powers to uphold Virginia's legislation providing for

---

[813] *Id.*

[814] 2 Va.Cas. 447, 4 Va. 447, 1824 WL 1072, Va.Gen.Ct, June Term 1824.

whipping of offenders. Four years later, in ***Commonwealth v. Wyatt***[815], the Virginia Supreme Court held that whipping was "odious, but cannot be said to be *unusual.*"

Several other cases have gone to the highest court of a state on this issue. For example, the Supreme Court of the Territory of New Mexico addressed the issue in ***Garcia v. Territory of New Mexico***[816], where the court sentenced a mule thief to thirty stripes, as provided for by statute. The court stated the following:

All punishment is more or less cruel, and the kind of punishment to be inflicted upon criminals to induce reformation and repress and deter the thief from a repetition of his larcenies has generally been left to the sound discretion of the law-making power.

The word cruel, as used in the amendatory article of the constitution, was no doubt intended to prohibit a resort to the process of torture, resorted to so many centuries as a means of extorting confessions from suspected criminals, under the sanction of the civil law. It was never designed to abridge or limit the selection by the law-making power of such kind of punishment and suppression of crime. If a father, without the charge of cruelty, may administer stripes to his vicious and disobedient child, may not the supreme power of a territory, state, or nation administer the same kind of punishment to its vicious and lawless citizens? However averse the court may be to this mode of punishment, it can not authorize the court in disregarding and annulling the law providing for the punishment of this crime, and, until repealed, it is the duty of the court to enforce it.

In addition, the Tennessee Supreme Court, in ***Cornell v. State***[817], held, in 1881, that corporal punishment could be imposed, but only if sanctioned either by the legislature or "a law or regulation made for the government of the convicts by the county court in due form, at a regular session, or the governing authorities of the corporate town by whom the work-house has been established." The Arkansas Supreme Court reached a

---

[815] 6 Rand. 694, 27 Va. 694, 1828 WL 860, Va.Gen.Ct, November Term 1828.

[816] 1 N.M. 415, 1 Gild. 415, 1869 WL 2421, N.M.Terr., January Term 1869.

[817] 74 Tenn. 624, 1881 WL 4276, 6 Lea 624, Tenn., April Term 1881.

similar conclusion in 1884.[818] In contrast to these decisions, at least two courts stated, in dicta, that the use of the whipping post was cruel. Nevertheless, the weight of the evidence supports the conclusion that the Framers did not consider whipping to be a cruel and unusual mode of punishment.

The most significant state court decisions originated in Delaware. In 1963 the Supreme Court of Delaware issued two opinions directly addressing whether a state may statutorily permit or mandate whipping as a form of punishment.[819] In 1961 Franklin Cannon pled guilty to grand larceny. He was sentenced to three years imprisonment and a whipping of twenty lashes. The sentence was suspended to probation, but it was reinstated after the defendant violated the terms of his probation. He appealed the sentence to the Supreme Court of Delaware. Mr. Cannon challenged the whipping portion of his sentence as violative of the Delaware Constitution and the Eighth Amendment.

The parties and the court agreed that whipping was not considered cruel and unusual at the time of the adoption of the Constitution. Within the context of analyzing the prohibition, under the Delaware Constitution, of cruel punishments, the court concluded that the framers of the Delaware Constitution intended to abolish punishments prohibited in England by the so-called Bill of Rights of England.[820] These were the cruel and barbarous punishments on occasion formerly imposed in England by the Crown. They were punishments considered at the time to be unnecessarily cruel and bordering upon outright torture such as breaking on the wheel, public dissection and the like.

The court concluded that whipping was not per se violative of the Delaware Constitution at the time of its ratification. Implicit in the court's decision was the

---

[818] Werner v. State, 44 Ark. 122, 131 (1884). In *Werner,* the Court held: Corporal punishment by the lash can be inflicted lawfully upon the convicts in the penitentiary for refusal to work, only under a rule or regulation made for that purpose by the board of commissioners; for all questions of discipline are deferred to their discretion by the Legislature, and it follows that the manner of punishment to be inflicted by way of correction must be prescribed by them.

[819] Balser v. State, 195 A.2d 757 (Del. 1963); State v. Cannon, 190 A.2d 514 (Del. 1963).

[820] *Id.*

extension of this reasoning to the Eighth Amendment. This extension, however, did not conclude the court's inquiry.[821]

Later that same year, the Delaware Supreme Court reaffirmed the rationale of ***State v. Cannon***[822] in ***Balser v. State***[823]. In *Balser,* a defendant convicted of robbery challenged his sentence to twenty lashes as being constitutionally repugnant upon the same theories as were asserted by the defendant in *State v. Cannon.* The court summarily disposed of the issue, referring to its decision in *State v. Cannon.* Again, however, the whipping did not take place. The court reversed the sentence on other grounds, ordered a resentencing, and the Governor of the State of Delaware removed the whipping portion of the sentence through a commutation of the sentence.

Corporal punishment has never been held by United States courts per se to violate the Eight Amendment. Courts routinely sentenced offenders to be whipped in early America. Courts that have considered whether whipping is cruel and unusual punishment have concluded that it is not. Finally, this conclusion is reinforced by the fact that whipping continued well beyond the lives of the Framers of the Constitution.[824] The conclusion that whipping was not considered cruel and unusual at the time of the adoption of the Eighth Amendment does not end the constitutional inquiry.

Reviewing a case in Iran: Mohsen Mofidi had been convicted of charges including possession of a medicine containing alcohol, consuming alcohol in the early 1980s, possession of a television satellite dish, and aiding and abetting his sister's "corruption" in having boyfriends. He was sentenced to 80 lashes, to be carried out on completion of a four-month prison sentence. On February 11th, the 25th anniversary of the revolution in Iran, the remainder of his prison sentence was suspended, and the flogging was scheduled to take place on the day of his release. It is reported that Mofidi was kept in extremely poor conditions at Qasr prison.

---

[821] *Id.*

[822] State v. Cannon, 190 A.2d 514 (Del. 1963).

[823] 7 Storey 206, 57 Del. 206, 195 A.2d 757, Del.Supr, November 27, 1963.

[824] Daniel Hall, *supra* note 716.

Judicial corporal punishments in Iran are cruel and unusual per se and unlawful because they entail key elements of torture or ill-treatment, including the deliberate infliction of severe pain and suffering as a punishment. The UN Human Rights Committee has stated that the prohibition of torture and ill-treatment under the International Covenant on Civil and Political Rights "must extend to corporal punishment."[825] Amnesty International opposes the punishment of flogging and has long called on the Iranian authorities to cease this practice.[826] Amnesty International continues to urge the government to conduct an immediate investigation into the death of Mohsen Mofidi and to make the findings public.

Therefore, it will ordinarily be a cumulative: If a punishment is unusually severe, if there is a strong probability that it is inflicted arbitrarily, if it is substantially rejected by contemporary society, and if there is no reason to believe that it serves any penal purpose more effectively than some less severe punishment, then the continued infliction of that punishment violates the command of the Clause that the State may not inflict inhuman and uncivilized punishments upon those convicted of crimes.

IV *Cruel & Unusual Due to the Doctrine of Proportionality*

1   Proportionality Analysis

Provisions against cruel and unusual punishment are aimed primarily at the kind of punishment imposed, not its degree. Nevertheless, where the degree of a sentence imposed on one convicted of crime is so disproportionate to the offense committed as to shock the moral sense of the community, the punishment is prohibited. In determining whether the degree offends a prohibition against cruel and unusual punishment, the courts will look to such matters as the nature of the offense, the character of the offender, the penalties imposed in the jurisdiction for other offenses, and the penalties imposed in other jurisdictions for the same offense.

The Proportionality Doctrine states, in part, that the Cruel and Unusual Punishment Clause requires some measure of proportionality in criminal cases between

---

[825] See www.ohchr.org/english/bodies/hrc.

[826] See www.amnesty.org.

the punishment imposed and the offense committed. This proportionality principle is not symmetrical. That is, proportionality doctrine forbids only those punishments that are disproportionately severe, not those that are disproportionately lenient.

There are three objective criteria from prior cases for resolving claims of disproportionality: (1) "the gravity of the offense compared to the severity of the penalty", (2) "the sentence imposed for commission of the same crime in other jurisdictions," and (3) "the sentence imposed upon other criminals in the same jurisdiction".[827]

Under Iran's law the infliction of punishment should be just and commensurate with the crime committed. Here justice is done only when the offender is appropriately punished without excess. It is an important aspect of Islamic law of crimes that whatever punishment is to be meted out to or inflicted on the offender for committing the crime should be proportionate to the harm inflicted by him without any excess.[828] For example in the case of False accusation of unlawful intercourse (Qadhf), anyone who commits it, according to the Holy Quran, is punished with 80 lashes.[829] It means if 80 lashes is awarded for this offence, the punishment is commensurate or proportionate to the harm inflicted. But if, the punishment awarded is 100 lashes or tongue removal then it is not proportionate to the harm inflicted. When punishment is inflicted in excess according to Quranic verses, this means transgressing beyond the limits set by God.[830]

Wisdom behind the amputation of the hand under Islamic law for the theft of property worth 1.4 Dinar or above is intended to provide an effective means of protecting people's property. The underlying reasoning the graver the punishment the more effective it is. The question remains whether amputating a hand for a property worth 1.4 Dinar can be held to compare with 500 Dinar for loss of a hand as retribution. It is not comparable to say one should lose his hand for stealing a property worth 1.4 Dinar as

---

[827] Stephen Parr, *supra* note 500.

[828] Mohammadreza Zafari, ***Origins of Criminal Justice in Islamic Law***, Tehran, Iran: Amirkabir Publication (1997) [In Farsi].

[829] Holy Quran, Soreh Noor, 4 verse.

[830] Yunesa Bambale, ***Crimes and Punishments under Islamic law***, p 8, Malthouse Press Limited, (2003).

equivalent to 500 Dinars as a retribution for the loss of a hand so damaged. If there is anything that the comparison tends to show, it is that they both provide protection to property and human life. In short, the 1.4 Dinar for cutting the hand and 500 Dinars as the Qisas for the loss of a hand are made completely for different purposes.

For example, the thief who steals food is not subject to amputation. Perhaps this could be extended to the thief who, while not literally starving, lives in poverty in a society where the majority of the wealth is concentrated in the hands of a privileged minority. Accounts could also be taken of psychological disorders, such as compulsive theft or lying, before deciding that Hodoud penalties were called for. The option of Taazir punishments and civil remedies is not foreclosed. The mentally disabled are exempt from responsibility for violating these laws. Since medical research shows alcoholism is a disease, punishment for the crime of drinking should be suspended conditioned on the convict seeking treatment for his illness. Likewise, children are not to receive the Hodoud penalties. Some Islamic law schools rule that puberty begins as young as age nine. Modern psychology, however, demonstrates that puberty itself is not the onset of adulthood, but an intermediate phase in human development. Therefore, it is plausible to decide that these penalties are only applicable to adults, not just inapplicable to children. This could spare teenagers who violate the law from the most severe penalties.[831]

The United States Supreme Court explained that the Founders understood the Cruel and Unusual Punishment Clause primarily as a protection against barbarous punishments such as whippings and ear removal. The punishment clause was intended to encompass new situations and contexts that the Framers could not have foreseen. "A principle, to be vital, must be capable of wider application than the mischief which gave it birth." As part of its analysis, the Court compared the punishment of *cadena temporal* with punishments for other crimes in the same jurisdiction and with the punishments for forgery in other jurisdictions. [832] This process of comparing sentences has become an integral part of current Supreme Court proportionality analysis.

---

[831] Edna Lewicki, *Need Word's Collide: The Hudad Crimes of Islamic Law and International Human Rights*, 13 NYILR 43 (2000).

[832] Drew Page, *Cruel and Unusual Punishment and Sodomy Statutes: the Breakdown of the Soldem v. Helm*, 56 U. Chi. L. Rev. 367 (1989).

The United States Supreme Court has not had occasion to apply these principles to statutorily authorized and judicially imposed whippings of criminal offenders as punishment for criminal conduct.

2 When is Whipping Appropriate?

For what crimes and what offenders is whipping appropriate? Proportionality analysis is fact-sensitive. The nature of a crime, the penological objectives underlying its punishment, and the particular facts of each case will determine whether a punishment is too severe. Therefore, it is not possible to draw generalized conclusions concerning the applicability of whipping under proportionality analysis. Consider the long-standing history of whipping in the United States, and Iran especially the fact that it continued well into the twenty first century should be considered. Presumably, evidence of jurisdictions that have considered, or are considering, whipping as a form of punishment would be taken into account. Otherwise, no jurisdiction could ever become the first of possibly many adopting jurisdictions.

We can conclude that disproportionality of punishment is a major flaw in Iran's criminal justice system. Otherwise this issue is arguable because flogging is not inherently cruel and inhumane. If properly regulated and proportionately imposed, flogging is equally as valid as paddling or capital punishment. Iran can begin to conform to international human rights standards without abolishing flogging. Although flogging is disproportionate penalty for property crimes such as vandalism and drug possession, it is probably proportionate for crimes against the person, including assault, rape, and domestic violence. One of most significant problems with flogging is that it is disproportionate punishment for property crimes. By restricting flogging to violent crimes against the person, Iran will retain this traditional punishment without further alienating the international community. International standards prohibit torture and ill-treatment, domestic law can not consider whipping appropriate even for applying flogging in crimes against the person.

3 Punishment Objectives v. Contemporary Standards

A Contemporary Standards of Decency

The evolving standards of decency that mark the progress of a maturing society are final resort for applying cruel and unusual punishment definition on corporal punishment statutes. An important reason why bodily punishment is thought of with repugnance is that they have been historically linked to the process of torture.

In many cases two terms are synonymous, often what one individual would call a just form of punishment another would term torture. In many vases the actual punishment which society imposed was preceded by torture.

Although some scholars believe corporal punishment may appear to be a barbaric solution to the problems of a civilized society, but some believe it is in fact a reasonable, rational alternative to the systemic prison overcrowding and rampant recidivism that are part of our current approach to crime and criminals.

The Supreme Court has held that the Eighth Amendment not only precludes the government from inflicting punishments believed by the Framers to be cruel and unusual but it also precludes punishments that are inconsistent with contemporary values. The Eighth Amendment is not "bound by the sparing humanitarian concessions of our forebears." Hence, the Court has taken a dual-interpretative position. In one sense, the Court has adopted an originalist point of view by holding that punishments intended by the Framers to be forbidden continue to be forbidden today. This appears to be true even if a punishment thought to be barbaric in 1791 were to become popular today. In a second sense, the Court has taken a progressive view in examining the Eighth Amendment in light of contemporary values and penological evidence. Punishment that transgresses today's "'broad and idealistic concepts of dignity, civilized standards, humanity, and decency'" offends the Eighth Amendment. Therefore, the government is prohibited from imposing a penalty that is inconsistent with "'the dignity of man.'" [833]

---

[833] Stephen Parr, *supra note* 500.

How does a reviewing court determine society's contemporary values? The court defers to the decisions of the people's representatives. The ***State v. Cannon*** [834] court stated the following:

What better way is there for the people to express an enlightened attitude toward the punishment of crime than through their elected representatives, the members of the General Assembly who, indeed, hold their office for the very purpose of expressing the will and beliefs of the people who elected them.

The court reasoned that the Delaware Legislature deserved deference in this context because it had historically responded to public opinion concerning punishments, as evinced by its abolition of the use of the pillory, drawing and quartering, death by burning, and other forms of punishment. The court, noting that Great Britain did not abolish whipping until 1948 and that Canada maintained whipping as a punishment until 1957, stated, "It does not seem to us that a punishment so recently in use in the country that leads the world in the administration of justice may be held to be a barbarity that, as a matter of constitutional law, must be deemed cruel and unusual."[835] The court also believed it was important that in no state had whipping been abolished by judicial decree; rather, it had been a legislative decision in every instance. Accordingly, the court held that whipping did not violate the state constitution or the Eighth Amendment. The court remanded the case to the trial court with instructions to conduct a hearing as to whether the defendant was mentally fit to receive the lashes. On remand the trial judge remitted the whipping portion of the sentence without a hearing.[836]

The debate over the application of the cruel and unusual punishment to the practice of corporal punishment includes that the words "cruel," "unusual," and "punishment" have changed their meanings. The debate surrounds whether the application of the Cruel and Unusual Punishments should be tied to perceptions of values and customs contemporaneous with its enactment, or whether that the principle must ever reflect current, evolving, presumably progressive, values.

---

[834] State v. Cannon, 190 A.2d 514, 514-15 (Del. 1963).

[835] *Id.*

[836] *Id.*

When the Delaware court invited the state legislature to abolish the punishment of whipping as inconsistent with contemporary mores (something the legislature did in 1973). And even in the harsh climate of the late 1980s, as firm as believer as Justice Scalia admitted that flogging had become too uncomfortable a practice not to be banned Nevertheless, it remarkable how difficult American lawyers have found it to uncover some clear argument against the practice of flogging, even at the height of the era of prison reform.[837] How whipping as a formal punishment that is not deeply rooted in Iran's cultural and background can be applied.

Similarly amputation for theft and brigandage are not punishments in every civilized society. In fact, for the state to tolerate them would run afoul of human rights norms which declare that no one should be deprived of his property without due process of law.

Thus, because personal dignity and humanity are highly valued in current societies, then punishments that violate these values would have to be deemed problematic and in contrast to the idealism embodied in the ban on cruel and unusual punishment.

B Penological Objectives

The father of modern criminology was ***Cesare Beccaria***, who, in 1764, wrote a famous treatise called on crimes and punishments. He pointed an accusing finger at the judges of his days because he said; their unbridled direction had led to the horrendous punishments of the 18th century: drawing and quartering, breaking on the wheel, and many other terrible punishments. Beccaria believed that the mind of a criminal needed to be changed and could be changed by punishing it rather than the body.[838] Unfortunately, systematic imposition of psychic punishments is impossible; mental punishment is

---

[837] James Whitman, *supra* note 145, p 189-190.

[838] Cesare Beccaria, On Crimes and Punishments, for a look at what is perhaps the first published opinion regarding the use of mental rather than physical punishment in a modernizing society. Note that Beccaria did arguably support corporal punishment at an early point in his career, but he shifted to a belief that imprisonment for life, with hard labor, was the best punishment available to civilized man.

possible only indirectly by the professional approach, so prison became the chosen alternative.

As to the supporting by legitimate penological purposes, **rehabilitation**, **deterrence**, **incapacitation**, and **retribution** are legitimate penological objectives. Whipping could potentially serve retribution, rehabilitation, and deterrence objectives; however, the evidence concerning whether whipping is an effective form of specific deterrence is inconclusive. Although the experts may disagree as to the value of corporal punishment in deterring crime, the same debate exists in regard to imprisonment and other forms of popular punishment. It is reasonable to believe that whipping will be as successful in preventing crime as imprisonment. Intuitively, however, it is easy to believe that whipping could serve as an effective general deterrent. Although rehabilitation and deterrence are the most popular penal objectives today, a punishment is also valid if it is an effective form of retribution. Undoubtedly, whipping can satisfy retribution objectives.[839]

Will corporal punishment *deter*?

Only two substantial studies on corporal punishment in criminal justice have been conducted. They were conducted in Delaware and England roughly forty years ago. The Delaware study was conducted by Professor Robert Caldwell in 1947, and published in his interesting book Red Hannah: Delaware whipping post. As I mentioned earlier Delaware was the last state in the United States to abolish whipping as a criminal punishment. Professor Caldwell compared the rate of the re-committal of 1- those criminals sentenced to whipping and who were not whipped, with 2- those criminals who were sentenced to whipping and who were whipped. On the basis of his findings, Calswell concluded that whipping should be abolished.[840]

The British research in to whipping displayed a similar bias. The report of the committee on corporal punishment was published by the Home Office in March 1938. Its conclusion was: "We are not satisfied that corporal punishment has that exceptionally effective influence as a deterrent which is usually claimed for it by those who advocate its use as a penalty… ." Social scientists conclusions were invariably that corporal

---

[839] *Id.*

[840] Robert Graham Caldwell, *supra* note 596.

punishment should be abolished because it could not be demonstrated to have a deterrent effect.[841]

Legislation enacting the punishment of whipping must be artfully drawn. Legislation providing for whipping that is intended to cause pain in excess of what is necessary to achieve the desired deterrence is unlawful. Accordingly, many of the early whippings in United States history would not be permissible today. For example, in 1715 Maryland adulterers were fined money and tobacco and were "whipped upon his or their bare bodies till the blood do appear, so many stripes (not exceeding thirty-nine) as the justices before whom such conviction shall be, shall adjudge." Similarly, canings, such as those administered to Michael Fay, would not meet Eighth Amendment standards because they often draw blood and cause offenders to lose consciousness.[842]

Although the effectiveness of whipping as a specific deterrent is unclear and additional research is necessary, it would be reasonable for a legislature to determine that retribution and general deterrence would be served. The fact that whipping is used in both the American home and school can be relied upon by a legislature as evidence of its value. The apparent success of whipping as a deterrent in other nations can also be used. Of course, criminal offenders are different than children, and the cultural differences between nations may make these analogies faulty. But the constitutional inquiry is limited to determining whether the decision to whip was made recklessly or maliciously. If, after whipping has been tried and tested the penological data evinces that it is not successful in achieving any one of the recognized penological objectives, and then the continuation of the punishment would be unnecessary. Accordingly, it is necessary to examine the punishment objectives that whipping may achieve.

As previously stated, ***retribution*** is a valid objective. In *Gregg v. Georgia*[843], the Court recognized retribution as a sound penological objective, and, in *Spaziano v. Florida*[844], the Court stated that "retribution is an element of all punishments society

---

[841] Graeme Newman, *supra* note 195, pp 127-136.

[842] *Id.*

[843] 424 U.S. 904, 96 S.Ct. 1095 (Mem), 47 L.Ed.2d 308, U.S.Ga., February 23, 1976 (NO. 74 6257).

imposes." But what is retribution? Retribution can be troublesome because it has vengeance at its core. It can be defined as "a disguised form of vengeance." Not all commentators assume that vengeance is bad. James F. Stephen claimed that the criminal law stands to the passion of revenge in much the same relation as marriage to sexual appetite.[845] Stephen assumed that by channeling vengeance through an organized justice system, unruly violence, which can be highly destructive, will be thwarted.[846] In this sense, the retribution rationale is validated. But what if society's passions are heightened due to a particularly heinous crime? Could the punishments intended to be prohibited by the cruel and unusual definition be practiced? Yes. Therefore, defining retribution as satisfying the public's need for revenge is not adequate. It may play a part, but it is not sufficiently limiting.

The nature of the crime and the resulting injuries and damages to individuals and the public will also be factors in determining the limits of retributive punishment. In *Tison v. Arizona*[847], the Court held that "the heart of the retribution rationale is that a criminal sentence must be directly related to the personal culpability of the criminal offender." True, this standard is vague, and the determination of whether a sentence serves rehabilitation, incapacitation, or deterrence objectives is more precise. But, few punishments will be based solely on retribution, and, when one is, the *Tison* standard provides courts with the discretion necessary to prevent cruelty. It is a safety net.

What more can retribution is? In previous times, punishment was thought to be for the benefit of the offender. It had religious significance and a secular purpose. Offenders "paid" their debt to society. David Starkweather noted that '"criminal behavior constitute[s] a violation of the moral or natural order . . . and, having offended that order, require[s] payment of some kind.' Therefore, a criminal is punished because he or she 'deserves' it.[848] This justification for punishment is appropriately called the principle of

---

[844] 516 U.S. 1053, 116 S.Ct. 722 (Mem), 133 L.Ed.2d 674, 64 USLW 3466, U.S.Fla., January 08, 1996 (NO. 95-6471).

[845] James F Stephen, *History of the Criminal Law of England (Making of the British Legal System)*, Routledge/Thoemmes P; 1 edition (December 4, 1996).

[846] *Id.*

[847] 454 U.S. 960, 102 S.Ct. 499 (Mem), 70 L.Ed.2d 376, U.S., November 02, 1981 (NO. 81-5634).

'just deserts.'" In the theory of "just deserts," both the offender and society benefit from the punishment. This latter objective is the one most thought of today--just deserts. So, maybe the limit of retributive justice is the amount of punishment necessary for an offender to make amends.

Can corporal punishment be administered without *humiliating* the offender? Most certainly it can. Because that corporal punishment has been used for centuries in many countries as an aid to, or a replacement for imprisonment by using it here, we could save money that is spent on prisons to achieve other social goals. By making the punishment public, we can add general and specific deterrent effects to the retributive effects already established. And by coupling the corporal punishment and shaming[849] to successfully reintegrate the offender into society. This will strengthen the long term specific deterrent effect on the individual and, eventually, the general deterrent effect on society as a whole. Corporal punishment would return the criminal justice system to its proper place as a small part of the system to promote the general welfare. And, not only could we begin to combat the crime problem of today, we could see more a profound reduction in youthful offenders and a greater impact on the generations to follow.[850]

Therefore, the infliction of violent punishment upon violent offender was entirely defensible from the point of view the ethics of retributive justice. While the infliction of economic punishments for economic crimes is the logical punishment from

---

[848] See David A. Starkweather, *Note, The Retributive Theory of "Just Deserts" and Victim Participation in Plea Bargaining,* 67 Ind. L.J. 853, 854-55 (1992).

[849] It is too early to tell how effective shame punishments will be in the long run. They have already had an enormous impact on offenders throughout the nation, including those in Kansas. It will be up to the lawmakers and courts to decide whether this reemerging form of punishment will continue to have a positive impact upon American jurisprudence. For certain crimes, such as drunk driving and prostitution solicitation, shame penalties are effective as a punishment as well as a deterrent. Yearning for social accountability, Judge Poe stated, unchastised wrongdoing and country club prisons, complete with color televisions and weight rooms, have left us a society replete with people who don't believe they ever will be held accountable for their actions. If they did, the streets of the United States would be safer in 1997 than they were in 1776. But they aren't. If we are to change America's criminals, it is time the punishment publicly fit the crime. Let those who would beat their wives, steal their neighbor's property and abuse children feel the sting of community intolerance, hear their names on our lips and pay the price in view of the public. Shame on them or shame on us.

[850] Whitney Wiedeman, *supra* note 784.

the point of view of retribution, for a number of practical and moral reasons this is not defensible, and that violent punishments are the most sensible solution.

The imprisonment as an *incapacitative* sanction may entail social costs that are not present with corporal punishment. This argument is based on two assumptions. First, some crimes may involve an undeterrable organ--that is, the undeterred bodily means to affecting a crime--only. Second, some corporal punishment may be used to incapacitate the particular organ temporarily.

As is widely known, corporal punishment has had a much longer history than imprisonment. Indeed, "eye for eye, tooth for tooth, hand for hand, foot for foot"[851] has been a familiar theme in both Christian and non-Christian societies. Various types of capital punishment--such as burning, strangulation, and beheading--represented the most severe forms of corporal punishment. Whipping, caning, castration, and dismembering of limbs were less damaging corporal punishments. We have to know why these corporal punishments, relative to imprisonment, are no longer popular--their social costs increased as civilization further developed. Capital punishment was not exercised for all crimes; instead, flogging and mutilation were adopted for some. Why? The old retributive theory or the modern economic theory of marginal deterrence can provide an answer; however, incapacitation as an alternative explanation will be emphasized here.[852]

Capital punishment and castration were alternatives used to stop adultery and rape, and a rational wealth-maximizing emperor would refrain from capital punishment so that the offender could still work and pay taxes. Thus, optimal incapacitation implies that both adulterers and rapists should be castrated but not beheaded. After castration was abolished in China, capital punishment was used to punish those who were convicted for the more serious cases of adultery and rape. In contrast, after the abolition of mutilation in 167 B.C., convicts who originally would have been mutilated were punished by flogging. Frequently, convicts received so many strokes that they were in effect beaten to death. As a result, many people, including informed intellectuals, considered both changes in criminal punishment (the abolition of castration and mutilation) to be cruel.

---

[851] Bible, Exod. 21:24.

[852] Whitney Wiedeman, *supra* note 784.

Therefore some scholars found that imprisonment is not optimal and that corporal punishment--for example, whipping, caning, castration, and other forms of punishment--can be optimal incapacitative measures against certain undeterrable criminal acts. The temporary incapacitation of the particular organ at fault would incur less social cost, compared to imprisonment or mutilation. With recent advances in biological, medical, and other technologies, it is not impossible to develop new ways to temporarily incapacitate some organs by way of injection or electric shock without creating long-term side effects. (Please refer to chart 5-4).

Chart 5-4 AN EXTENDED ANALYTICAL STRUCTURE OF OPTIMAL INCAPACITATION: EXAMPLES OF PUNISHMENT[853]

EXTENT OF BODILY INVOLVEMENT	DURATION OF THE PROPENSITY TO COMMIT AN OFFENSE	
	Temporary	Permanent
Whole body	Term imprisonment	Life imprisonment
		Capital punishment
Organ	Whipping	Mutilation
	Electric caning	Castration

Source: Steven S. Kan, *Corporal Punishments and Optimal Incapacitation*, 25 J. Legal Stud. 121 (January, 1996).

In sum, by using a utilitarian analysis of corporal punishment, I concluded that a reform of criminal punishment need not revert to bloody corporal punishment, without

---

[853] Table 1 presents an analytical structure for the determination of optimal incapacitative sanctions. Two characteristics of importance, namely the duration of the propensity to commit an offense and the extent of undeterred bodily involvement, are identified in the table. For illustrative purposes, the column heads indicate the permanent and temporary duration of the propensity to offend, while bodily involvement in effecting an offense, by organ or the entire body, is presented in the stub column. Optimal incapacitative punishments for the four resulting cases are shown. Let us first look at the cases in which the completion of an offense requires a deliberate coordination of the whole body. If the propensity to commit an offense is permanent, then life imprisonment or capital punishment is optimal, depending on which incurs the smaller social cost. If, however, the propensity to commit an offense is only temporary, then a corresponding length of imprisonment is optimal.

consideration of rehabilitation goal. Instead, retribution, deterrence, incapacitation, and rehabilitation are all legitimate objectives and adoption of any one penological theory is not possible. Also if the objective of a punishment is only to inflict pain or to rob the offender of his humanity, the punishment is improper per se because it is not founded upon a sound penological purpose.

Conclusion

Tracing the historical development of the cruel and unusual punishment concept has proven a long, involved, and at times complex process. This concept has become more and more important with the passing of each decade after the twentieth century.

Punishment is universal feature of contemporary societies. It would be a mistake to view cruel and unusual punishment as uniform response to particular types of misconduct. In fact how crimes are defined and their legal treatment reflects the prevailing social, cultural, political, economic, and historical conditions of a society at any given point in time. In some contexts punishment may be considerable normatively acceptable in some cultures. Even within the same country over time, the legal acceptance of particular punishments changes. For instance drug offenses in the United States were punishable by capital crime or capital crimes for adultery and sodomy after Islamic revolution in Iran.

A major difficulty is how to distinguish between cruel and unusual punishment in the United States and Iran. The most dramatic differences are related to the proportionality doctrine. Penal proportionality based on religious proportionality in Iran is completely different from the secular proportionality in the United States. For example fornication between non-Muslim man and Muslim woman would not pass secular proportionality doctrine. In the United States criminalizing sexual conduct, is related to harm caused for the society rather than virtue of Muslims.

Hanging as an execution method is not in practice in United States, however Iran routinely hangs capital offenders. This profound clash of attitudes was not the result of some difference in degree of civilization. It was the result of differences in traditions of status.

This book is about two societies on both sides of the world. I do not mean to suggest these societies should adapt uniform aspects of penal system. There is no reason to expect that other societies will all take the same turns. There is nothing inevitable about either the Iranian or American path. Not all societies necessarily evolve countries with mild punishments practices. This claim would be false as degradation process and practice of harsh punishments in contemporary Iran demonstrates.

In the first chapter of my book, I traced the development of the norm prohibiting cruel and unusual punishment and its relationship to different kinds and degree of punishments in general. The prohibition of cruel and unusual punishment for the first time had been expressed as early as 1641 in the Massachusetts Body of Liberties, and reiterated in such instruments as the English Bill of Rights of 1689, the French Declaration des droits de l'homme et du citoyen of 1789, and the American Bill of Rights. Internationally the first time this prohibition was included in the Universal Declaration of Human Rights in 1948. As the decades and centuries wore on, the notion that the "cruel and unusual" phrase restricted the degree of punishment was deemphasized. Emphasis was placed on the idea that the phrase restricted the mode of punishment. Many scholars and jurists believed that the cruel and unusual punishment inhibition restricted only certain modes of punishment. After years finally the idea of the prohibition restricted the degree and excessive punishments as well as modes of punishment. Therefore imposition of disproportionate sentences is forbidden in violation of cruel and unusual punishment.

The second chapter examined the death penalty as cruel and unusual per se. In recent years a frontal assault has been launched on the death penalty. The abolitionists and retentionists have been locked in a heated debate over whether the evolving standards of decency have now reached the point where the death penalty is per se prohibited under cruel and unusual definition. When the drafters of the Universal declaration of Human Rights first declared the prohibition of cruel, inhuman, and degrading treatment and punishment in 1948, nobody felt that the capital punishment came within the scope of that norm. Thus the law is in transition. Specialized treaties now exist that supports abolition of death penalty. It is too early to say that capital punishment is deemed contrary to customary international human rights law.

In the third chapter I examined execution methods in detail. Effort was devoted to an examination of various methods from hanging, stoning and lethal injection. Early acceptance of the death penalty focused on the mode of infliction of capital punishment. As for the methods of execution, there seems to be an important element of cultural relativism. Since a pattern is present, one of a constant if ephemeral search for a technique of killing that is free of suffering, humiliation and mutilation.

Failing to eliminate cruel and unusual methods of imposing the death penalty, abolitionists then challenged the death penalty as excessive, as described in chapter four, for non-murder crimes. Later, cruel punishment came to include notions relating to the humanity of the process itself. Even a penalty that was felt to be proportionate to the crime might still be cruel and unusual. This modern view has come to dominate judicial thinking on the nature cruel and unusual punishment.

Corporal punishments were examined in chapter 5. Today some methods of corporal punishment exist in statutes in Iran and United States. Although the United States Supreme Court has officially upheld corporal punishment, many states have outlawed it by statute. But the question about cruelty is ambiguous. In the twenty first century there are partial voices in Iran and United States. Compared with prison, it is difficult to see how corporal punishment is cruel. We must distinguish carefully among corporal punishments all corporal punishments are certainly not the same. Biased voices believe that if corporal punishment can be shown not to cause any lasting damage to the body, expect that its hurts then, how we can conclude that this punishment is cruel. In spite of its barbarous nature, corporal punishment proponents at least want to limit its imposition in the following ways:

- Acute corporal punishment should be introduced to fill the gap between the severe punishment of prison and non-punishment of probation.

- For the majority of property crimes, the preferred corporal punishment is that of electric shock because it can be scientifically controlled and calibrated. Shock is less violent in its application when compared with other corporal punishment such as whipping.

- For violent crimes in which the victim was terrified and humiliated and for which a local community dose not wish to incarcerate, a violent corporal punishment should be considered, such as whipping. In these cases, humiliation on the offender is seen as justifiably deserved.

A harsh penal system long on degradation and short on mercy without considering the canon law led us to conclude that may be punishment is the way we want. If not there is certainly nothing to stop us from trying to overcome the traditions that have brought us to this point. In the United States in contrast to Iran the abolition movement towards cruel and unusual punishment has been essentially religious.

The change in the penal systems of Iran and United States carefully by considering International law should bring about real change in punishments much grander cultural traditions. Punishment is not simply a legal administrative entity but also "an expression of state power, a statement of collective morality, a vehicle for emotional expression, an economically conditioned social policy, an embodiment of current sensibilities, and a set of symbols which display a cultural ethos and help create a social identity."[854]

The norm prohibiting cruel and unusual punishment is unique, because its interpretation is so closely related to public attitudes. What we really need to reestablish is the policy of punishment itself. It would be an exaggeration to suggest that mild punishment is coming soon in Iran or United States. Hopefully authorities will continue to accept responsibility of policing penal systems where conditions reach subhuman levels.

The most severe punishment of the unsuccessful never deters the successful from repeating his crime, or even the potential miscreant from becoming a criminal. When the methods of punishment employed by the state are so efficient and certain that anyone thinking of committing a criminal offense is well aware that detection and consequent punishment are almost inevitable, the conquest of crime will be well on the way to accomplishment, but not before.

This book is a comparative analysis about the cruel and unusual punishment, but it is also concerned deeply with human rights. Never before has law evolved and developed between national and international tribunals wrestling with similar facts and essentially identical norms.

---

[854] David Garland, ***Punishment and Modern Society: A Study in Social Theory***, p 287, Oxford: Clarendon Press (1990).

Although international law consistently prohibits torture and cruel, inhumane, or degrading punishment, the question remains what kind or degree of punishment fits in that category of punishment. The governing human rights treaties which define the concept reflect Western standards of just punishment. Nevertheless, in Iran, as well as in a number of other countries, corporal punishment is considered a legitimate form of deterrence by legal authorities and public.

One final point, the criminal sanction is indispensable; we could not, now or in the foreseeable future, get along without it. Yet we often resort to it in far too indiscriminate a way, thereby weakening some of the important bases upon which its efficacy rests and threatening social values that transcend the prevention of crime. In spite of difficulties for the abolition of cruel and unusual punishment, there are solutions to limit its application:

1. The role of the legislature in the interpretation of cruel and unusual punishment provides guidance that is helpful in determining the subjective components of the concept. For example, judges in one country may frequently invoke legislative patterns in other countries as evidence that legislation in their country is out of step with evolving standards of decency. Therefore trends in international law and comparative studies would help to abolish of harsh punishments.

2. The Executive is also one of the features of legal systems that despite legislation would be helpful. The executive refuses to authorize the imposition of cruel and unusual punishment. Many countries have not abolished capital punishment, they still have capital crimes in their law but it is no longer carried out.

3. The role of juries and judges in sentencing is crucial to maintaining a link between contemporary community values and the penal system. Except for mandatory harsh punishments, it may further reduce the imposition of cruel and unusual punishments.

Table of Cases

Akron v. Rowland, 67 Ohio St. 3d 374, 1993-Ohio-222, 618 N.E.2d 138 (1993).

Aldridge v. Commonwealth, 2 Va.Cas. 447, 4 Va. 447, 1824 WL 1072, Va.Gen.Ct, June Term 1824.

Atkins v. Virginia, 536 U.S. 304, 311-12 (2002).

Beard v. State, 262 Ind. 643, 323 N.E.2d 216 (1975).

Boyde v. California, 494 U.S. 370, 400 (1990).

Branch v. Texas, 403 U.S. 952 (1971).

Brennan v. State, 754 So.2d 1(Fla.1999).

Buell v. Mitchell, 274 F.3d 337 (6th Cir. 2001).

Burger v. Kemp, 483 U.S. 776, 107 S.Ct. 3114 (1987).

Campbell & Cosans v. United Kingdom, 48 Eur. Ct. H.R. (ser. A) (1982).

Campbell v. Wood, 18 F.3d 662 (9th Cir.1994).

Coker v. Georgia, 433 U.S. 584, 592 (1977)

Commonwealth v. Wyatt, 6 Rand. 694, 27 Va. 694, 1828 WL 860, Va.Gen.Ct, November Term 1828.

Cornell v. State, 74 Tenn. 624, 1881 WL 4276, 6 Lea 624, Tenn., April Term 1881.

Edding v. Oklahoma, 455 U.S. 104, 102 S.Ct. 869 (1982).

Furman v. Georgia, 408 U.S. 238, 377 (1972).

Graham v. West Virginia, 224 U.S. 616 (1912).

Gregg v. Georgia, 428 U.S. 153, 183 (1976).

Hudson v. McMillian, 503 U.S. 1, 28 (1992).

Hunt v. Smith, 856 F.Supp. 251 (D.Md. 1994).

In re Kemmler, 136 U.S. 436 (1890).

Ireland v. United Kingdom, 25 Eur. Ct. H.R. (ser. A) at 66 (1978).

Jackson v. State, 516 So. 2d 726, 738 (Ala. Crim. App. 1985).

Jurek v. Texas 428 U.S. 262 (1976).

McDonald v. Massachusetts, 180 U.S. 311 (1901).

Moore v. Missouri, 159 U.S. 673 (1895).

Papachristou v. City of Jacksonville, 405 U.S. 156, 92 S. Ct. 839, 31 L. Ed. 2d 110 (1972).

Penry v. Lynaugh, 492 U.S. 302 (1989).

People v. Ferguson, 60 Mich. App. 302, 230 N.W.2d 406 (1975).

People v. Gilmore, 37 A.D.2d 912, 325 N.Y.S.2d 455 (4th Dep't 1971).

People v. Weger, 251 Cal. App. 2d 584, 59 Cal. Rptr. 661 (2d Dist. 1967).

Powell v. State of Tex., 392 U.S. 514, 88 S. Ct. 2145, 20 L. Ed. 2d 1254 (1968).

Proffitt v. Florida 428 U.S. 242 (1976).

Resweber, 329 U.S. 459, 463, 67 S.Ct. 2159, 2163 (1985).

Robinson v. Caalifornia, 370 U.S. 660, 82 S. Ct. 1417, 8 L. Ed. 2d 758 (1962).

Roper v. Simmons, 540 U.S. 1160, 1160 (2004).

Solem v. Helm, 463 U.S. 277, 291-92 (1983).

Stanford v. Kentucky, 492 U.S. 361, 369 (1989).

State v. Cannon, State v. Cannon, 190 A.2d 514 (Del. 1963).

State v. Farrow, 118 N.H. 296, 386 A.2d 808 (1978).

State v. Iaukea, 56 Haw. 343, 537 P.2d 724 (1975).

State v. Pugh, 369 So. 2d 1308 (La. 1979).

State v. Stetson, 317 So. 2d 172 (La. 1975).

Thompson v. Oklahoma, 487 U.S. 815, 108 S.Ct. 2687 (1988).

Tyrer v. United Kingdom, 26 Eur. Ct. H.R. (ser. A) At 15, 17 (1978).

Weems v. United States, 217 U.S. 349, 368–72 (1910).

Wilkerson v. Utah, 99 U.S. 130 (1878).

Woodson v. North Carolina, 428 U.S. 280, 96 S. Ct. 2978, 49 L. Ed. 2d 944 (1976)

Workman v. Com., 429 S.W.2d 374, 33 A.L.R.3d 326 (Ky. 1968).

Table of Cases, Charts & Figures 275

Table of Charts & Figures

Figure 1-1: Practice of torture and cruel, inhuman, and degrading treatment in the world by year, 1985-2005.

Figure 2-1 States with Death Penalty (38) and the Number of Executions Since 1976.

Chart 2-1 Capital Crimes based on Islamic Penal Code of Iran.

Chart 2-2 Capital crimes in Islamic Penal Code of Iran based on recidivism.

Figure 2-2 Executions in Iran during 2005 & 2006.

Chart 2-3 Criminal Statute Prohibiting Sodomy in Iran.

Chart 2-4 Criminal Statute Prohibiting Lesbianism in Iran.

Figure 2-3 Executions Rate in Iran Based on Capital Offenses during 2005 & 2006.

Chart 3-1 Overview of the Execution Method during 2005

Figure 3-1 Public v. Private Executions in Iran.

Figure 4-1 Juvenile executions in the world (since 1990).

Figure 4-2 Executions of child offenders since 1990 in the world.

Figure 4-3 Juvenile executions in U.S.A since 1990.

Figure 4-4 Juvenile executions in the United States since 1977.

Figure 4-5 Juvenile executions in U.S.A since 1977(by states).

Figure 4-6 Juvenile executions in U.S.A by race of defendants / victims (since 1977).

Figure 4-7 Juvenile Executions in Iran & U.S.A (since 1990).

Chart 5-1 Flogging In Islamic Penal Code Of Iran.

Figure 5-1 Frequency of flogging as a discretionary punishment in Islamic Penal Code (1997) in compare to Discretionary statute (1984).

Chart 5-2 Mutilation in Islamic Penal Code of Iran.

Chart 5-3 Corporal punishment in the Quran and tradition.

Chart 5-4-An Extended Analytical Structure of Optimal Incapitication: Examples of Punishment.

Bibliography

Alperin, Howard; *Length of Sentence as Violation of Constitutional Provisions Prohibiting Cruel and Unusual Punishment,* 33 ALR3d.

Adolf, Peter S. Killing Me Softly: *Is the Gas Chamber, or any Other Method of Execution, "Cruel and Unusual Punishment?"* 22 HASTINGS CONST. L.Q. 815, 842 (1995).

Aflatooni, Arastoo; *Law of Ancient Iran, Iran Publication,* Tehran, Iran (1947) [In Farsi].

Alnoovi; *Sahihe Moslem,* Lebanon: Dar 'Ketab Arabi Publication, 1407 Lunar Hejira [In Arabic].

Alotta, Robert; **Civil** *War justice: Union Army Executions under Lincoln,* White Mane publishing, PA, U.S. (1989).

Amin, Hassan; *The History of Law in Iran,* The Encyclopedia of Iran Publications, Tehran, Iran (2004).

Anderson, J.N.D. *Homicide in Islamic Law,* 13 Bull. of The School of Oriental & African Stud. 811, 815 (1951).

Asghari, Abdoreza; *Age of Criminal Responsibility in Islam,* Razavi university law review, (2000) [In Farsi].

Aslan, Reza; *The Problem of Stoning in the Islamic Penal Code: AN Argument for reform,* UCLA J. Islamic & Near E. L. 91, (Fall/Winter 2003-2004).

Bahrami, Mohammad; *Islamic Jurisprudence and Legal Analysis of Hodoud punishments are to be prevented in case of doubt,* 5 Legal viewpoints Journal, (1376 Solar Hejira) [In Farsi].

Bahrampour, Firouzeh; *Note and Comment: The Canning of Michael Fay: Can Singapore's Punishment withstand the Scrutiny of International Law,* 10 Am. U.J. Int'l L. & Pol'y 1057(1995).

Bambale, Yunesa; *Crimes and Punishments under Islamic law,* Malthouse Press Limited, (2003).

Beccaria, Cesarre, *On Crimes and Punishments,* Translated with an introduction by Henry Paolucci, Bobbs-Merrill, Indianapolis, U.S. (1963).

Bentham, Jeremy; ***Principles of Penal Law***, in The Works of Jeremy Bentham 365, 401 (John Bowring ed., 1843).

Berkowitz, Beth; ***Symposium: Rethinking Robert Cover's Nomos and Narrative: Negotiating Violence and the Word in the Rabbanic Law***, 17 Yale J. L. & Human 125 (Winter 2005).

Berkson, Larry Charles; ***The Concept of Cruel and Unusual Punishment***, Lexington Books (1975).

Bernard Schwartz, ***The Bill of Rights: A Documentary History,*** pp 231-79, New York: McGrew Hill Book Co. (1971).

Bessler, John D. ***Televised Executions and the Constitution: Recognizing a First Amendment Right of Access to State Executions,*** 45 Fed. Comm. L.J. 355, 441 n.53 (1993).

Bishop, Anthony N. ***The Death Penalty in the Unites States: An International Human Rights Perspective***, 43 S. Tex. L. Rev. 1115 (2002).

Blum, Steven A. ***Public Executions: Understanding Cruel and Unusual Punishments Clause,*** 19 Hastings Const. L.Q. 413 (Winter 1992).

Bohm, R. "***Deathquest: An Introduction to the Theory and Practice of Capital Punishment in the United States***," Anderson Publishing (1999).

Bois, Mary; ***History of Zarathushtrian Religion***, Translation by Homayoon sanatizadeh, Toos Publication, Tehran, Iran, 1997. [In Farsi].

Bookspan, Phyllis; ***Too young to Die: Evolving Standard of Decency and the Juvenile Death Penalty in America***, 21 Delaware Lawyer 19 (Winter 2003-2004).

Bowers, William and Pierce Glenn; ***Legal Homicide: Death as Punishment in America***, Northeastern University press, Boston, U.S. (1984).

Bowers, William; ***Executions in America***, Lexington Books, MA, U.S. (1974).

Bradford, William, "***An Enquiry How Far the Punishment of Death is Necessary in Pennsylvania***", American Journal of Legal History 12 (1968).

Bukhari; Mohammad Ibn Esmaeil; ***Sahih Bokhari***, *vol.* 6, Hadith No. 25, Lebanon: Dar 'Fekr Publication (1401 Lunar Hejiri) [In Arabic].

Caldwell, Robert Graham; *Red Hannah, Delaware Whipping Post*. University of Philadelphia press, pp 69-82(1947).

Chapin, Bradley *Criminal Justice in Colonial America 1606-1660*, Athens: University of Georgia Press (1983).

Claus, Laurence; *The Antidiscrimination Eight Amendment*, 28 Harv. J.L. & Pub. Pol'y 119 (Fall 2004).

Cokley, Michael A. *Whatever Happened to that Old Saying "Thou Shall No Kill?" A Plea for the Abolition of the Death Penalty*, 2Loy. J. Pub. Int. L. 67(2001).

Compbell, James; *Revival of the Eight Amendment: Development of Cruel-Punishment Doctrine by the Supreme Court*, 16 Stand. L. Rev. 996 (July 1964).

Denno, Deborah W. *Is Electrocution An Unconstitutional Method of Execution? The Engineering of Death over the Century*, 35 WM. & MARY L. REV. 551, 554 (1994).

Duff, R.A. *Punishment, Dignity and Degradation*, 25 Oxford J. Legal Stud. 141 (spring 2005).

Durkheim, Emile; *The Division of Labor in Society,* George Simpson trans., The Free Press (1933) (1893).

Durkheim, *Two laws of Penal evolution*, 21, in M. Gane, ed., The Radical sociology of Durkheim and Mauss (London, 1992).

Ebadi, Shirin; *Children Rights*, Tehran, Iran: Kanoon publication, (1996) [In Farsi].

Ebrahimi, Eesa; *Philosophy of Punishment in Islam*, 38, Bar Association Journal, Tehran: 1333 Solar Hejira, [In Farsi].

Eckhert, Amy; *"Unlawful Combatants" or "Prisoner of War": The Law and Politics of Labels*, 36 Cornell Int'l L.J. 59, 66 (2003).

Edwards, Lori; *Critique of the Juvenile Death Penalty in the United States: A Global Perspective*, 42 Duq. L. Rev. 317, winter, 2004.

Emam Malek, *Motan*, Lebanon: Dar 'ehyae Torase Arabi Publication, 1985[In Arabic].

Emmerson, B and Ashworth, A; *Human Rights and Criminal Justice*, pp 479-514, Sweet & Maxwell London (2001).

Entessar, Nader; *Criminal Law and the Legal System in Revolutionary Iran*, 8 Boston College third World law Journal, p 91-102, (winter 1988).

Fitzpatrick, Joan & Miller, Alice; *International Standards on the Death Penalty: Shifting Discourse*, 19 BROOK. J. INT'L L. 273, 278 (1993).

Flanders, Chad; *Shame and the Meanings of Punishment*, 54 Clev. St. L. Rev. 609 (2006).

Frase, Richard S. *Excessive Prison Sentences, Punishment Goals, and the Eighth Amendment: "Proportionality" Relative to What?*, 89 Minn. L. Rev. 571, 574 (2005).

Galliher, John F. *Abolition and Reinstatement of Capital Punishment During the Progressive Era and Early 20th Century*, 83 J. CRIM. L. & CRIMINOLOGY 538, 541 (1992).

Glass, Robert F. *Roper v. Simmons: A Dead-End for the Juvenile Death Penalty*, Mercer Law Review Summer (2006).

Goldouzian, Iraj; *General Criminal Law*, Tehran, Iran: Mizan Publication, (1999) [In Farsi].

Goldouzian, Iraj; *Special Criminal Law*, Tehran, Iran: Mizan Publication, (1999) [In Farsi].

Gorji, Abolghasem; *Legal Injunctions of the Quran*, Iran, Tehran: Mizan Publication (2004).

Granucci, Anthony; *"Nor Cruel and Unusual Punishments Inflicted:" The Original Meaning*, 57 Cal. L. Rev. (1969).

Gray, F.C. *Remarks on the Early Laws of Massachusetts Bay, reprinted in Collection of the Massachusetts Historical Society* (n.p., 3d Series 1843).

Gross, Oren; *Are Torture Warrants Warranted? Pragmatic Absolutism and Official Disobedience,* 88 Minn. L. Rev. 1481, 1506 (2004).

Hall, Daniel; *When Canning Meets the Eighth Amendment: Whipping Offenders in the United States*, 4 Widenr J. Pub. L. 403 (1995).

Harding, Roberta M. *The Gallows to the Gurney: Analyzing the (Un) constitutionality of the Methods of Execution*, 6 B. U. PUB. INT. L. J. 153, p 135-136 (1996).

Hatfield, Steven A. *Criminal Punishment in America: From the Colonial to the Modern Era*, 1 USAFA J. Leg. Stud. 139 (1990).

Hatfield, Steven *Criminal Punishment in America: From the Colonial to the Modern Era*, 1 USAFA J. Leg. Stud. 139, 1990.

Herman, Lawrence; *The Unexplored Relationship Between the Privilege Against Compulsory Self-Incrimination and the Involuntary Confession Rule* (Part 1), 53 Ohio St. L. J. 101, 147 (1992).

Hoffman, Paul; *The Blank Stare Phenomenon: Proving Customary International Law in U.S. Courts*, 26 Ga. J. Int'l & Comp. L. 181 (1995-1996).

Humphrey, John P. *The Universal Declaration of Human Rights, in Human Rights: Thirty Years After the Universal Declaration* 29, B.G. Ramcharan ed. (1979).

James, Ryk & Jones, Rachel Nasmyth; *The Occurrence of Cervical Fractures in Victims of Judicial Hangings*, 54 FORENSIC SCI INT'L 81, 90 (1992).

Javan, Mosa; *Zoroaster laws or Vandidad of Zoroaster's holy book,* Iran, Tehran (1953) [In Farsi].

Joyner Christopher C. & *Dettling* John C., *Bridging the Cultural Chasm: Cultural Relativism and the Future of International Law*, 20 CAL. W. INT'L L.J. 275, 275 (1990).

Kan, Steven S. *Corporal Punishments and Optimal Incapacitation*, 25 J. Legal Stud. 121(January, 1996).

Karami, Mohammad bagher; *Introduction on Criminal Justice System in ancient Iran*, Khate sevvom (1380)[in Farsi].

Kogan, Terry; *Legislative Violence Against Lesbian and Gay Men*, 1994 Utah L. Rev. 209 (1994).

Kopelmanas, Lazare; *Custom as a Means of the Creation of International Law*, 18 Brit. Y.B. Int'l L. 127, 129 (1937).

Kreimer,Seth F. *Allocational Sanctions: The Problem of Negative Rights in a Positive State*, 132 U.PA.L.REV. 1293, 1387 (1984).

Lacey, Forrest; *Vagrancy and Other Crimes of Personal Condition,* Harvard Law Review 66 (May 1953).

Lane, Roger; *Capital Punishment: In Violence in America*, vol 1, ed. Ronald Gottesman, Charles Scribner's Sons, New York, U.S..(1999).

Ledbetter, Garry . *The International Norms: An Interpretation of the "Evolving Standard of Decency"*, 2 San Diego Justice J. 263 (1994).

Lewicki, Edna;. *Need Word's Collide: The Hudad Crimes of Islamic Law and International Human Rights*, 13 NYILR 43 (2000).

Lippman, Matthew and McConville, Sean and Yerushalmi, Mordechai; *Islamic Criminal Law and Procedure: An Intriduction.* New Yory: Praeger publication (1988).

Lyons, Lewis; *The History of Punishment*, The Lyons press, Guilford, CT (2003).

Mackey Philip English;, *Hanging in the Balance: the Anti Capital Punishment Movement in New York State*, 1776-1861, (1982).

Macnair, M. *The Early Development of the Privilege Against Self-Incrimination*, 10 Oxford J. Legal Studies 66, 72 (1990).

Madani, Arefeh; *Execution of Criminal Sanctions*, Tehran: Majd publication, 1374 Hejira [In Farsi].

Manley, Steven; *The Constitution. The Punishment of death, and Misguided Originalism*, 1999 L. Rev. M.S.U. D.C.L. 913 (1999).

Matikan-e- Hazar Datastan: **The Digest of a Thousand Points of Law**, translated by Sohrab Jams, Published by Houshang Anklesaria, Bombay, India (1937).

Matura, Jeffrey C. *Campaign Finance Reform Symposium: Note: When Will It Stop? The Use of the Death Penalty for Non-Homicide Crimes*, 24 J. Legis. 249 (1998).

Meron, Theodor; *The Geneva Conventions as Customary Law*, 81 Am. J. Int'l L. 348 (1987).

Merskey, H *Pain: Psychological and Psychiatric Aspects,* London: Baillere (1967).

Miethe; Terance and Lu, Hong; *Punishment: A Comparative Historical Perspective*, Cambridge University Press (2005).

Mishali, Jessica; ***Roper v. Simmons--Supreme Courts Rellance on International Law in Constitutional Decision-Making,*** Touro Law Review (2006).

Mohammadi, Abolhassan; ***Islamic Criminal Law***, Tehran: University publication (1374 Solar Hejira).

Mohhaghegh Helli, ***Sharaye*** 'Islam, (translation by Abdo 'Ghani Ebn Abi Taleb),. [InFarsi].

Morse, Alice Earle; ***Curious Punishments of Bygone Days***, Chicago: Herbert S. Stone and Company (1896).

Mousavi, Abas; ***Torture: In the Iranian, UN and Criminal Policy***, Khat-E-Sevom publishing, Tehran, Iran (2003) [In Farsi].

Newman, Graeme; ***Just and Painful: A Case for the Corporal Punishment of Criminals, Macmillan Publishing Company,*** (1983).

Ogg, David; ***England in the Reigns of James II and William III 175***, Oxford Univ. Press (1955).

Ozimek, Mark Alan; Note, ***The Case for a More Workable Standard in Death Penalty Jurisprudence: Atkins v. Virginia and Categorical Exemptions under the Imprudent "Evolving Standards of Decency" Doctrine,*** 34 U. Tol. L. Rev. 651, 684 (2003).

Page, Drew; ***Cruel and Unusual Punishment and Sodomy Statutes: the Breakdown of the Soldem v. Helm***, 56 U. Chi. L. Rev. 367 (1989).

Parr, Stephen; ***A New Perspective on the Cruel and Unusual Punishment Clause***, 68 Tenn. L. Rev. 41 (2000).

Paust, Jordan J. ***Human Dignity as a Constitutional Right: A Jurisprudentially Based Inquiry into Criteria and Content,*** 27 How. L.J. 145, 176 (1984).

Pirnia, Hassan; ***History of Ancient Iran***, Donyaye Ketab Publication, Tehran, Iran, (1982) [In Farsi].

Pittman, R. Carte; ***The Colonial Constitutional History of the Privilege Against Self-Incrimination in America,*** 21 Va. L. Rev. 763, 768 (1935).

Powers, Edwin; ***crime and Punishment in Early Massachusetts:*** 1620-1692, Boston: Beacon Press, (1966).

Ravandi, Morteza; *Revolution of Law and Administration of Justice*, Tehran, Iran (1988) [In Farsi].

Razi, Hashem; *Ancient Religion of Iran*, Asia Publication, Tehran, Iran (1963) [In Farsi].

Razi, Majid; *Avesta Era*, Asia Publication, Tehran, Iran, (1963) [In Farsi].

Robertson, James; *Houses of the Dead: Warehouse Prisons, paradigm change, and the Supreme Court*, 34Hous. L. Rev. 1003 (1997).

Rose, Sara L. Comment: *"Cruel and Unusual Punishment" Need Not Be Cruel, Unusual, or Punishment*, 24 Cap. U.L. Rev. 827 (1995).

Rosen, Sonia & Journey, Stephen; *Abolition of the Death Penalty: An Emerging Norm of International Law,* 14 Hamline J. Pub. L. & Policy 163, 164 (1993).

Rosenberg, Irene Maker; *Of God's Mercy and the Four Biblical Methods of Capital Punishment: Stoning, Burning, Beheading, and Strangulation*, 78 Tul. L. Rev. 1169, (March, 2004).

Roth, Mitchel P. *Crime and Punishment: A History of the Criminal Justice System*, Thomson Wadsworth, CA, U.S. (2005).

Rothenberg, Laurence E. *International Law, U.S. Sovereignty, and the Death Penalty*, 35 Geo. J. Int'l L. 547 (2004).

Saharsky, Nicole; *Consistency as a Constitutional Value:*
A Comparative Look at Age in Abortion and Death Penalty Jurisprudence, 85 Minn. L. Rev. 1119 (April 2001).

Sanders, Scott; *Scarlet Letters, Bilbo's and Cable TV: Are Shame Punishments Cruel and Unusual or are they Viable Option for American Jurisprudence?* , 37 Washburn L.J. 359 (1998).

Saneiee, Parviz; *General Criminal Law,* Iran, Tehran: Ganje Danesh Publication (Fall 1992).

Schabas, William A. *Symposium: Religion's Role in the Administration of the Death Penalty Islam and the Death Penalty*, 9 Wm. & Mary Bill Rts. J. 223.

Schabas, William A. *The death Penalty as Cruel Treatment and torture*, Northeastern University press (1996).

Schabas, William A. *The International Sourcebook on Capital Punishment*, Northwestern University press (1997).

Schneider, Victoria; and Smykla, John Ortiz; *A summary analysis of executions in the United States*, Anderson Publishing, Cincinnati, U.S. (1991).

Schreiber, Ariane M. *States that Kill: Discretion and the Death Penalty– a Worldwide Perspective*, 29 Cornell Int'l L.J. 263 (1996).

Sech, Robert J. *A Proposal for Thoroughly Evaluating The Constitutionality Of Execution Methods,* 30 Val. U. L. Rev. 381 (1995).

Shahid avval, *Lomeh Demeshghieh*, (translation by Ali Shyravani), Qom: Dar 'Fekr Qom publication, 1376 Solar Hejira, [In Farsi].

Shuster, Kenneth; *Halacha as a Model for American Penal Practice: A Comparison of Halachic and American Punishment Methods*, 19 Nova L. Rev. 965(1995).

Sigler, Mary; *Contradiction, Coherence, and Guided Discretion in the Supreme Court's Capital Sentencing Jurisprudence,* 40 Am. Crim. L. Rev. 1151, 1155 (2003).

Sohn, Louis; *The New International Law: Protection of the Rights of Individuals Rather than States*, 32 Am. U. L. Rev. 1, 17 (1982).

Stacy, Tom; *Cleaning up the Eighth Amendment Mess,* 14 Wm. & Mary Bill Rts. J. 475 (December 2005).

Starkweather, David A. *Note, The Retributive Theory of "Just Deserts" and Victim Participation in Plea Bargaining,* 67 Ind. L.J. 853, 854-55 (1992).

Stephen, James F; *History of the Criminal Law of England (Making of the British Legal System)*, Routledge/Thoemmes P; 1 edition (December 4, 1996).

Stewart, David; *The Torture Convention and the Reception of International Criminal Law within the United States*, 15 Nova L. Rev. 449 (spring 1991).

Streib, Victor; *Sentencing Juvenile Murderers: Punish the last Offender or Save the next Victim*, 26 U. Tol. L. Rev. 765 (summer 1995).

Tubb, Kristin O'Donnell; *Freedom from Cruel and Unusual Punishment,* Greenhaven press (2005).

Vahedi, Ava; *Criminal Justice System of Iran in Sassanian Era*, Tehran, Iran: Mizan Publication, (2001) [In Farsi].

Wernick, Steven J. *Constitutional Law: Elimination of the Juvenile Death Penalty Substituting Moral Judgment for a True National Consensus*, Florida Law Review April (2006).

Whiteman, James; *Harsh Justice: Criminal Punishment and the Widening divide between America and Europe*, New York: Oxford University Press (2003).

Whitman, James Q. *SYMPOSIUM: Model Penal Code: Sentencing: A Plea Against Retributivism,* 7 Buff. Crim. L. R. 85 (2003).

Wiedeman, Whitney; *Special Issue: Juvenile Justice and the Criminal Law: Comment: Don't Spare the Rod: A Proposed Return to Public, Corporal punishment on Convicts*, 23 Am. J. Crim. L. 651(1996).

Wyman, James H. *Vengeance is Whose?: The Death Penalty and Cultural Relativism in International Law*, Journal of Transnational Law and Policy (Summer 1997).

Zafari, Mohammadreza; *Origins of Criminal Justice in Islamic Law*, Tehran, Iran: Amirkabir Publication (1997) [In Farsi].

Zimring, Franklin & Hawkins, Gordon; *Dangerousness and Criminal Justice*, 85 MICH. L. REV. 481 (1986).

Zimring, Franklin; *The Contradiction of American Capital Punishment*, Oxford University press, NY, U.S. (2003).

Zimring, Franklin; *The Hardest of the Hard Cases: Adolescent Homicide in Juvenile and Criminal Courts*, 6 Va. J. Soc. Pol'y & L. 437(Spring 1999).

Zimring, Franklin; *Youth on Trial: A Development perspective on juvenile justice*, edited by Thomas Grisso & Robert G. Schwartz, University of Chicago Press, (2000).